AF594588

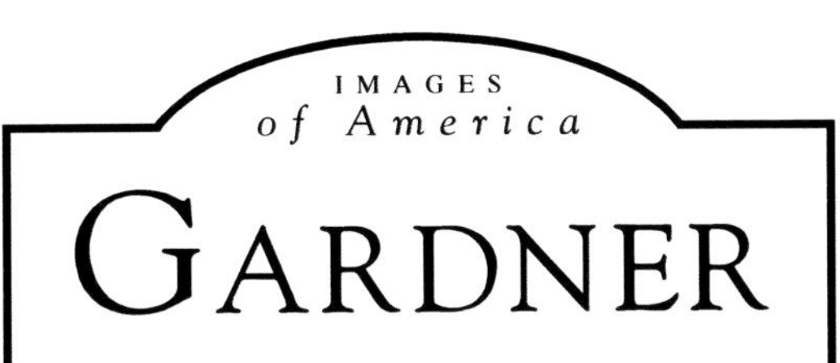
IMAGES
of America
GARDNER

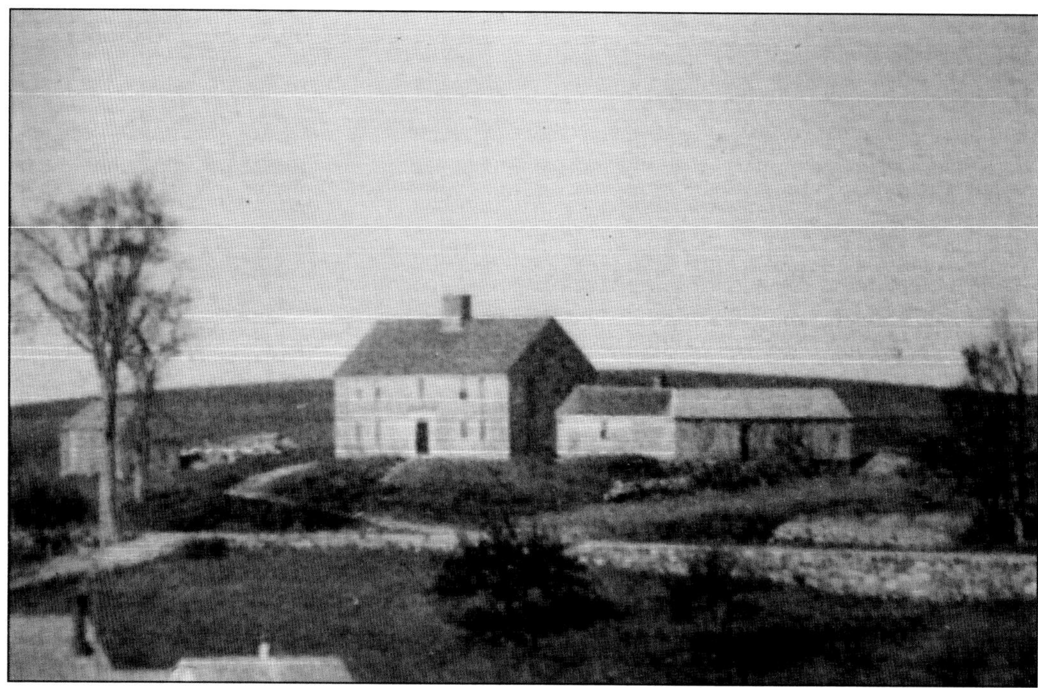

When Elisha Jackson, Gardner's first settler, settled on 400 acres in Narragansett No. 2, he built this home and public house in 1764 on the south side of "Jackson Hill" where the Post Road passed by. During the Revolutionary War Elisha served as a captain. He was the first town moderator and first chairman of selectmen. A stone on Kendall Hill, donated by John R. Conant (a descendant of Elisha), and a bronze tablet given by the DAR mark the site of his tavern.

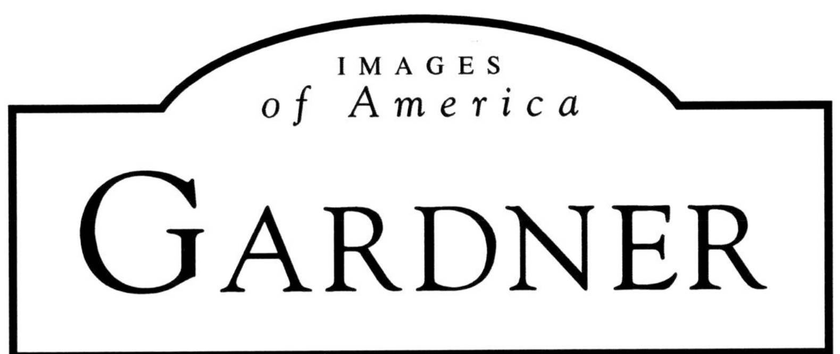

South Gardner Historical Society

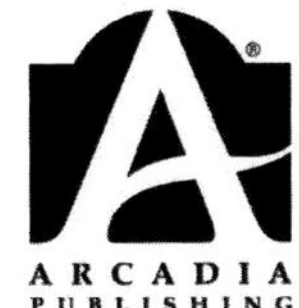

ISBN 978-0-7385-8845-2

Published by Arcadia Publishing
Charleston, South Carolina

Printed in the United States of America

For all general information contact Arcadia Publishing at:
Telephone 843-853-2070
Fax 843-853-0044
E-mail sales@arcadiapublishing.com
For customer service and orders:
Toll-Free 1-888-313-2665

Visit us on the Internet at www.arcadiapublishing.com

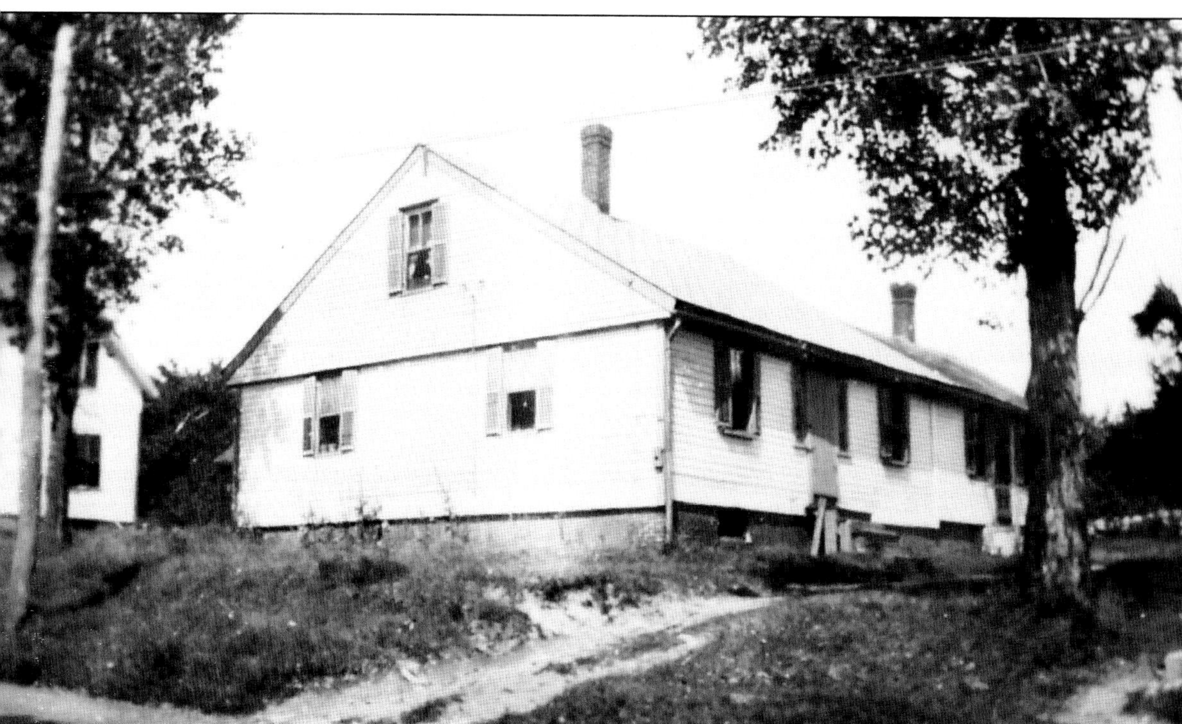

The John Glazier home and public house was the site of the first town meeting and organization of the first church. John Glazier carried the petition for the formation of Gardner to the legislature in Boston. He was on the first board of selectmen and board of assessors. Originally built on the top of Glazier (now Reservoir) Hill, the house was moved to near the junction of Cherry and Cedar Streets. It was eventually moved again, this time to 20 Lennon Street where it stands today.

Contents

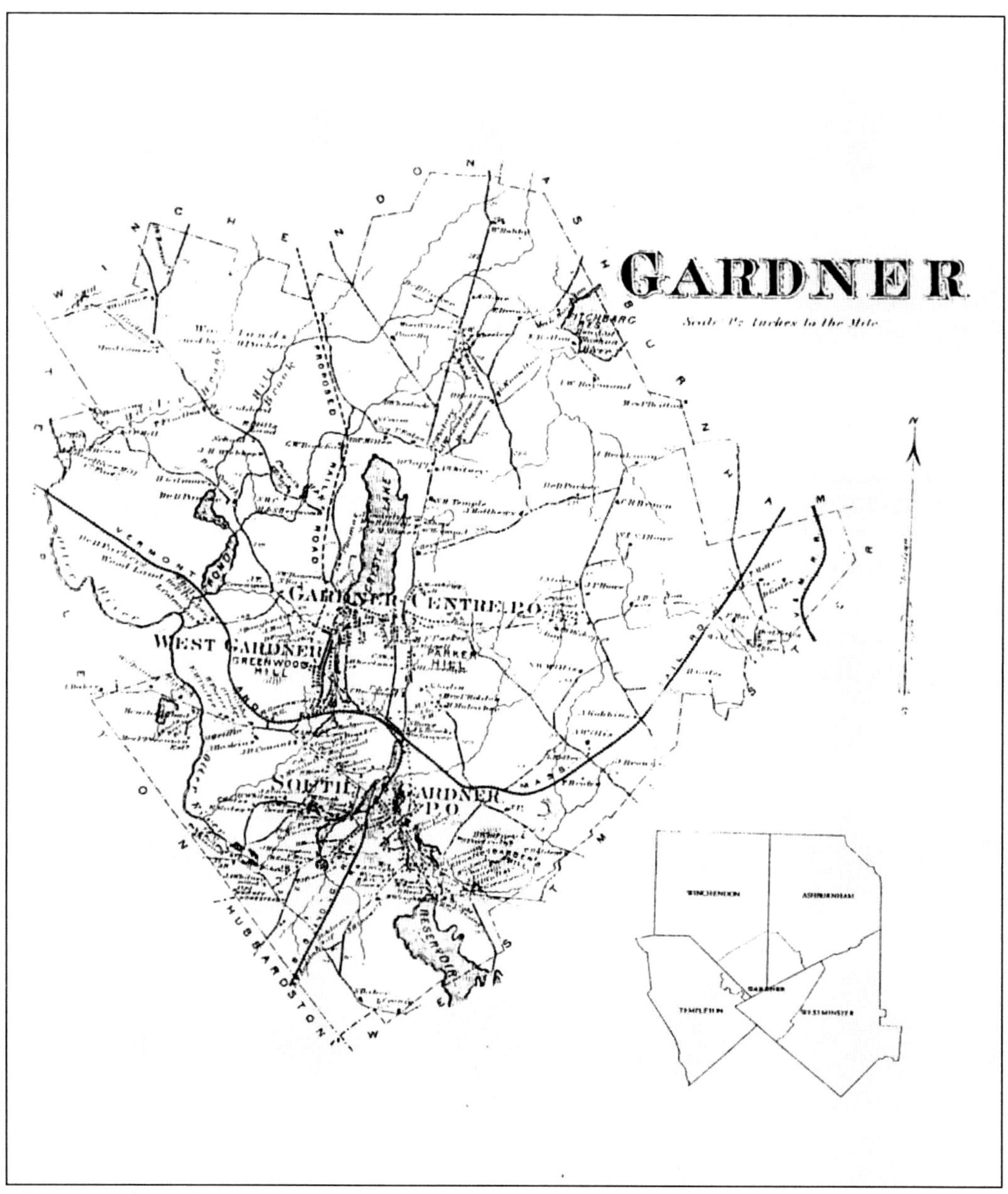

The map of Gardner as it appeared in Beer's *Atlas of Worcester County* of 1870. The small inset map indicates how Gardner was formed from the towns of Ashburnham, Templeton, Westminster, and Winchendon.

Introduction

Gardner, named after Revolutionary War hero Colonel Thomas Gardner, was born on June 27, 1785, when the legislature accepted a petition for incorporation with sixty-one signatures carried by John Glazier. The early settlers cited "great hardships and forteagues," especially on the women and children attending public worship in their respective towns.

Land was to be taken from Ashburnham, Winchendon, and Westminster in the original petition, with the addition of an area from Templeton soon to follow. Preliminary discussions in the four towns had been held as early as 1774, but the Revolutionary War put this planning on hold.

The first recorded settler to the area was Elisha Jackson, who built his home and tavern on Jackson Hill in 1764, on what was then the county road of 1754 from Lancaster to Paquoag (Athol). Elisha's 400 acres were originally a land grant in Narragansett No. 2 to his grandfather Edward Jackson of Woburn.

Elisha Jackson was elected moderator at the first town meeting held on August 15, 1785, at the home of John Glazier. At the next meeting in September 1785, town officers were elected. At Gardner's third town meeting in October, only four months after incorporation, the elected officers acted to build a meeting house and hire a preacher as dictated by the laws of the day.

Elisha Jackson and Beulah Taylor had ten children, five boys and five girls, all growing up to become active citizens. Elisha served as a captain in the Revolutionary War at various times, and served upon a local committee created to "deal with tories."

In common with other early colonial settlers, the first inhabitants of Gardner lived off the land, and their first enterprises were water-powered saw and gristmills, with carding and fulling to ensue. They brought with them trades that helped to develop the burgeoning new community. For instance, the Reverend Jonathan Osgood, Gardner's first minister, was a tanner by trade who practiced medicine as well. Seth Heywood, David Nichols, and Jude Sawyer were skilled blacksmiths. Joseph Bacon and Andrew Beard were skilled carpenters. Jonathan Bancroft and Jonas Richardson were shoemakers who visited households to ply their trade "whipping the cat." Potash works throughout the area served the tanner well.

Gardner's chair-making fame began in 1805 when James M. Comee, using hand tools and a foot lathe, commenced manufacturing chairs at his home on Pearl Street. He took in several apprentices who would later fan out into outlying districts to form their own small shops.

Elijah Putnam commenced the fabrication of cane seats in 1832, while others were using wood, flag, or rush seating.

The Heywood brothers began to make chairs in a little shed at Gardner Centre in 1826, while Stephen Taylor did the same in a small section of the Merriam carding and fulling mill in South Gardner. Heywood's would later become the largest chair manufacturer in the world.

Transportation was a problem in the early days of chair-making and giant chair racks (wagons) brought the finished product to Boston, Providence, and other major outlets. The arrival of the Vermont and Massachusetts Railroad to Gardner in 1847, and of the Boston, Barre, and Gardner line in 1871, eased the movement of raw materials into, and finished products out of, Gardner.

In 1855 fifteen major chair factories were operating in Gardner, and by the end of the nineteenth century, when steam had replaced most of the water power, further companies would join the list of producers. About this time Gardner came to be known as the "Chair Town" of the world, and a giant Mission Chair would welcome visitors at the Union Railroad Station in Depot Square.

Early industrial diversification began to show itself when Edward Goodrich Watkins joined his father, Gardner Watkins, at Heywood Brothers and Company to develop a time clock for that business. In 1902 Edward and Associates incorporated the now famous "Simplex Time Recorder Company." They are presently known not only for their time recorders, but also for fire protection and other sophisticated environmental control systems.

The Florence Stove Company, successors to the earlier Central Oil and Gas Stove Company, came onto the scene in 1924 and conducted a large business until 1957, when the plant closed.

Gardner has also been known for its famous silver shops and craftsmen. Frank W. Smith began to manufacture sterling silver in 1886 near the corner of Walnut and Chestnut Streets, and soon boasted one of the finest-equipped factories in the country. The weather vane of the factory is made in the shape of a knife. The Stone Silver Shop was established in 1901 on Winter Street by Arthur J. Stone, known as the "Dean of American Silversmiths." Mr. Stone, at age ninety and in failing health, sold his business to Henry E. Heywood, and later Heywood's son, Jerome A. Heywood, continued on until the mid-1950s. Both Arthur J. Stone and Frank W. Smith have examples of their craft exhibited on tours and in major museums throughout the world.

Many diversified industries have now taken over where once chair manufacturing held sway. Only S. Bent and Brothers, Nichols and Stone, and C.H. Hartshorn of the early companies remain, while a few smaller enterprises carry out the tradition of yesterday.

The Gardner Seal, designed by Harrison Cady—a native son and internationally-known illustrator—shows Colonel Thomas Gardner in the center, with the initials of donor towns around him and a small chair at the top. In the background are Crystal Lake and Mount Monadnock. The seal illustrates graphically the present day logo "Greater Gardner."

One

South Gardner: The Village

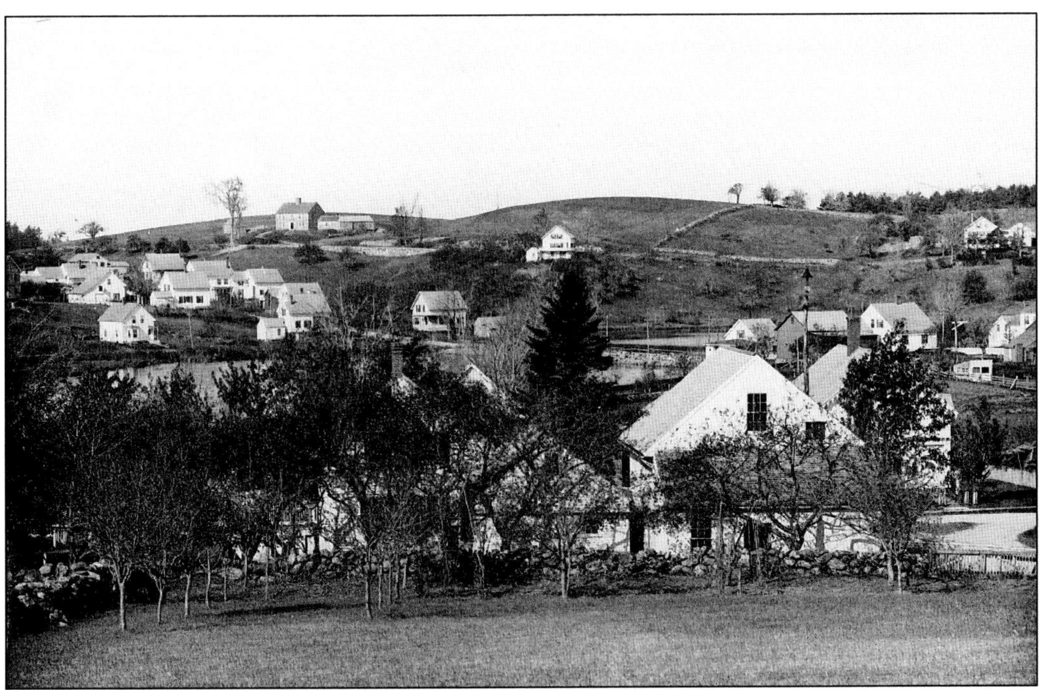

Jackson Hill was later called Conant and then Kendall. This is a Warren P. Allen photograph taken from Prospect Hill (Nutting Street) about 1885. Union Street crosses the lower section of the picture. Across the center is upper and lower Bent's Pond. At right is Gates Crossing on the Boston, Barre, and Gardner Railroad. The 5th Massachusetts Turnpike (West Broadway) crosses the picture near the center between ponds. The Jackson Tavern is on hill at the upper left, along the old County Road (Post Road), presently Kendall Street.

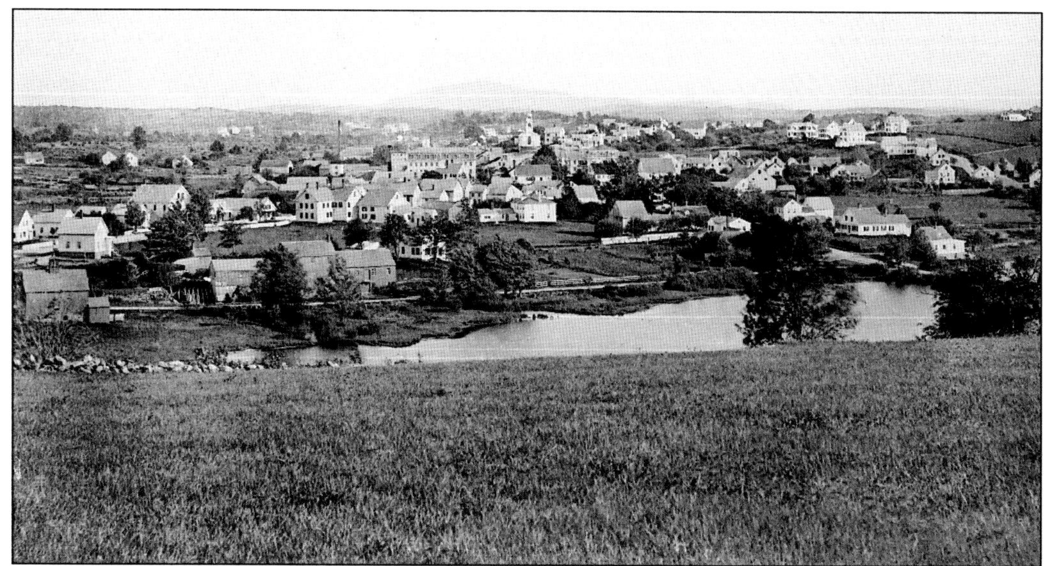

South Gardner Village seen here from Kendall's Hill, earlier known as Conant and sometimes Jackson Hill. The square white building in the direct center was the home of William Bickford, South Gardner's second settler, who came from Reading about 1771 and settled in what was then Westminster. Aaron Greenwood, famous in the town's history for his surveying and diary, lived in the Bickford house during the mid and late 1800s. The Bickford saw and gristmill on the factory site at the lower left, above the pond, was the first in the township.

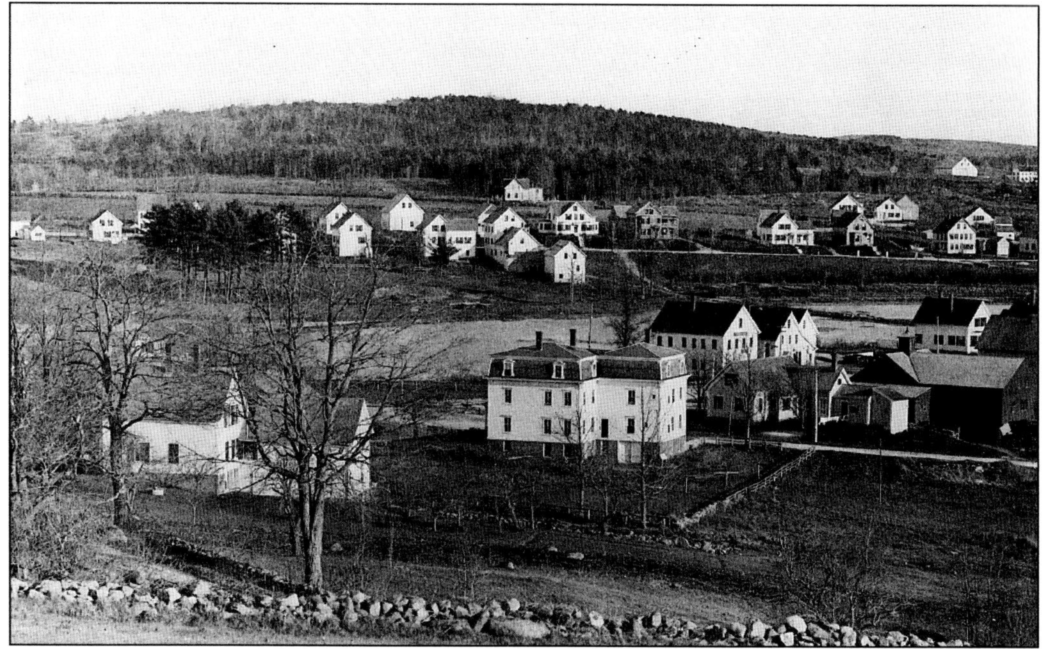

At right center is the shop of L. Sawin & Son, carriage manufacturers, later the Denney Manufacturing Company. The pond at the center is the present site of Pearson Boulevard. Summer Street, Pierce Road, and the causeway then connecting Summer to South Main at the Pierce Shop can be seen in the background. In the far upper right is the Jabez Partridge Farm (now Anderson's).

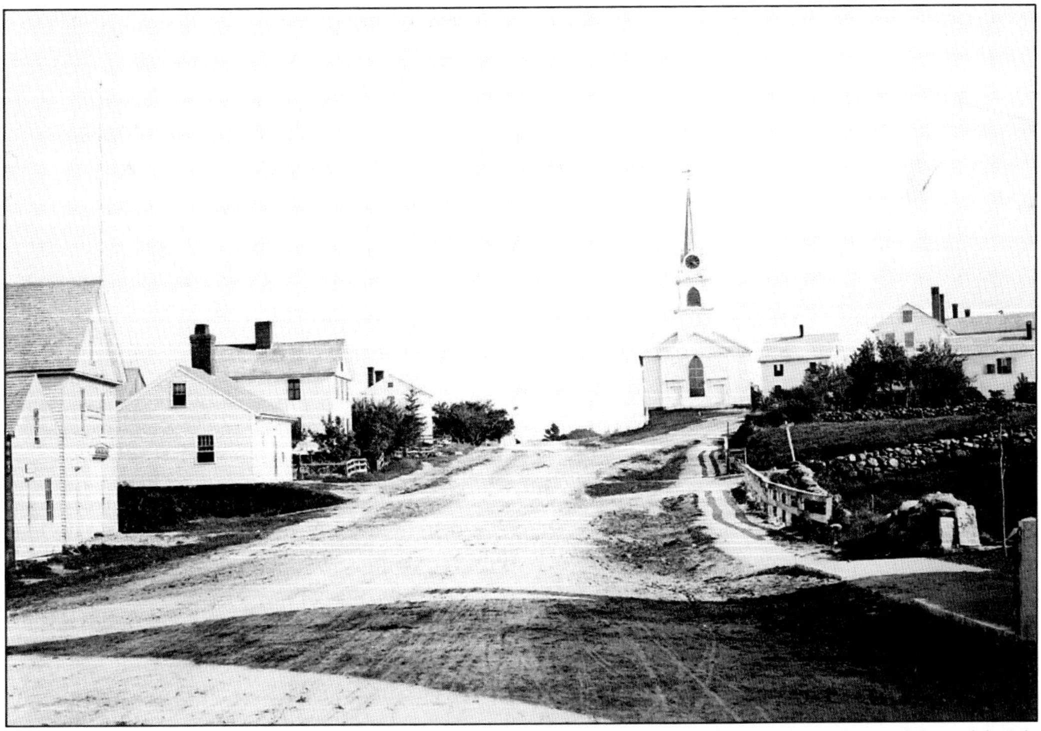

In the background is the First Baptist Church at the corner of East Broadway (the old 5th Massachusetts Turnpike) and High Street (old County Road). Band concerts were once held on the grassy triangle in front of the church. An Abijah M. Severy Memorial Stone erected by the South Gardner Historical Society and dedicated on November 11, 1979, now stands at the site as well as a flag pole erected in 1917 by a committee of firemen from Station No. 1.

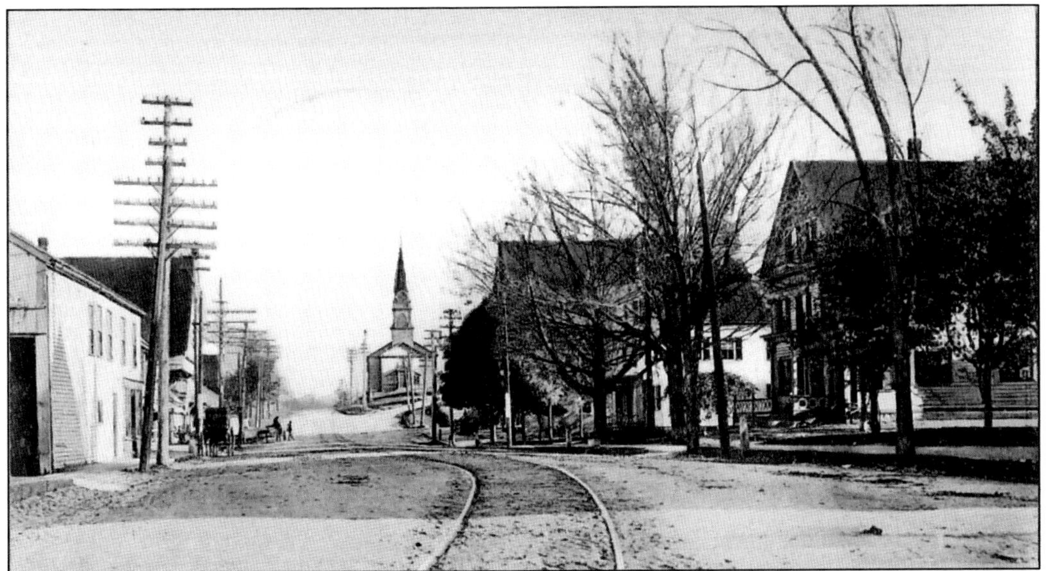

West Broadway looking east. On the left side is the South Gardner Hotel barn and S.W.A. Stevens' store. The trolley tracks are part of the Gardner, Westminster, and Fitchburg Street Railway.

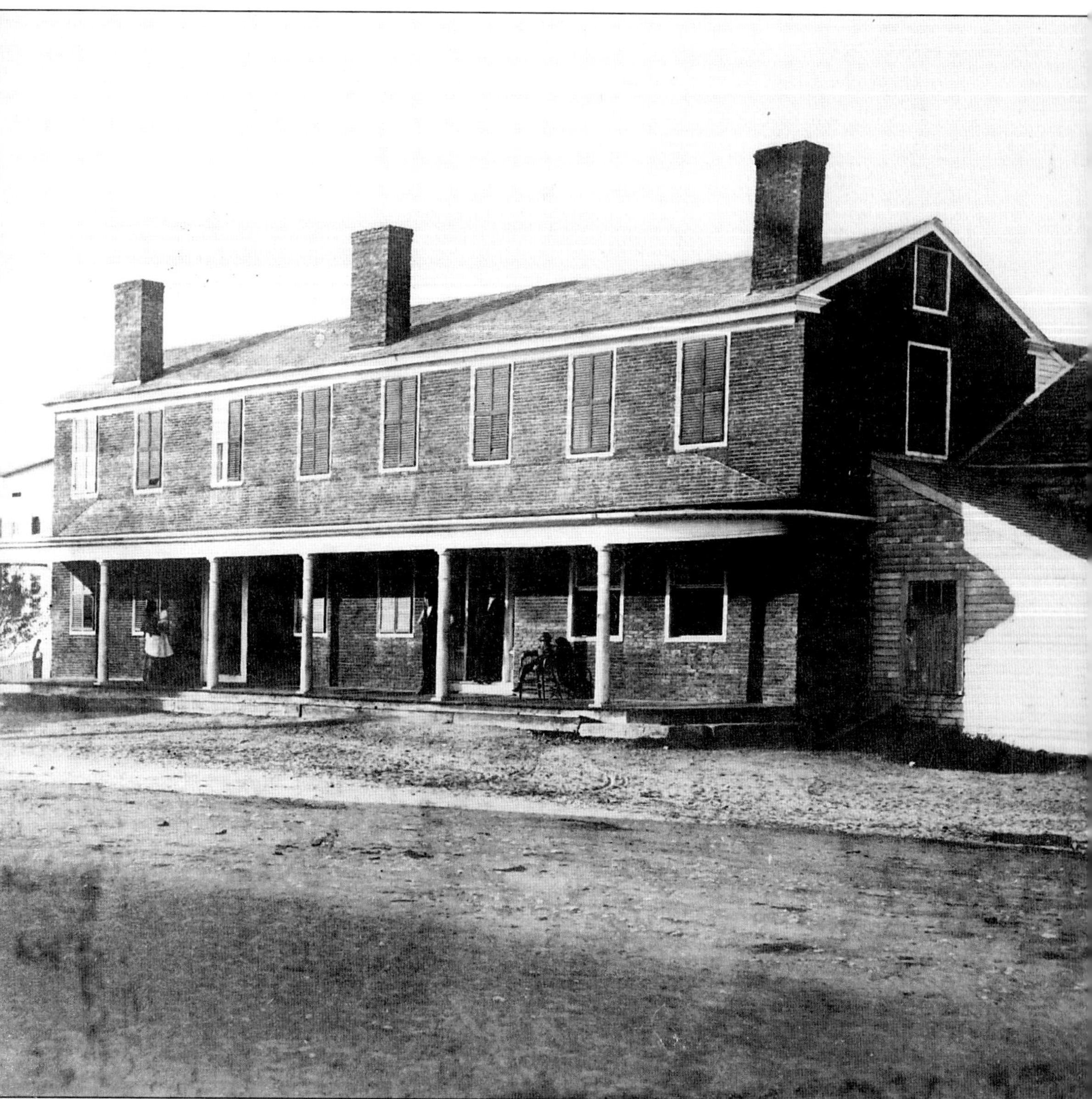

The South Gardner Hotel was built shortly after the 5th Massachusetts Turnpike was constructed in 1799. A first proprietor was probably Adam Noyes. Here also was an early post office on the stage route from Boston and Lowell to Brattelboro, Vermont, and other points west. Well-known later proprietors were Abel Stevens, Calvin Conant, N. Stockwell, L.H. Horton, Reed and Spencer, and Joseph Blouin. Mr. Blouin found inscribed on a roof board in the hotel barn "AP X111 186," probably dating the barn April 13, 1806.

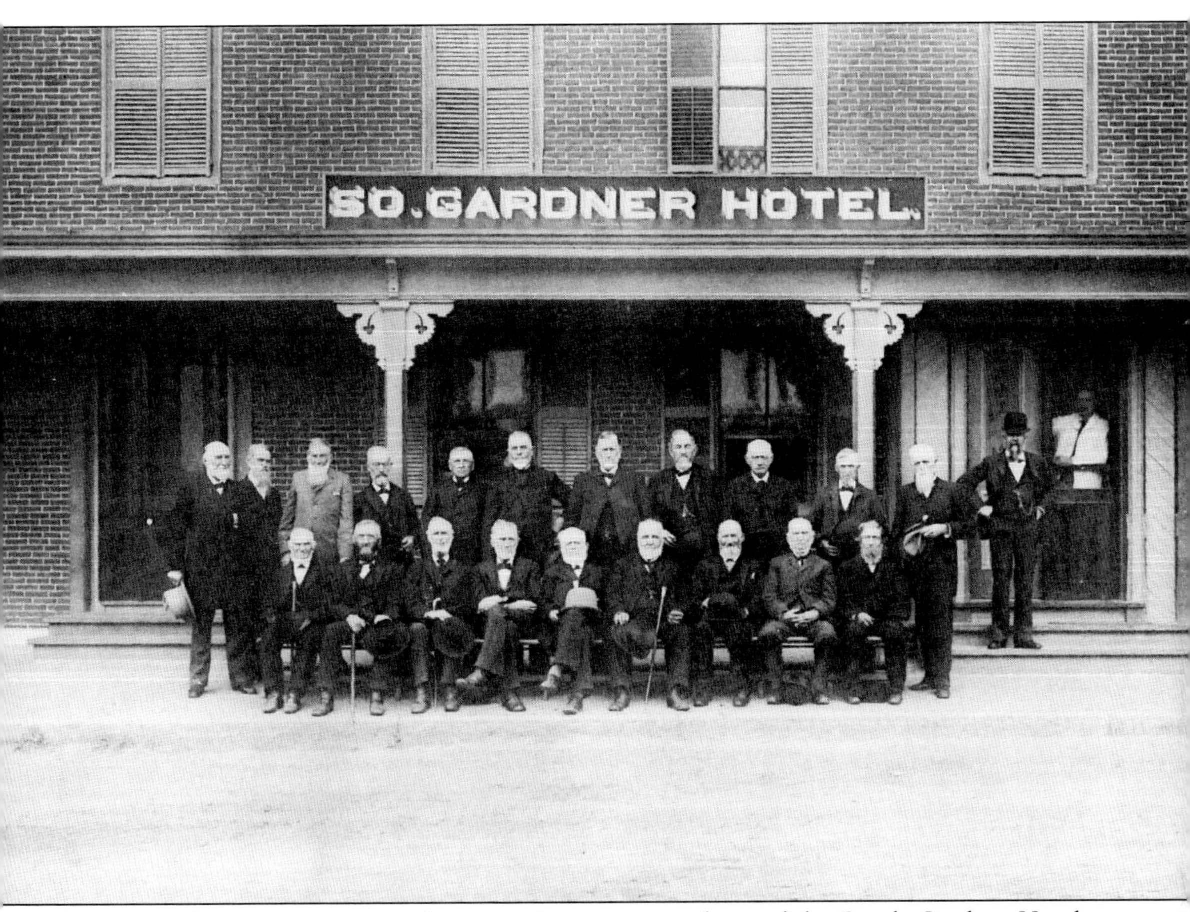

A picture of a reunion of stage drivers and teamsters in front of the South Gardner Hotel, on September 23, 1892. Among those present were Rodney Wallace (Fitchburg), William S. Briggs (Keene, N.H), Elbridge Clark (Keene, N.H.), L.S. Penniman (Blackstone), George Davis (Shirley), A.B. Gale (Harvard), Horace N. Pratt (Boston), C.D. Gale (Spencer), Elliott Swan (Worcester), Charles Whitney (Ashburnham), S.W.A. Stevens (South Gardner), A.L. Wright (Pepperell), John Starkey (Brattleboro, Vt.), Captain David Kendall (South Gardner), Sylvanus Wood (Fitchburg), William Woodbury (Fitchburg), Joseph Maynard (Somerville), Henry L. Lawrence (Fitchburg), Laton Martin (Keene, N.H.), and Benjamin Brown (Townsend).

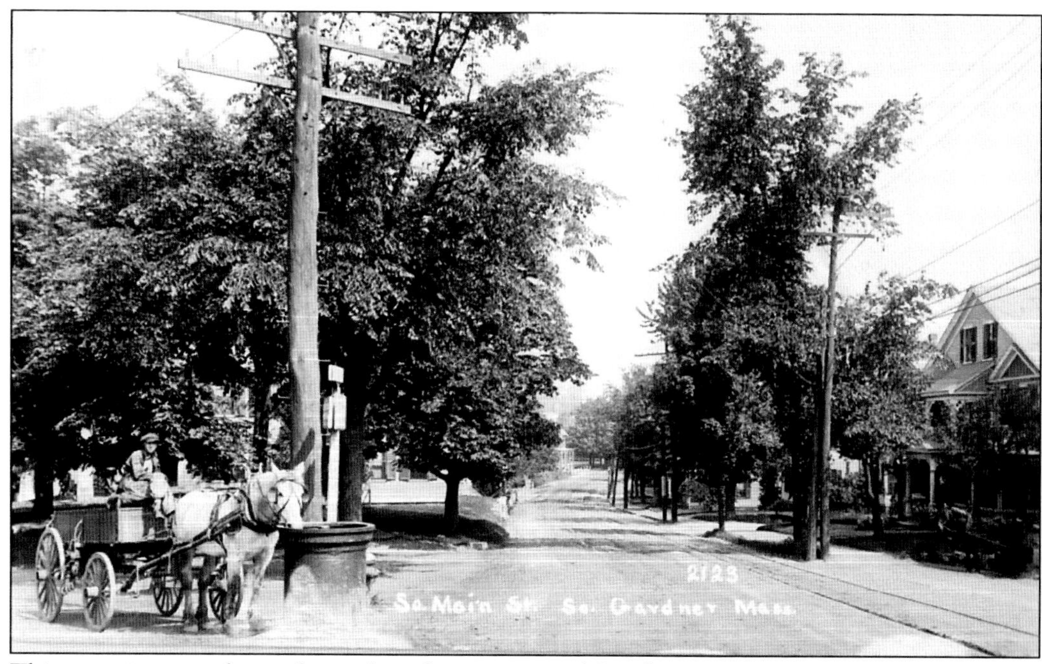

This watering trough was located at the junction of South Main Street and West Broadway. Directly behind the trough was the home of John Milton Moore, well-known town father, school committeeman, and chairmaker in the south village. At the right is the home of former state representative Fred Blake.

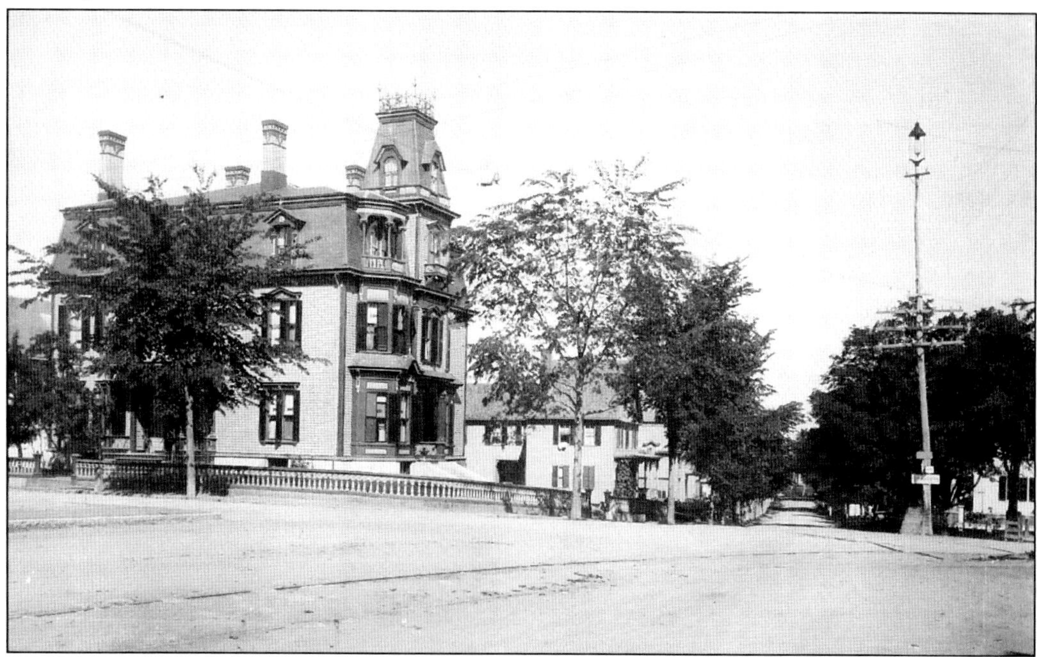

The Victorian, a show place built by Sylvester K. Pierce at the corner of Union Street and West Broadway in 1875 across from the site of the old S.K. Pierce Chair Shop, stands today as in yesteryear minus its showy iron fence. Early on this site was the house moved to 21 Union Street, then owned by S.K. and kept for years in the Pierce family.

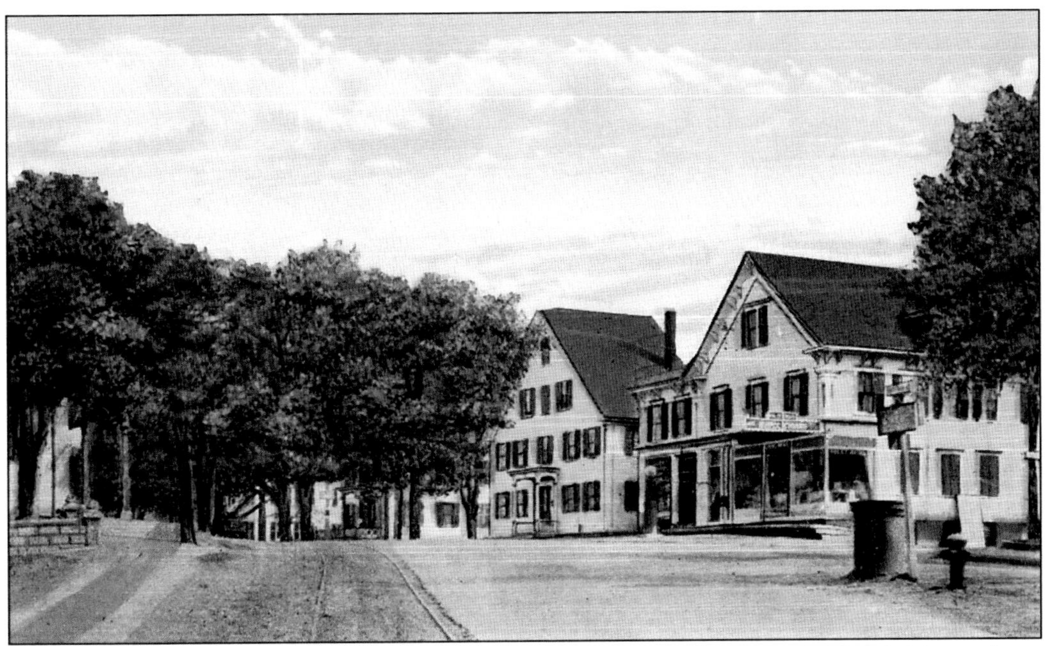

Willard B. Fowler opened his first drug store at the O.L. Wickes site, 58 South Main, about 1912. Shortly thereafter he removed to 3 East Broadway where the business operated through December 1944. His wife Jennie S. was the licensed pharmacist.

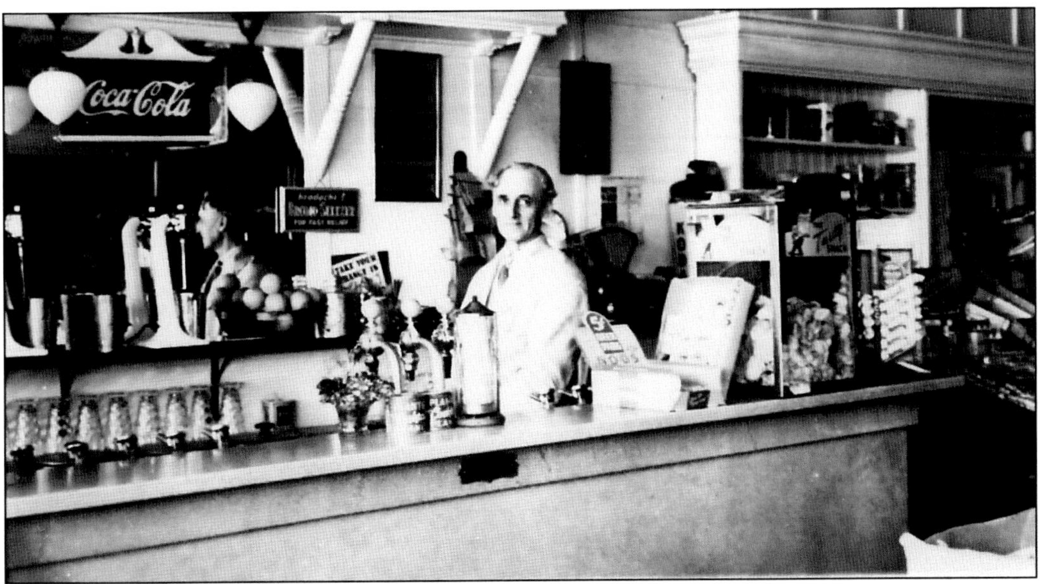

Clarence "Deak" Fowler was behind the counter at Fowler's Drug Store for many years. He was the son of the Fire Chief Albert Fowler. Deak Fowler was not related to Willard Fowler.

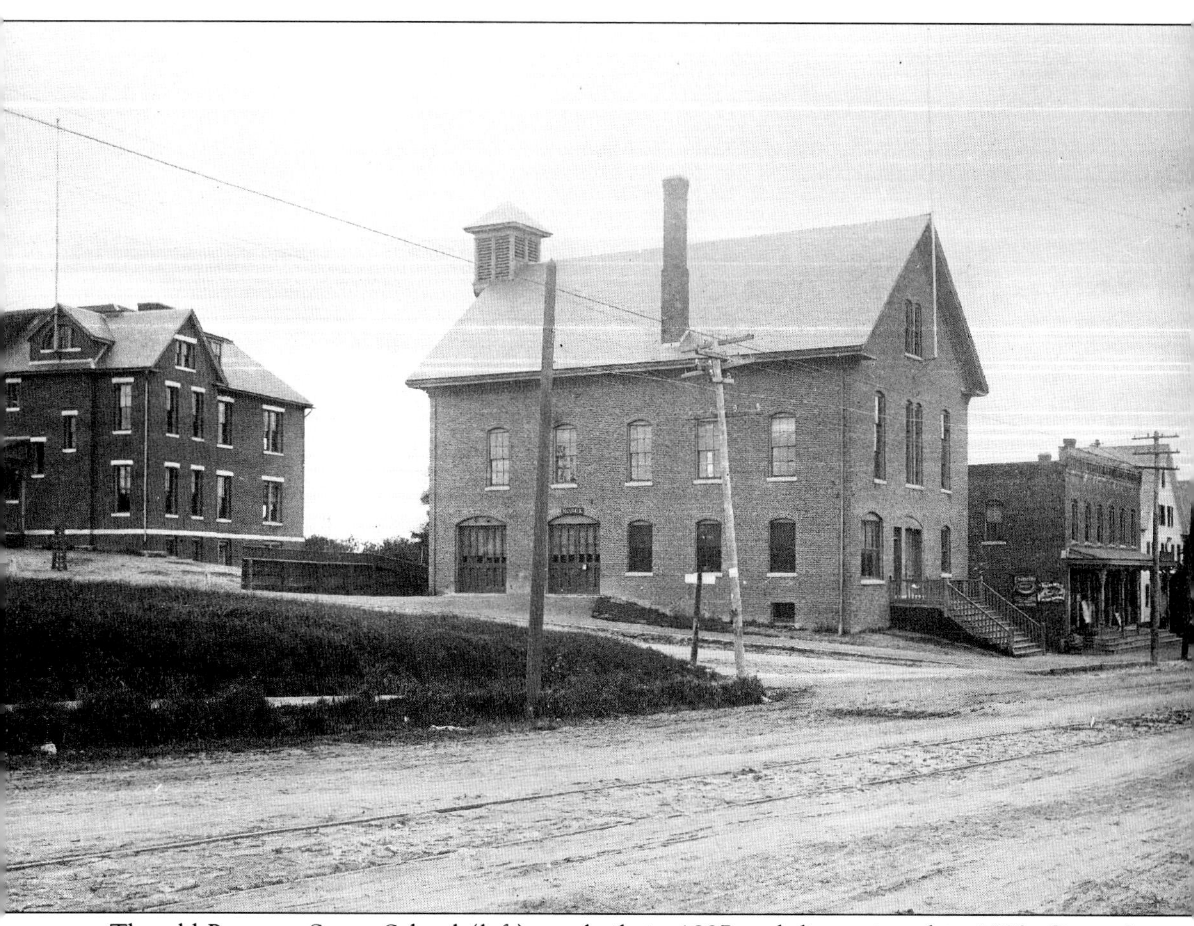

The old Prospect Street School (left) was built in 1887 and discontinued in 1923. Citizen's Hall was built in 1881 to provide an engine house for the fire department as well as a suitable hall for public use. The town appropriated $4,000 and citizens of the village raised $3,000 by subscription. The hall on the second floor had a capacity of 450. The basement held a lockup plus storage space. The building was torn down in 1934.

B. D. C.

There will be a

VARIETY ENTERTAINMENT!

—AT—

CITIZEN'S HALL,

SOUTH GARDNER,

SATURDAY EVENING, MAY 15th '86.

Under the Auspices of the

BOY'S DRAMATIC CLUB.

COME ONE! COME ALL!

ADMISSION, 10 cts. CHRILDREN UNDER 12, 5 cts.

NO RESERVED SEATS.

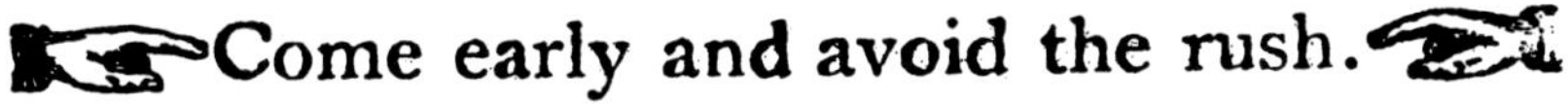

The Proceeds to go for the benefit of an Asylum for hypocrites.

DOORS OPEN AT 7-30. COMMENCES AT 8.

REMEMBER THE DATE.

W.H. TRAVERS, Job Printer.

A broadside illustrates one of the many entertainments that were staged at Citizen's Hall.

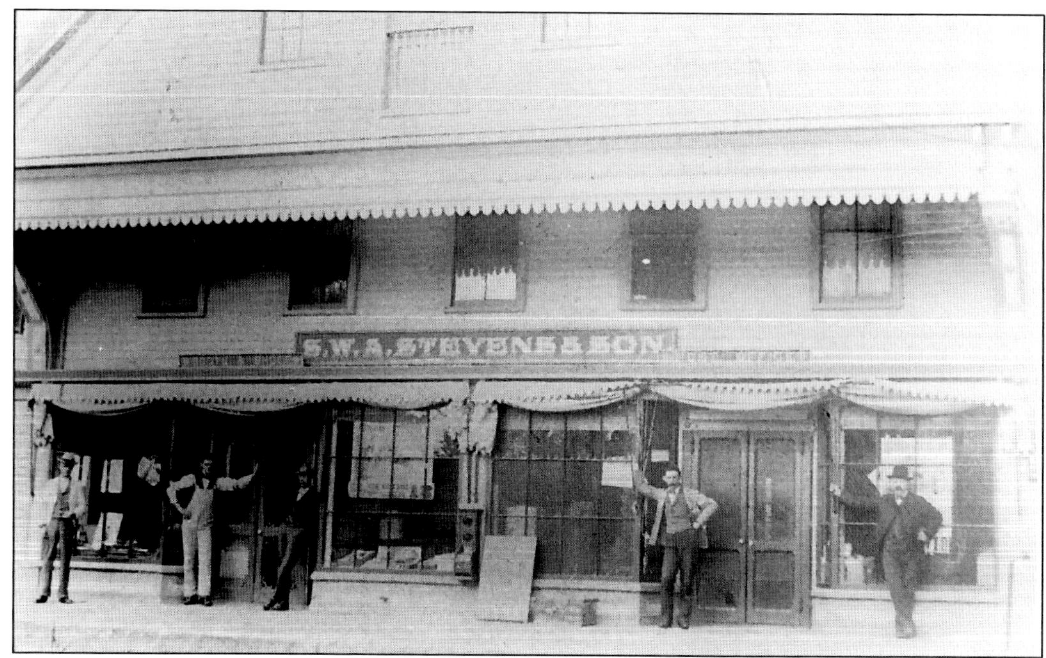

The S.W.A. Stevens & Son Store. The building was erected about 1825 by Captain Henry Whitney and occupied by Clement Jewett, Gardner's first postmaster, who operated it as a country store. Simeon Willard Ambrose Stevens became involved in the business 1850. In 1868 he became sole proprietor of the establishment. Simeon was appointed postmaster in 1854 under the administration of Franklin Pierce. The business at the corner of Chelsea and East Broadway was thriving after World War I and at present is the headquarters of the Gardner DAV.

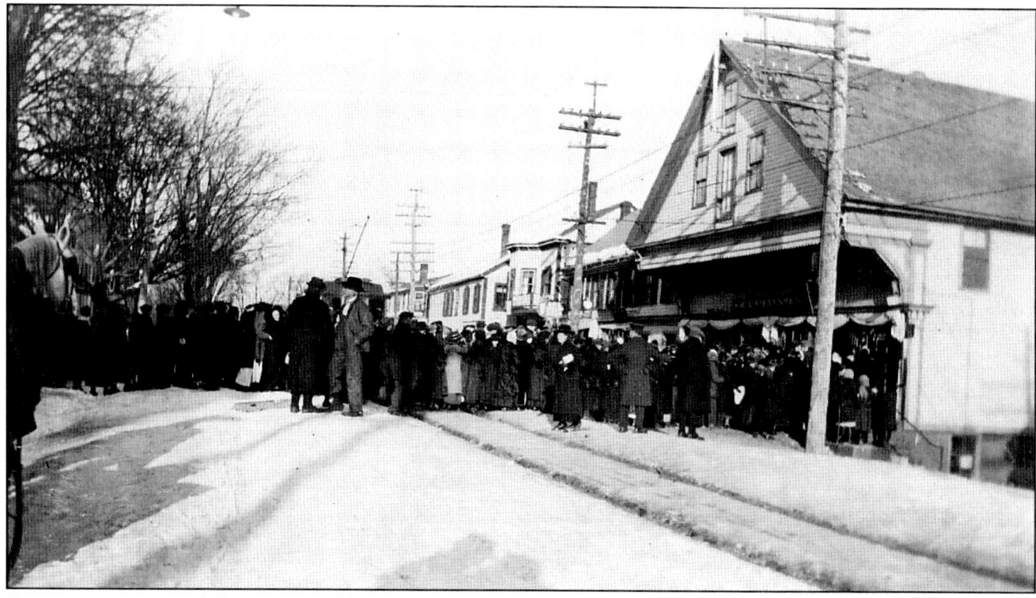

Sugar was rationed during World War I. Inhabitants were allowed a coupon for a certain amount of sugar at the local grocery store. Here we see them lined up outside S.W.A. Stevens' store. Note the rolled snow and dug-out trolley line.

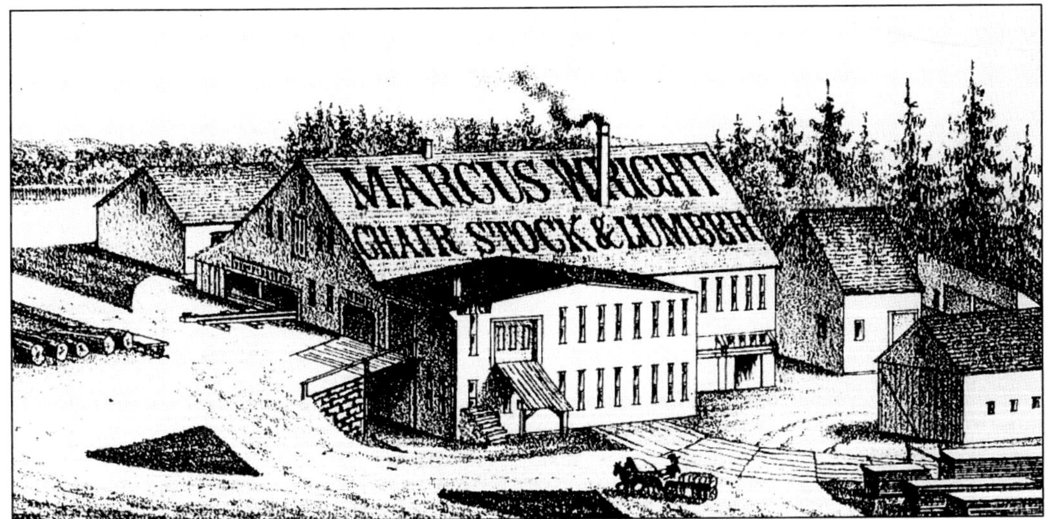

The M. Wright Saw Mill, located on the site of the first Jonathan Greenwood sawmill. Later this was the site of the famous Arcadia Ballroom. It was located by the present South Gardner flood control dam on Wright's reservoir off High Street.

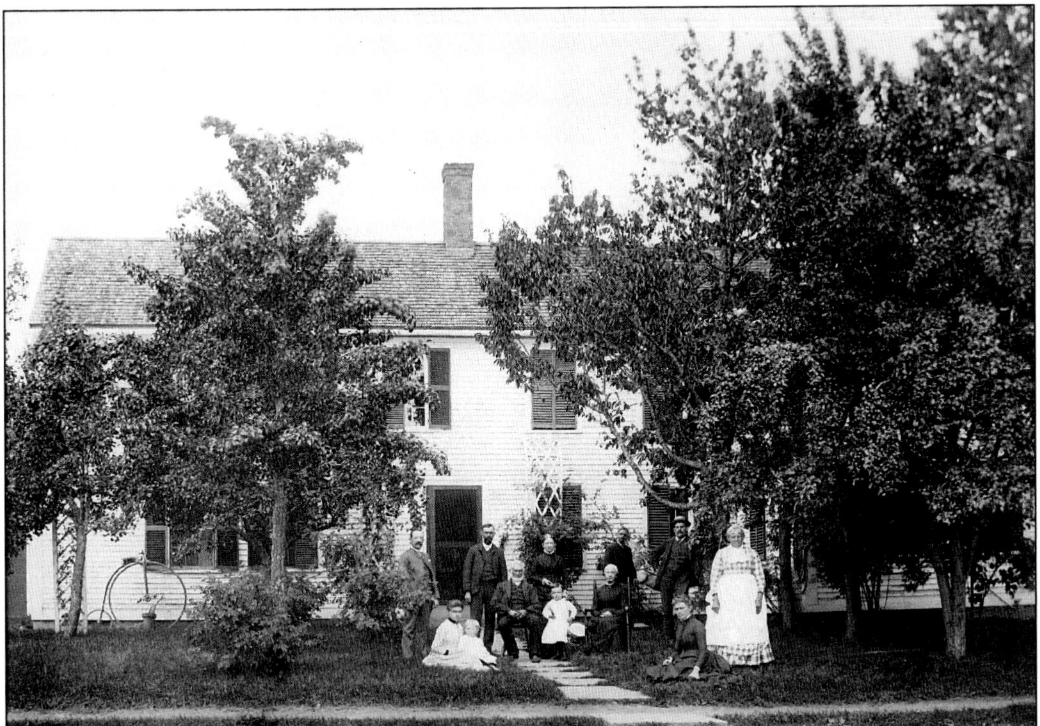

The house standing at the corner of High and Charles Streets was the home of Calvin S. Greenwood and David Wright, proprietors of the Greenwood and Wright Chair Shop. The house is on the 1855 pictorial map of Gardner. Pictured, from left to right, are: (front) Gertrude Read Knowlton, Mildred Ames, David Wright, Stanley Knowlton, Mrs. D. Wright, Nellie Ames, and a maid; (back) Jerome Ames, Charles C. Read, Mrs. C.C. Read, Charles F. Read, and Alex Knowlton.

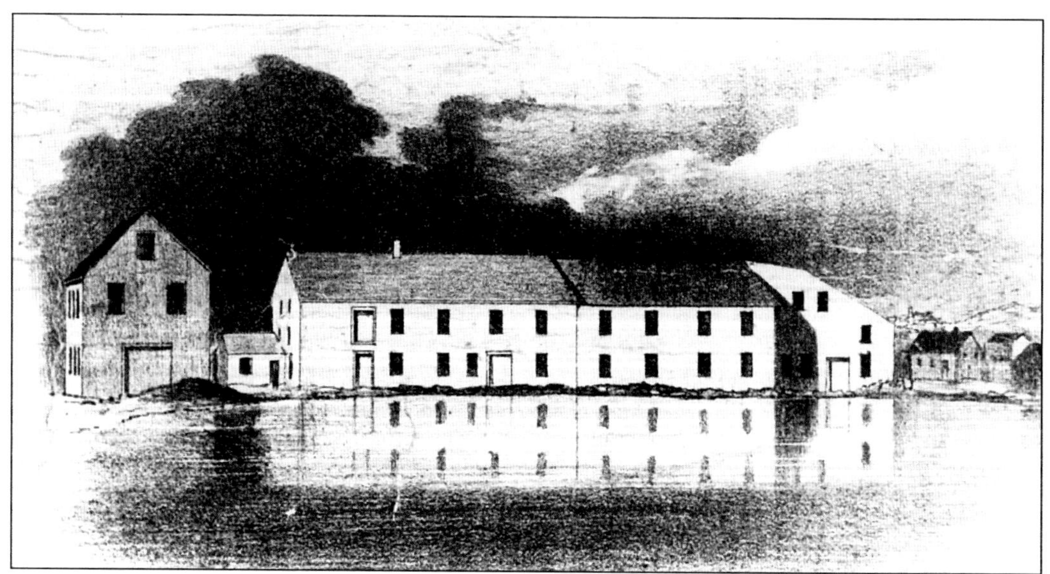

Greenwood and Wright's upper shop, established in 1837 by David Wright and Calvin S. Greenwood, sits directly across East Broadway from the First Baptist Church. The building was later occupied by E.H. Mahoney's Chair Shop, still later by the Thayer Furniture Corporation, and most recently by the Data Cable Guide Company.

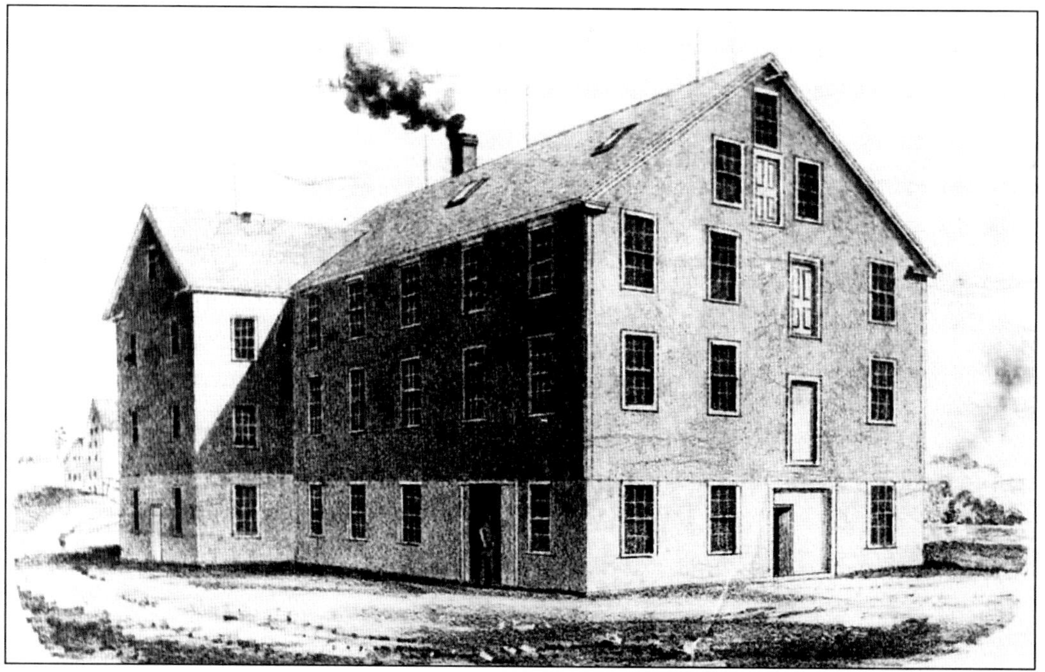

Greenwood and Wright's lower shop was located on the east side of Chelsea Street where Modern Contract furniture is presently situated. It was originally a nail-making operation in 1808. About 1829 Colonel Ephraim Williams operated a fulling and carding mill here. The next operation on the site was chair stock and furniture manufacturing. This was followed by Wright and Moore, Wright and Read, and many others.

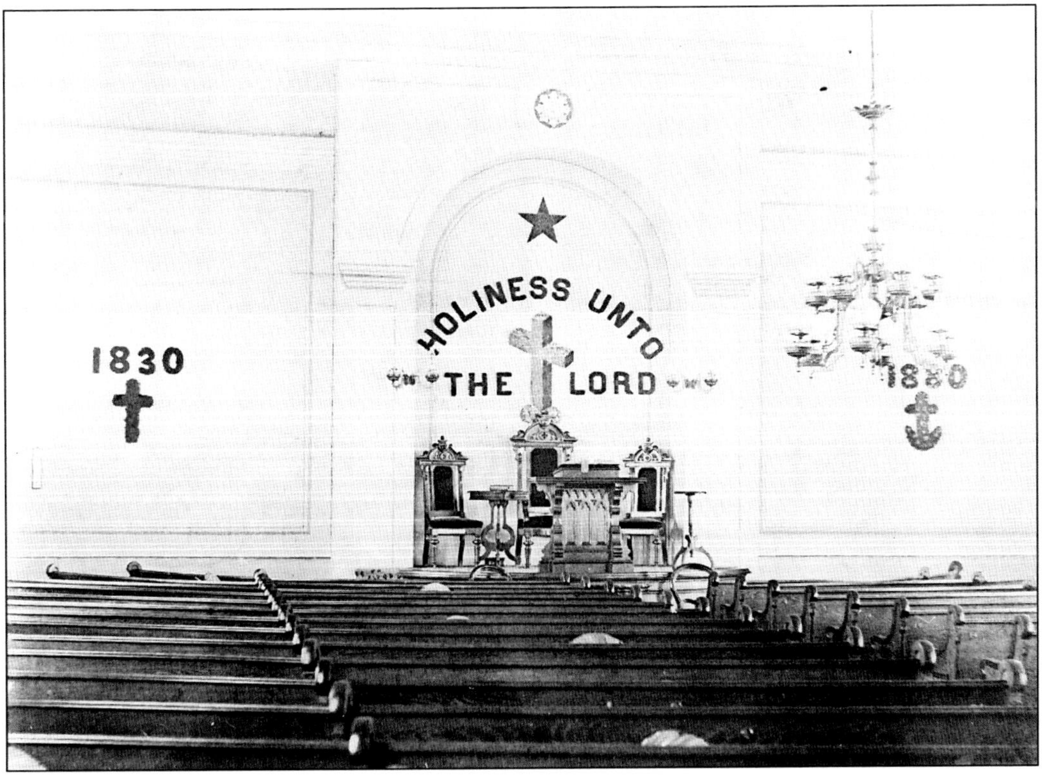

The interior of the First Baptist Church as it was decorated for its 50th anniversary. The church was organized in 1830 at the house of Sullivan Jackson. At this time hymns were lined and accompanied by a bass violin.

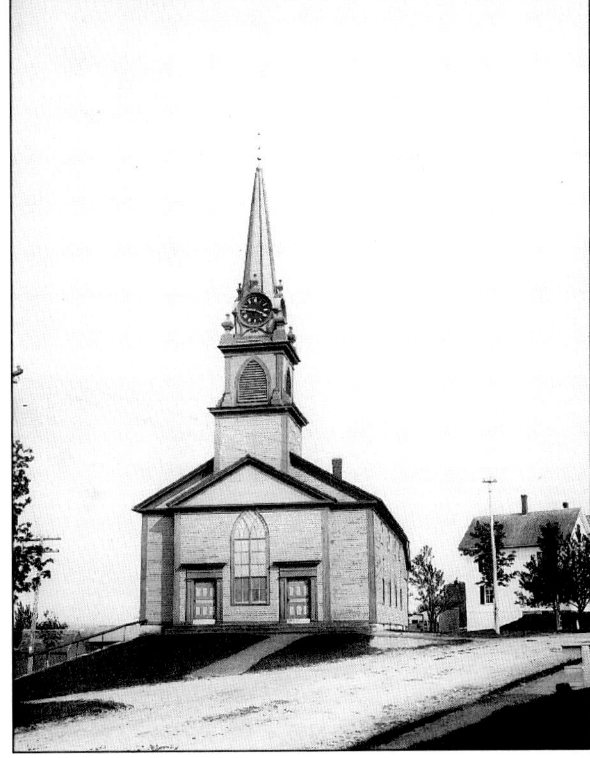

The exterior of the First Baptist Church as it looked after extensive renovation in 1872. Note the two doors entering into the vestibule.

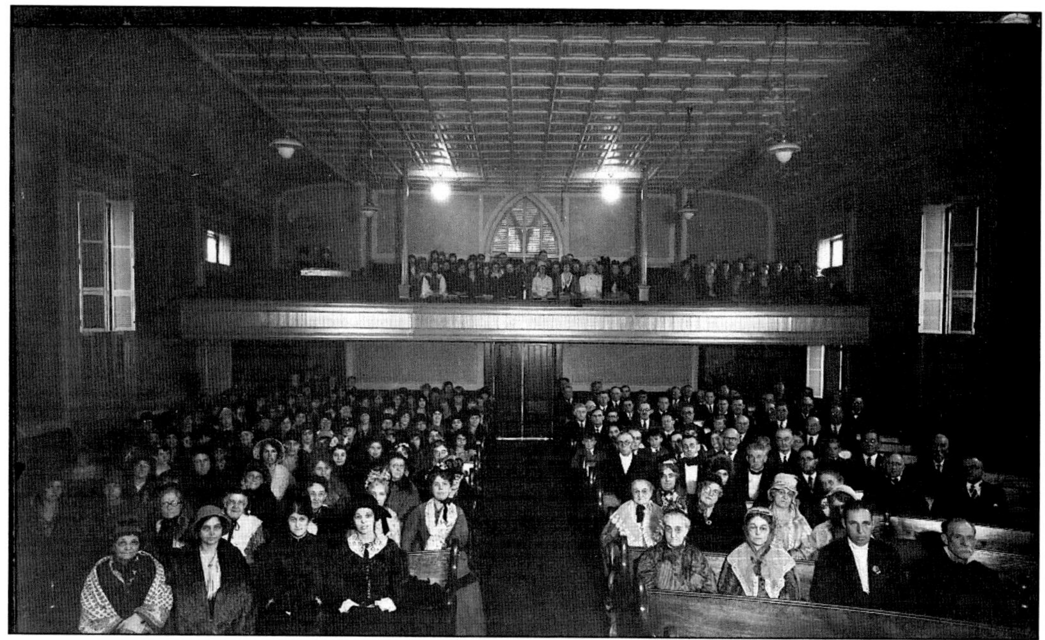

The members of the First Baptist Church, dressed in period costumes to commemorate the 100th anniversary of the founding of the church, in 1930.

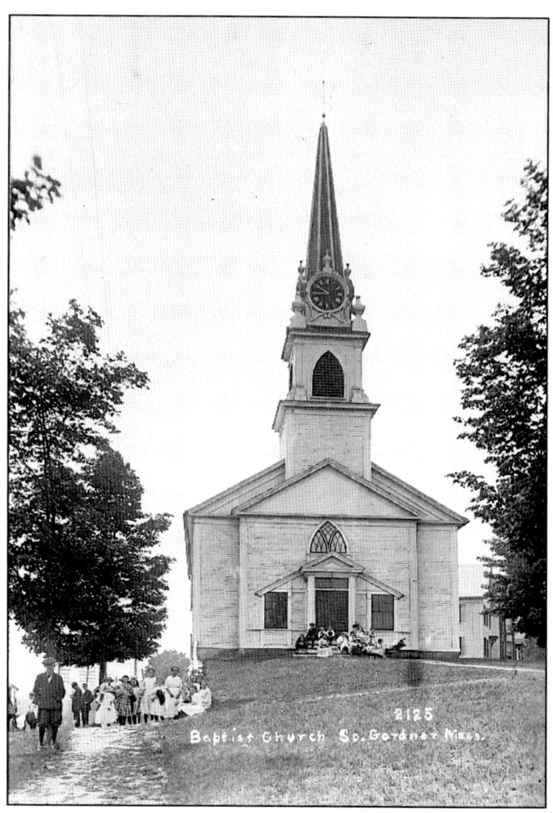

The exterior of the First Baptist Church much as it looks today with the single entrance. A Sunday school class is waiting for a trolley of the Gardner, Westminster, and Fitchburg Street Railway to take them to Whalom Park, for a Sabbath day picnic.

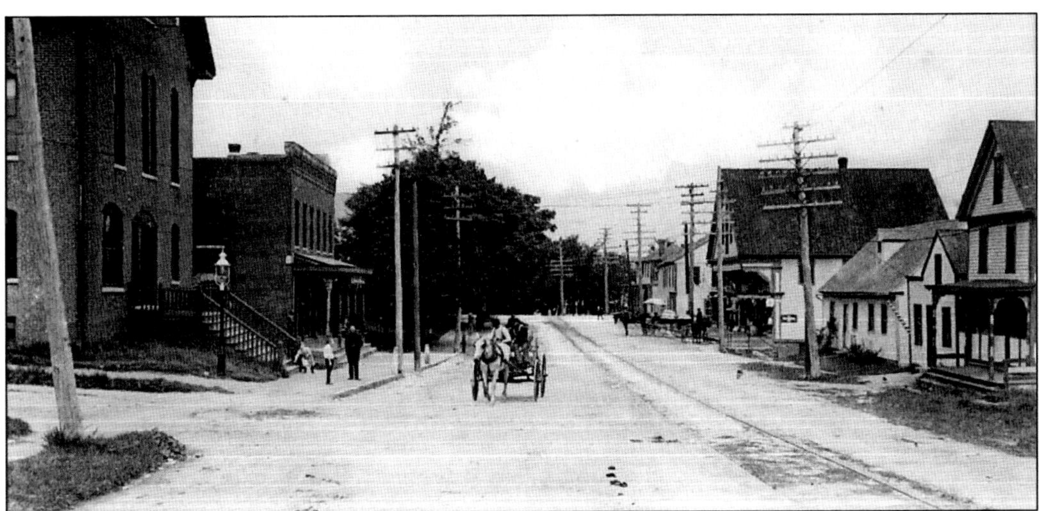

South Gardner Square, looking west on East Broadway. Citizen's Hall and N. Alzingre's store are on the left. On the right are two houses followed by a building, part of which was the old toll house when this was a toll road. The toll house was on the opposite side of the road. Beyond this is the S.W.A. Stevens Store.

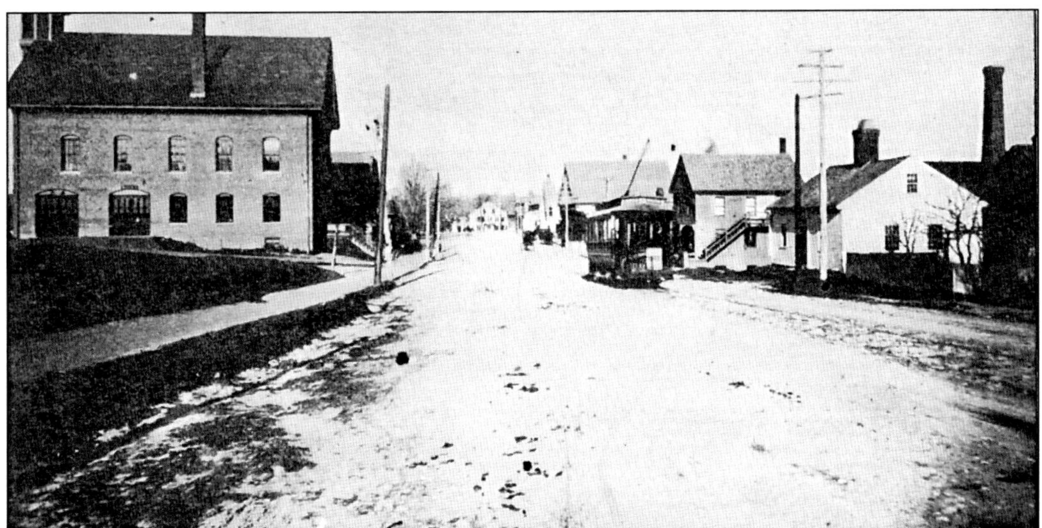

Citizen's Hall, with the doors to the section used by the fire department visible on the left. The trolley is passing through South Gardner on its way to Westminster, Fitchburg, or perhaps Wachusett Park.

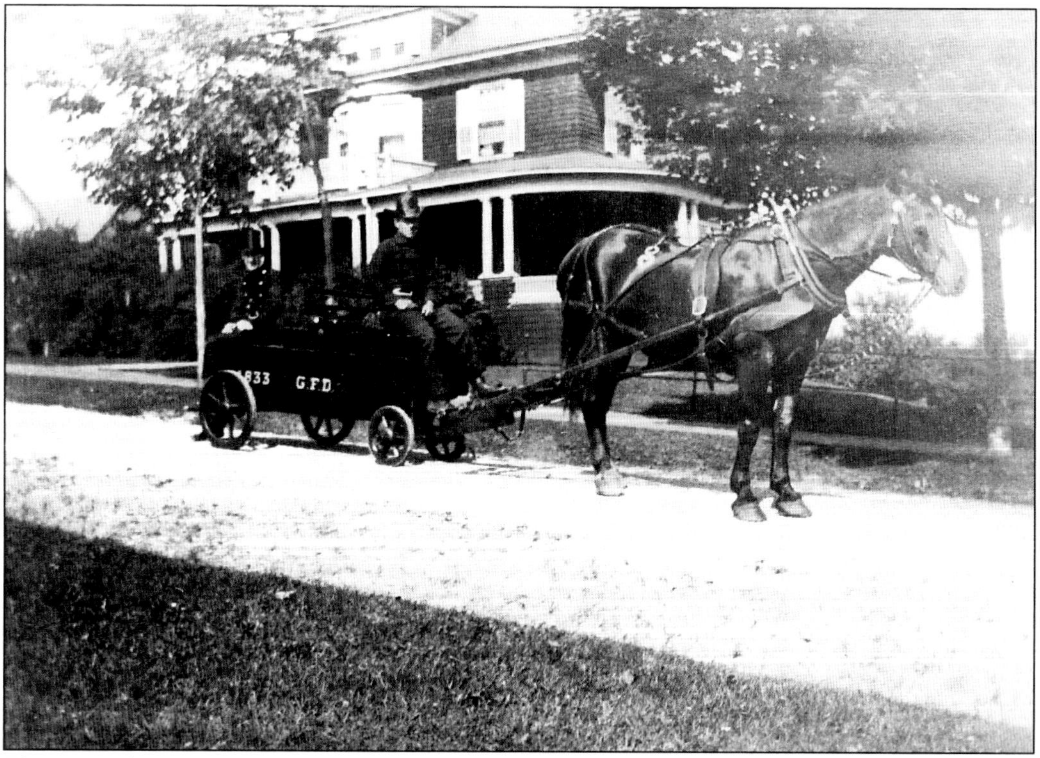

The Pine Plug, a rotary tub purchased for the town of Gardner in 1833 by Abijah M. Severy, Walter Greenwood, and Adam Partridge, was one of two similar machines purchased at that time. The Pine Plug was stationed in South Gardner; the other machine was placed in Gardner Centre. Gardner is fortunate to still possess the Pine Plug.

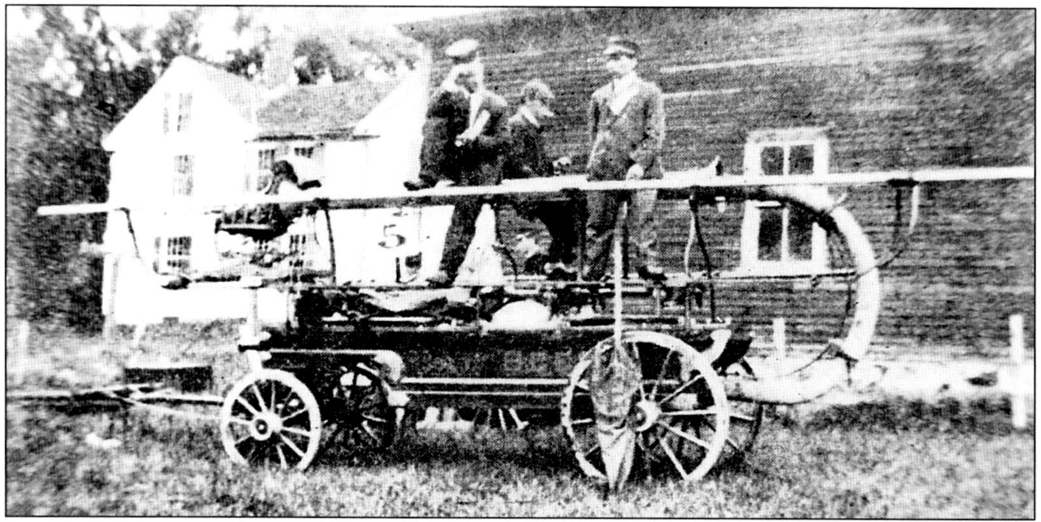

The Baw Beese Pumper was built by the Button & Co. in 1857. The engine was named for a chief of the Pottawattamic tribe. In 1878 the Baw Beese was purchased in Jackson, New York, by C.O. Bent, for use as a sporting engine. In 1895 the engine was the champion of New England, with a hosing distance of 230 feet, 9-1/2 inches. In 1918 the Baw Beese was sold to Quincy, Massachusetts.

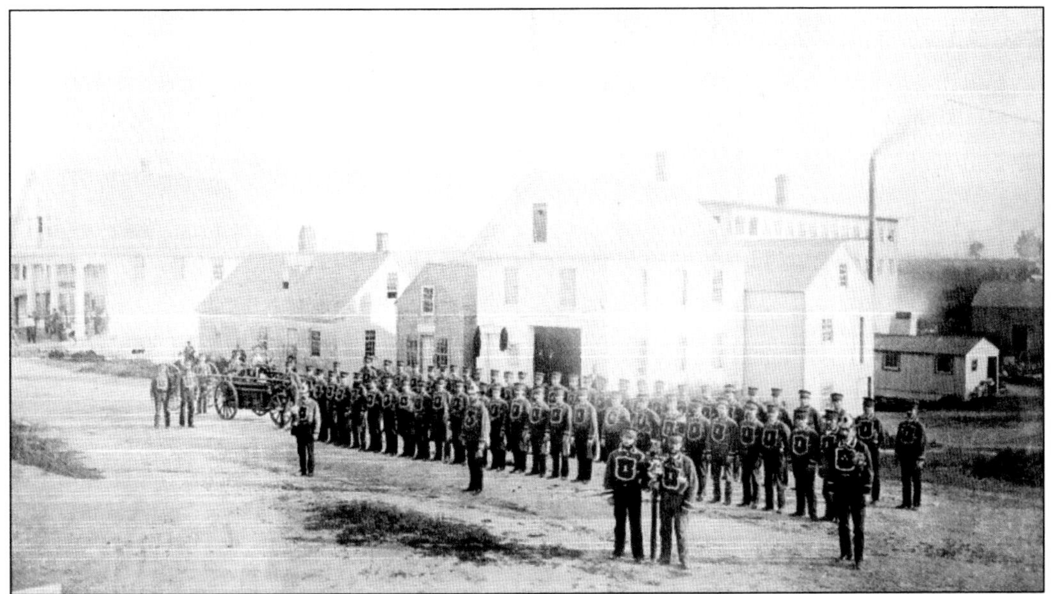

Cataract Company No. 1 stands with their machine in front of the old engine house on East Broadway, across from the present fire station. The Union Hall was located on the second floor of the engine house. The Cataract was purchased in 1852. Behind the station is the Wright and Read chair factory. To left is a dwelling house, a part of which was a toll house on the 5th Massachusetts Turnpike. On the far left is the store and post office of S.W.A. Stevens.

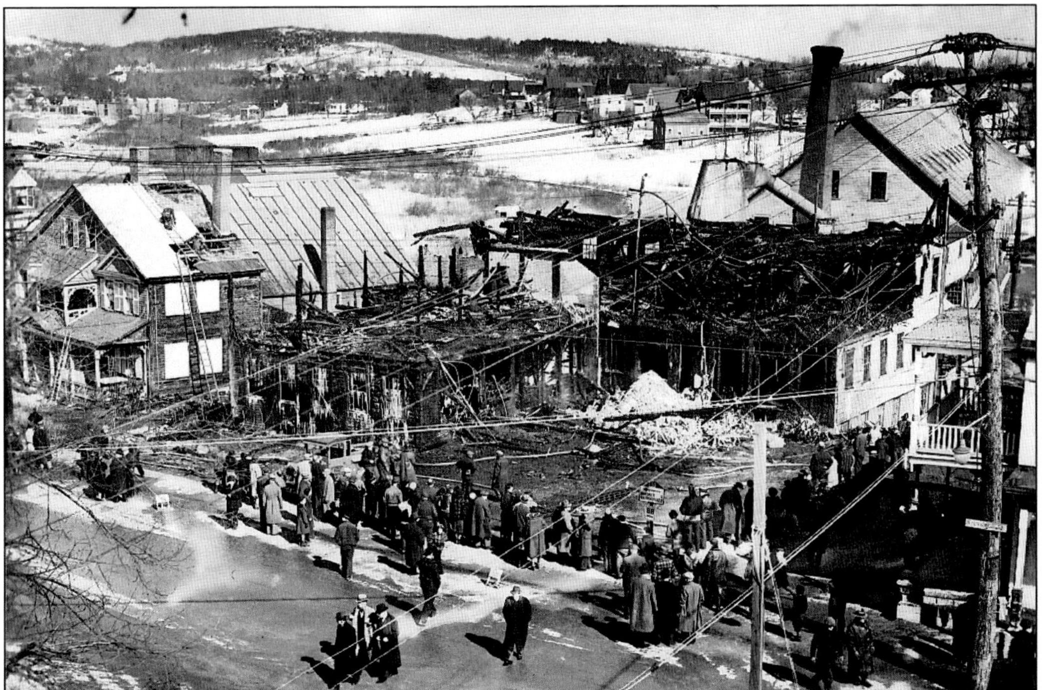

The old S.K. Pierce factory used by the Greenwood-Carlton Corp. burned on February 25, 1938. The property loss was $100,000. The intense heat cracked the plate glass window in Fowler's Drug Store across the street.

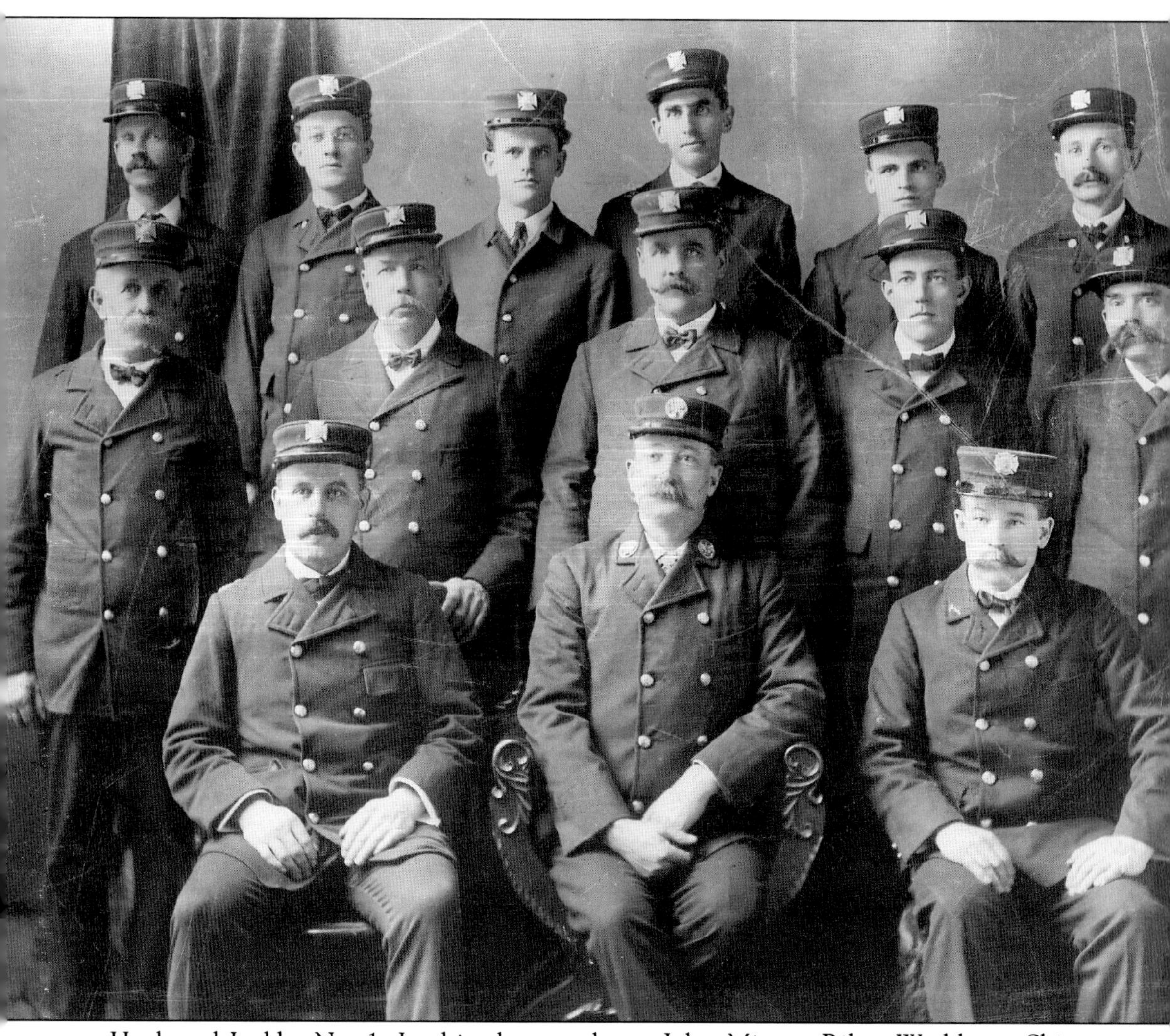

Hook and Ladder No. 1. In this photograph are John Minott, Riley, Washburn, Shippee, Richards, unknown, Wheeler, unknown, Seaver, C. Gordon, G. Gordon, Timpany, Chief Fowler, and Fairbanks.

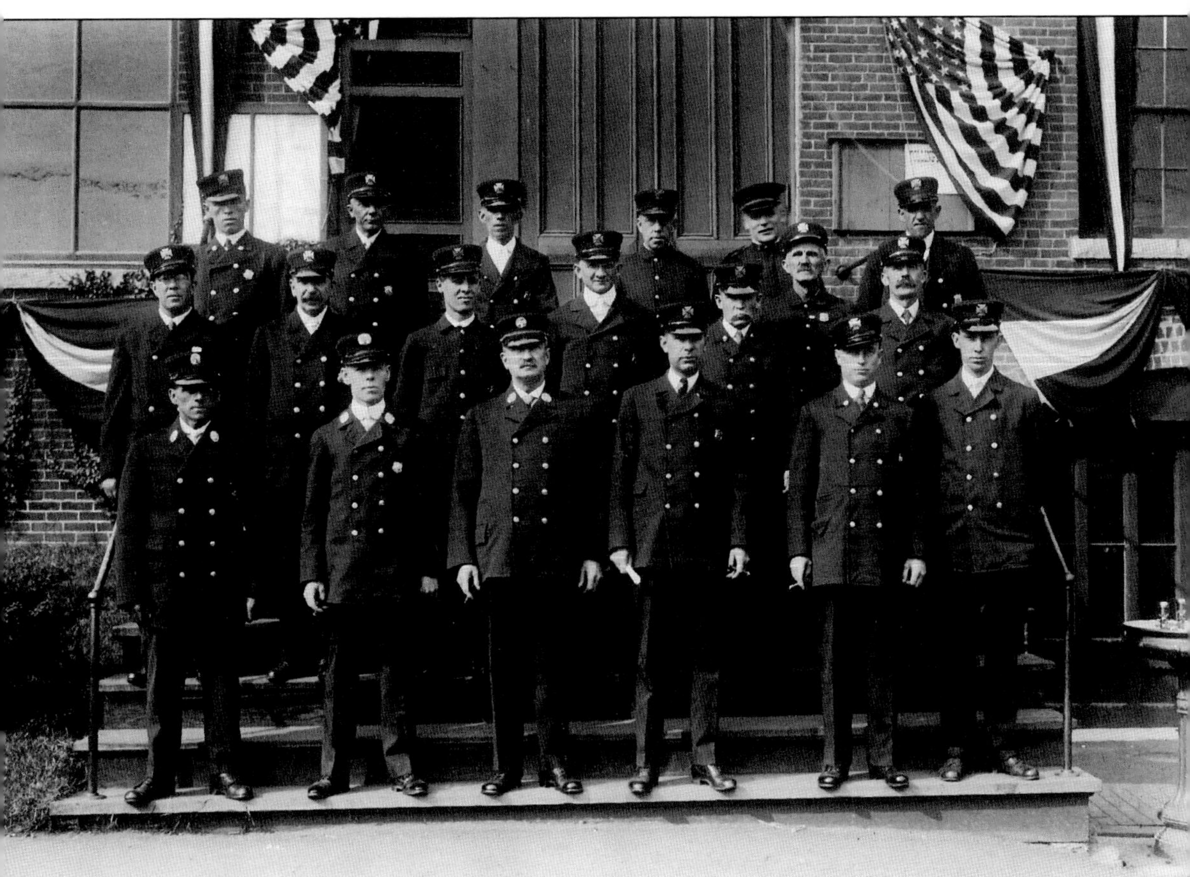

Hose Company No. 1. Pictured are McInerny, Smith, G. Fisher, Waite, Richards, L. Fisher, Cote, Fales, Morley, Holt, Fairbanks, Buckwold, Glendenning, H. Fisher, Hines, Chief Fowler, Martin, A. Fairbanks, and Huckins.

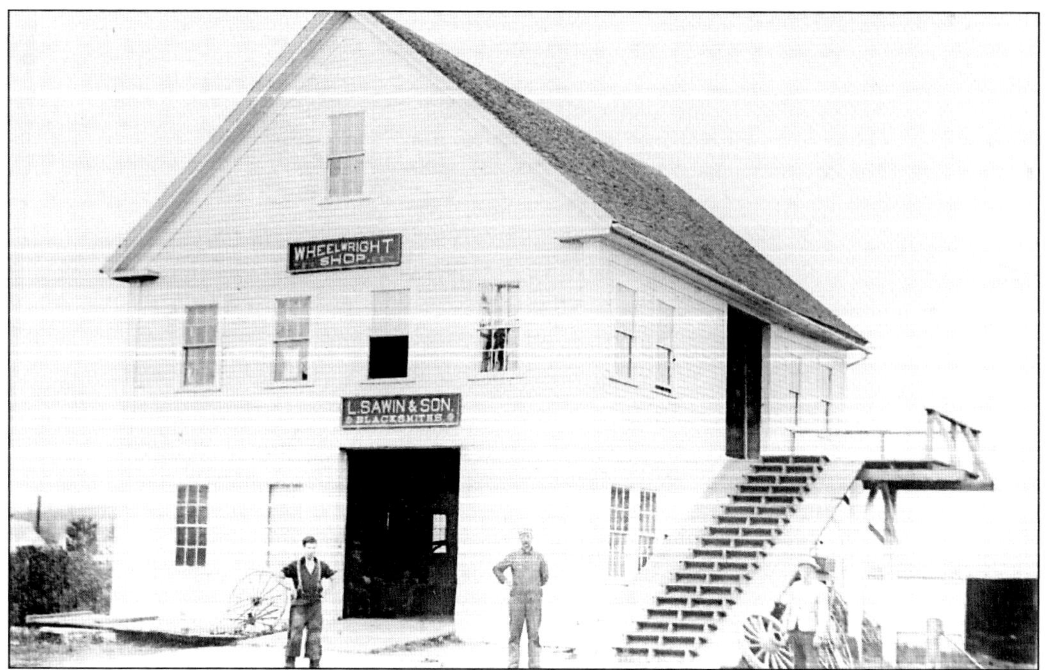

L. Sawin and Son, located on 129 South Main Street. From left to right are Lucius French, Eugene Saunders (blacksmith), and Lyman Sawin (proprietor). Several businesses were carried on in this building, including that of a blacksmith, a wheelwright, and a carriage manufacturer. Albert H. Barron ran a carriage-painting shop (the South Gardner Carriage Company) on the second floor. Pulley blocks hauled carriages up the ramp to his business. The company built a snow roller for the town in 1894. The 3,000-pound roller required 6 horses to pull it.

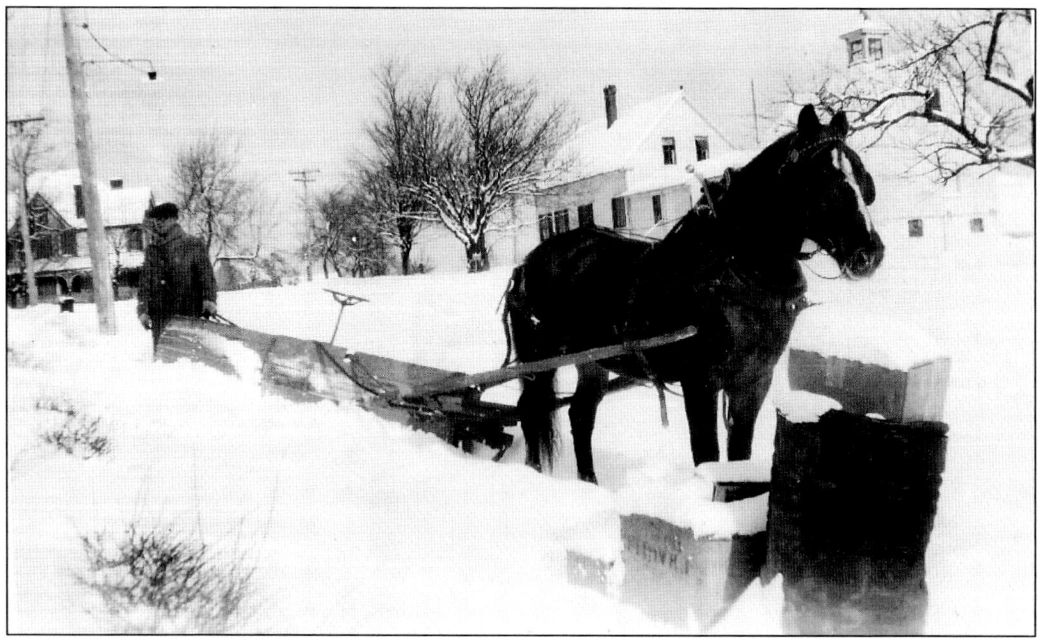

A horse-drawn sidewalk plow at work plowing the sidewalks on Prospect Street. The driver was Mike Bowker; the horse was either Barbara or Eva.

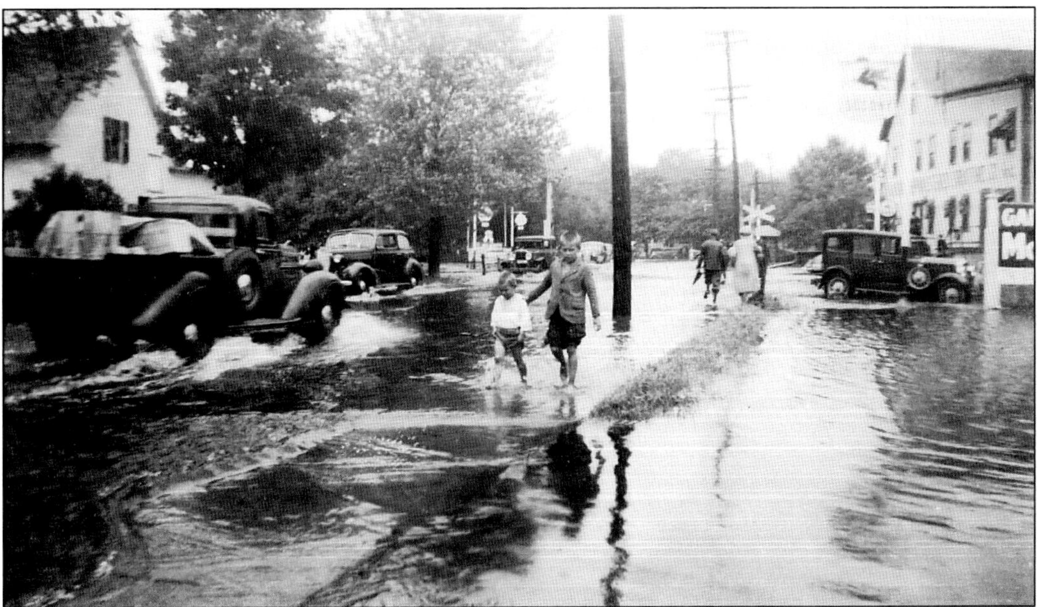

Flooding caused by the Hurricane of September 1938 on South Main Street at the Denney Manufacturing Company, near the junction of Kendall, Travers, and South Main Streets.

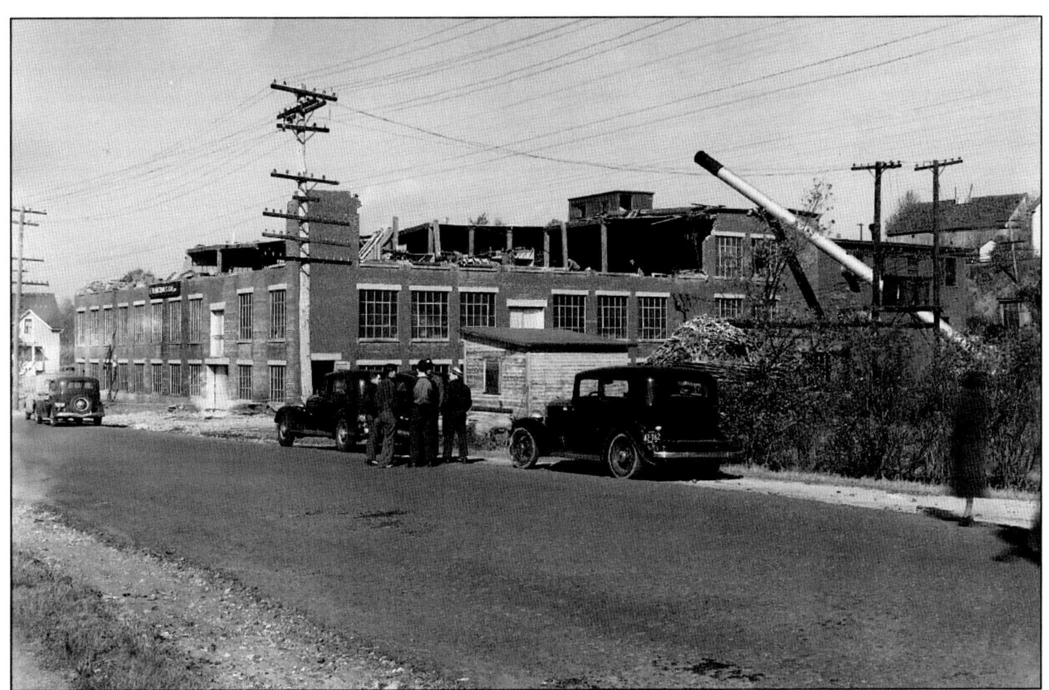

Damage done by the Hurricane of 1938 to the F.A. Nichols plant, West Broadway.

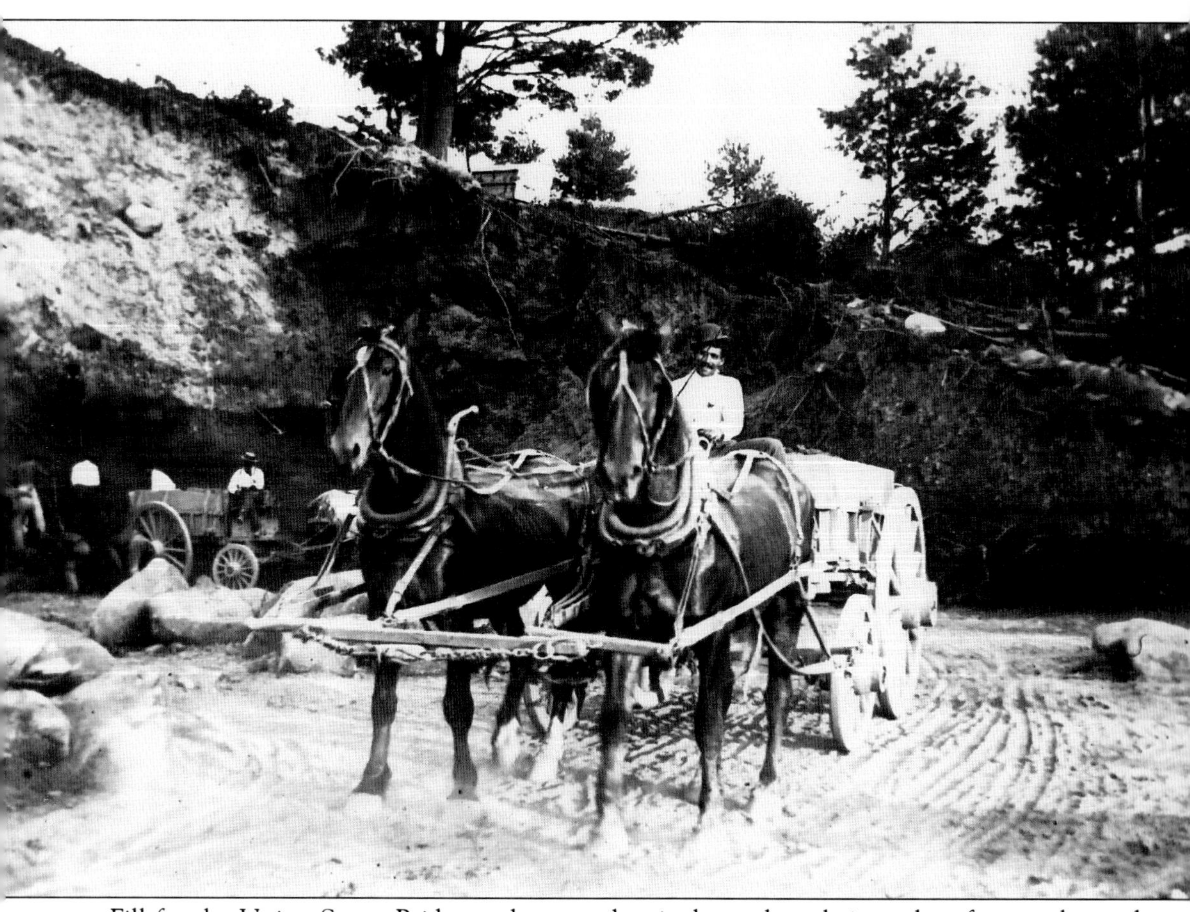

Fill for the Union Street Bridge and approaches is shown here being taken from a clay and gravel bank in 1900. The scene is a side hill about 100 yards south of the bridge, off the present Clairmont Street. Originally a grade crossing of the Boston, Barre, and Gardner Railroad set the scene near the junction of Union Street and the old Hubbardston Road.

Two

Gardner Centre: Uptown

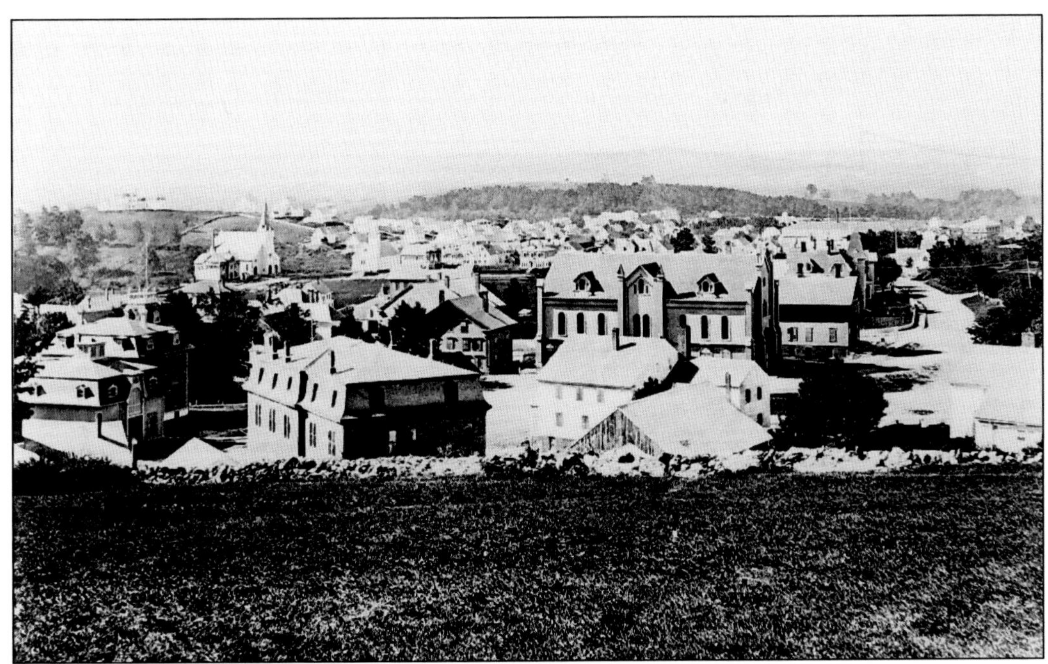

A view from Reservoir Hill looking down into Gardner Centre. This views shows the Town Hall (right center), Caswell's Block (right, next to the Town Hall), and Central Street.

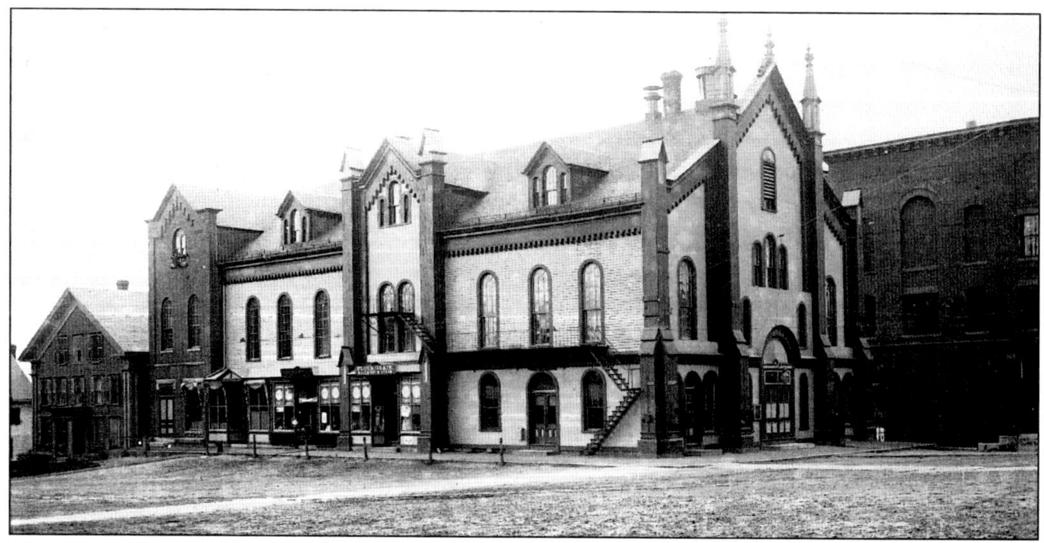

The Town/City Hall was built in 1859–60 and occupied the corner of Central and Elm Streets. The Heywood house, which originally stood here, where the Heywood brothers first began their chair business, was moved down Elm to number 13. A brick addition was added to the building in 1883. The interior contained an upper and lower hall, at which many functions were held. The building burned down on August 28, 1944.

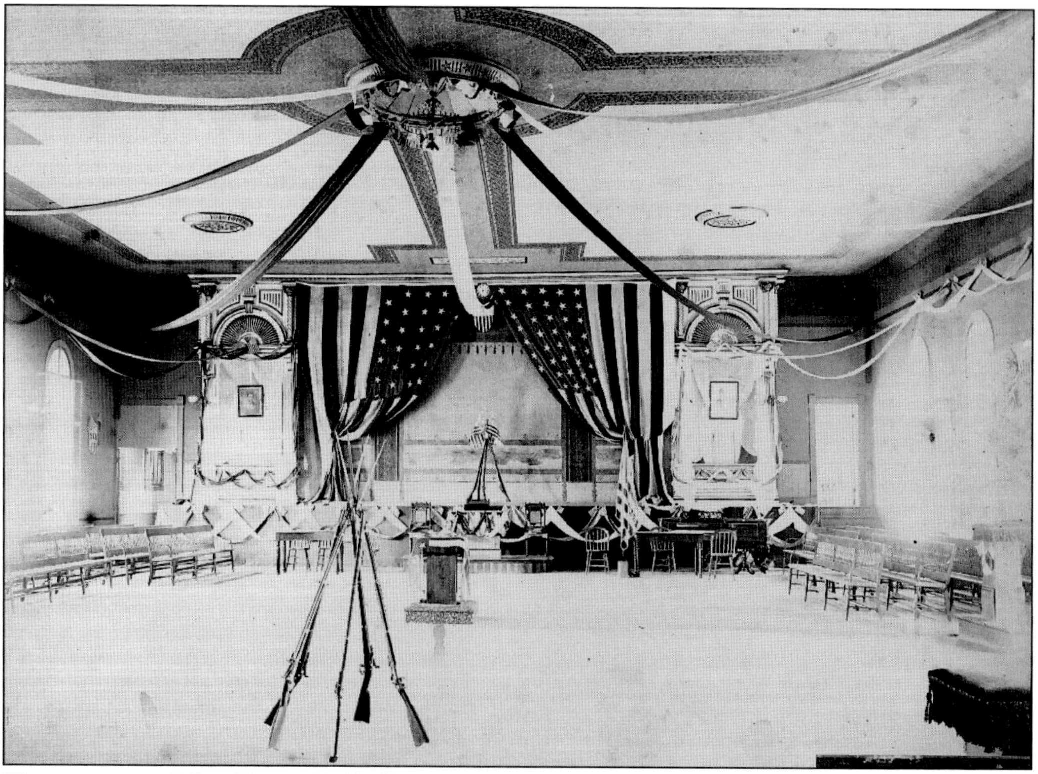

The interior of the Town Hall illustrating one of the many functions that were held in the building. It was used as the National Guard armory for a short time before and during World War II.

TOWN HALL - GARDNER

FAST DAY EV'G,

April 12, 1877

GRAND INSTRUMENTAL

CONCERT!

BY THE GARDNER

SERENADE BAND

PROGRAMME.

1. Fantasia. (Queen's Messenger.)............. *Godfrey.*
2. Song. ("Only Love can Tell.")............... *Tours.*
3. Andante. Alto Horn Solo................... *Graffula.*
4. Polka. Mazurka.......................... *Ringleben.*
5. Miserere. From Ill Trovatora.................. *Verdi.*
6. Fantasia. On Moody and Sankey's Sacred Songs.
7. Serenade. Song Without Words............... *Drach.*
8. Andante. Peace of Mind................... *Sponholtz.*
9. Galop. "The Boss."................... *Heilbreicht.*

The Town Hall hosted many types of entertainment.

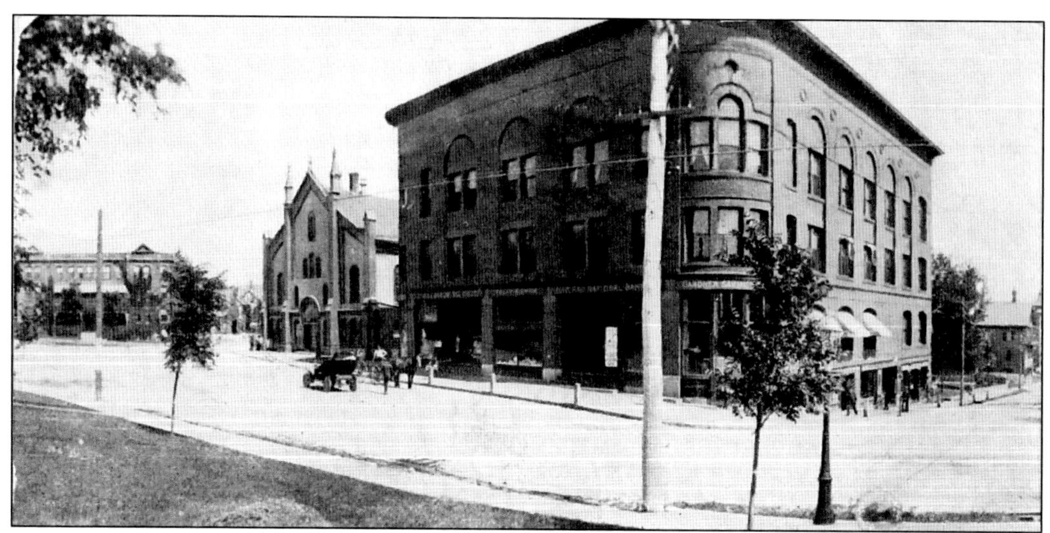

Gardner Centre showing the Syndicate Block, the Town/City Hall, and the Windsor House.

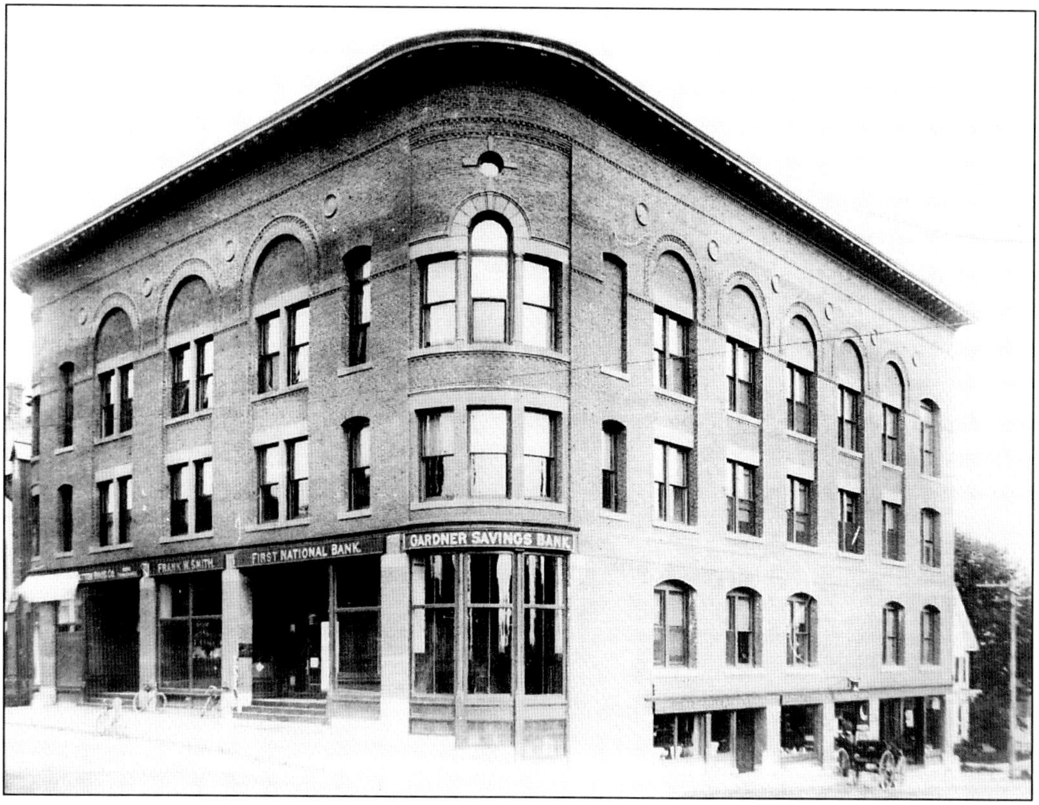

The Syndicate Block was built in 1895–96. It stood on the corner of Central and Chestnut Streets. The Caswell Block was moved down Chestnut Street to make way for this building. During construction one of the walls collapsed. The building was dedicated in October 1896. Among its tenants were the Mason's, the Gardner Boat Club, the F.W. Smith Store, the Gardner Savings Bank, and others. The building burned in May 1982 and lost its upper two floors.

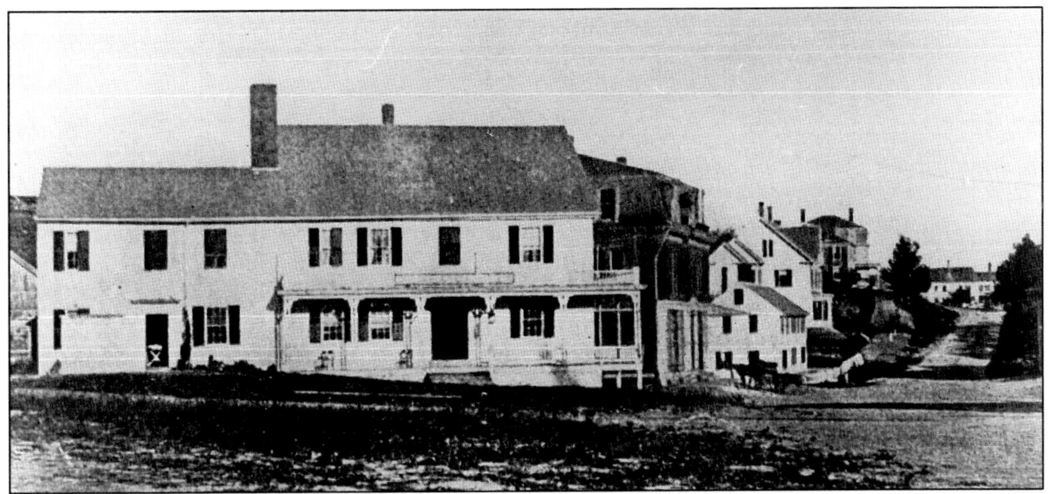

The Central House was located on the corner of Green and Pearl Streets, and it served as the first hotel in Gardner Centre. In 1882 it was purchased by Amos Morrel and moved to 94 Green Street, where it still stands, to make way for the Windsor House.

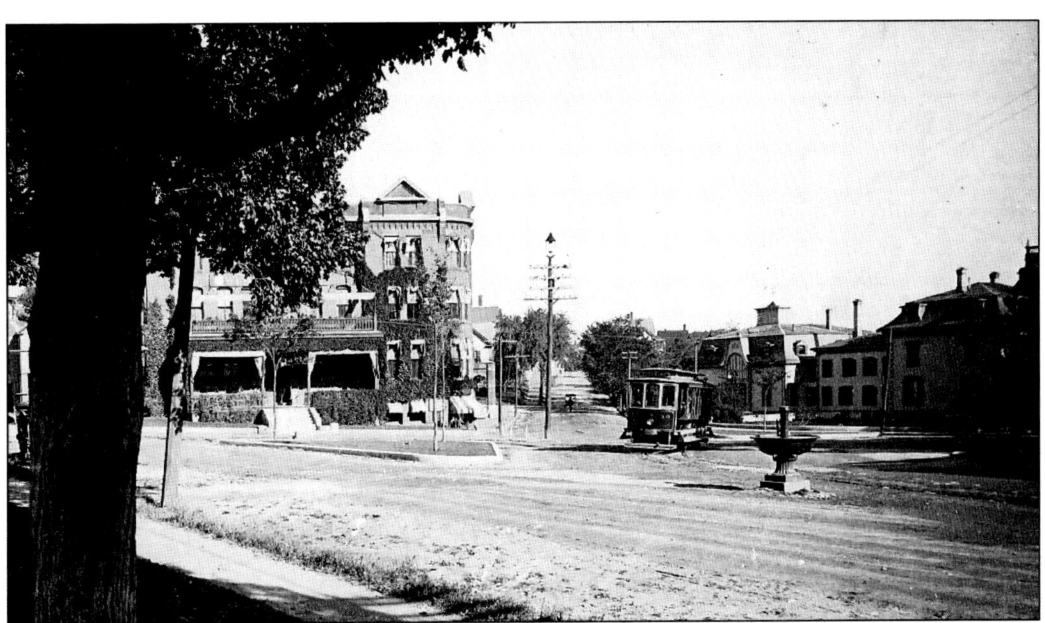

Gardner Centre showing the Windsor House and one of the trolley's going through the square.

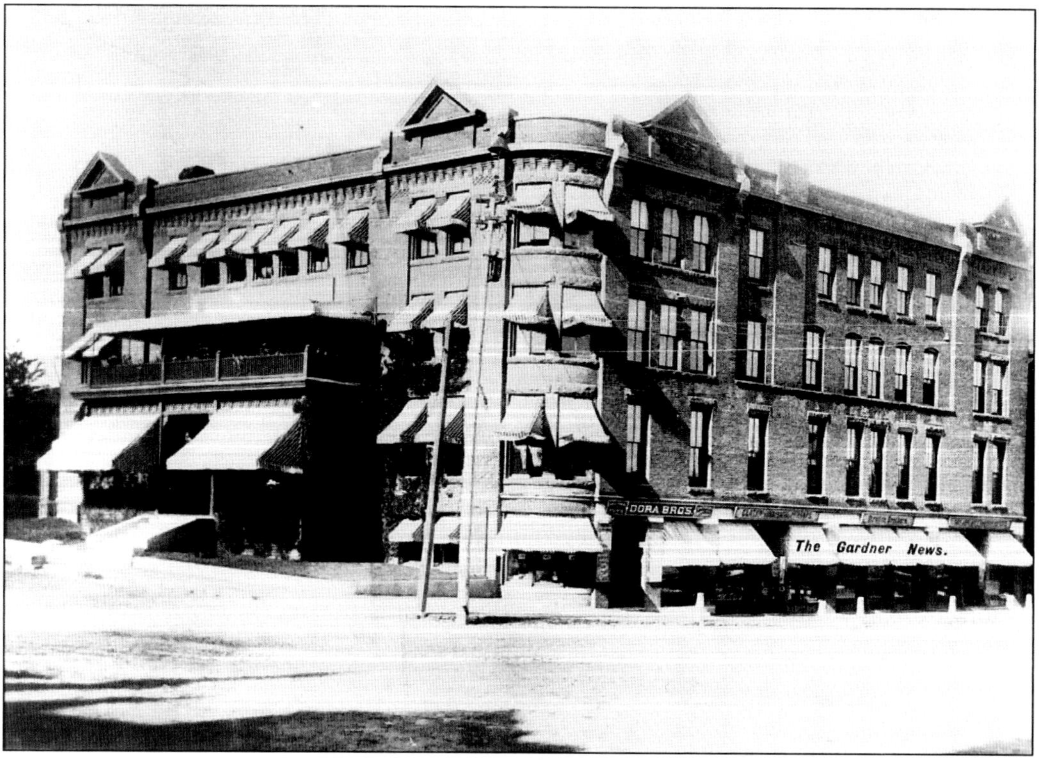

The Windsor House was located on the corner of Green and Pearl Streets. This 100-room hotel was said to be the finest establishment of its kind outside of Boston when it was built in 1882–83. The building burned on March 1, 1917.

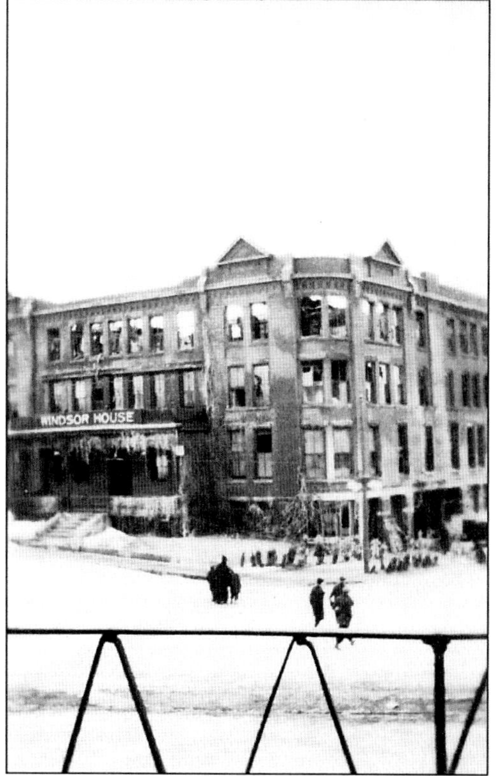

The ruins of the Windsor House after it was destroyed by fire on March 1, 1917. The fire was rung in at 5:55 p.m., and with the help of many people including Ashton Derby, Dr. A.S. Cleaves, and Albert L. Potter, many of the pictures and furnishings of the lobby and dining room were saved. Albert L. Potter saved the flag from the lobby and took it to Mayo's Drug Store.

The Evangelical Congregational Church was situated on Green Street. It was formed when a group of like-minded individuals left the First Congregational Church. This building first served the Evangelical Congregational Church; after the reunion of the two churches, it served them both until 1879, when the new brick structure was completed. The building was subsequently moved to 55-57 Green Street and Volney W. Howe built his home on the spot, 27 Green Street.

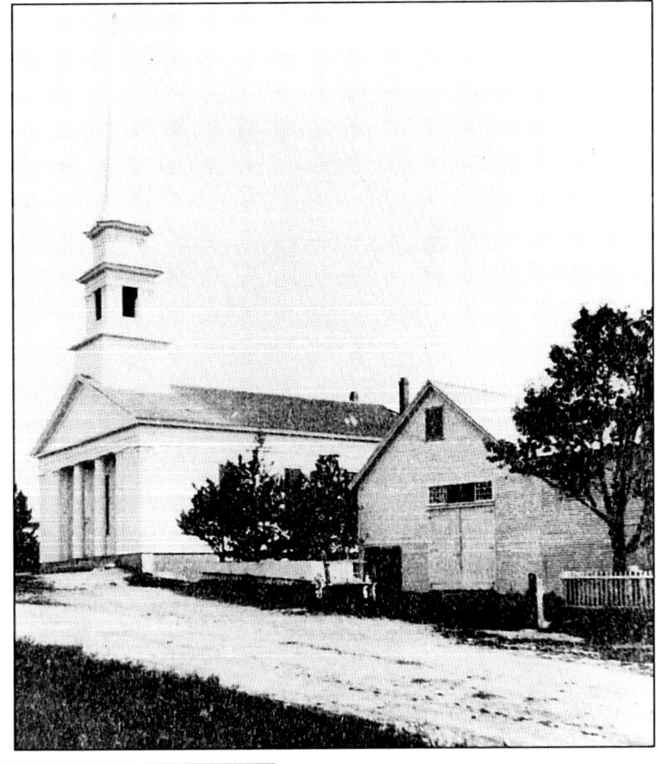

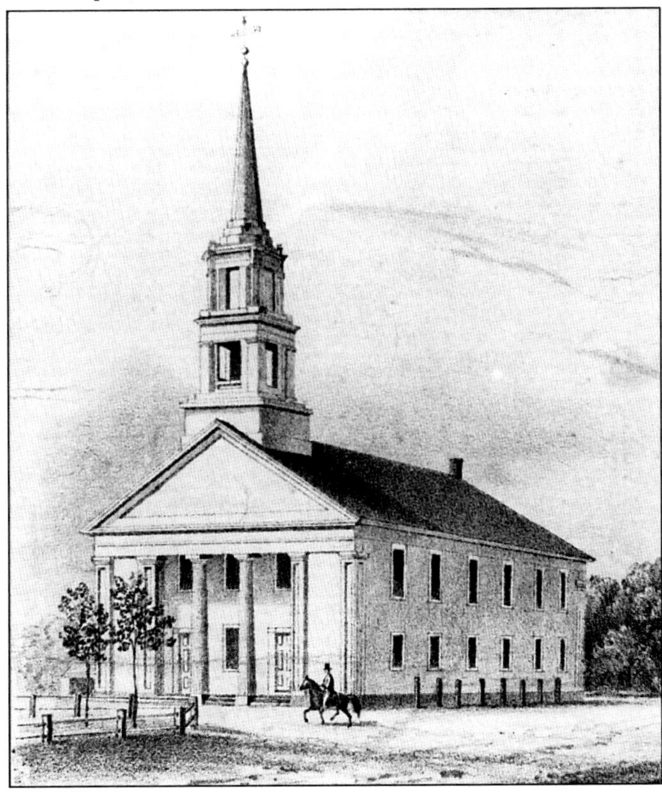

The First Congregational Church was built between 1787 and 1791. From 1791 until 1859 it served both as a church and as a town meeting place. In 1830 a schism took place: one group formed the Evangelical Congregational Church (see above), while the other continued to meet in the First Church. A reconciliation took place in 1868, and the reunited church met in the Evangelical Congregational Church building. A new brick church was completed in 1879. The old church was moved to Chestnut Street, where it was destroyed by fire in 1893.

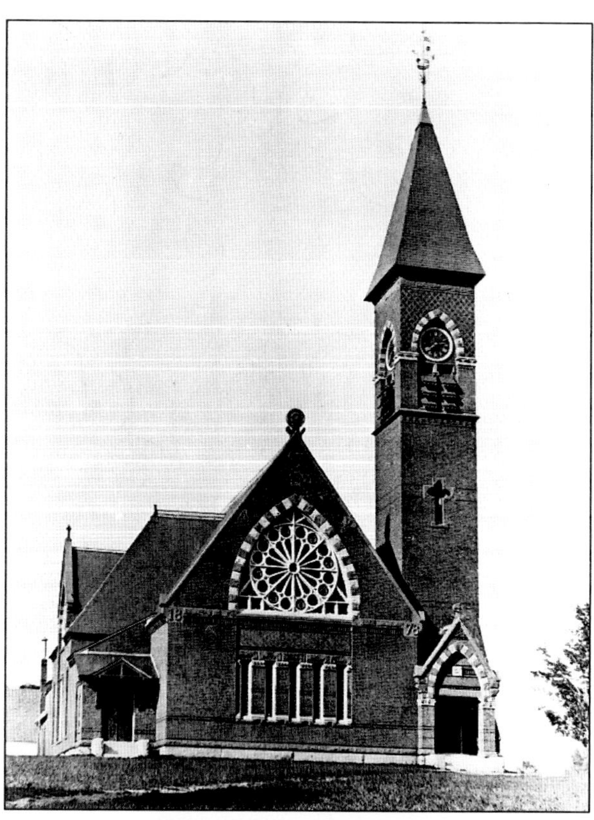

The First Congregational Church was built in 1878–79. The brick structure was designed by Fuller and Delano architects from Worcester. The building, with modifications, stands on Central Street between Green Street and Woodland Avenue.

The interior of the First Congregational Church soon after its completion in 1879.

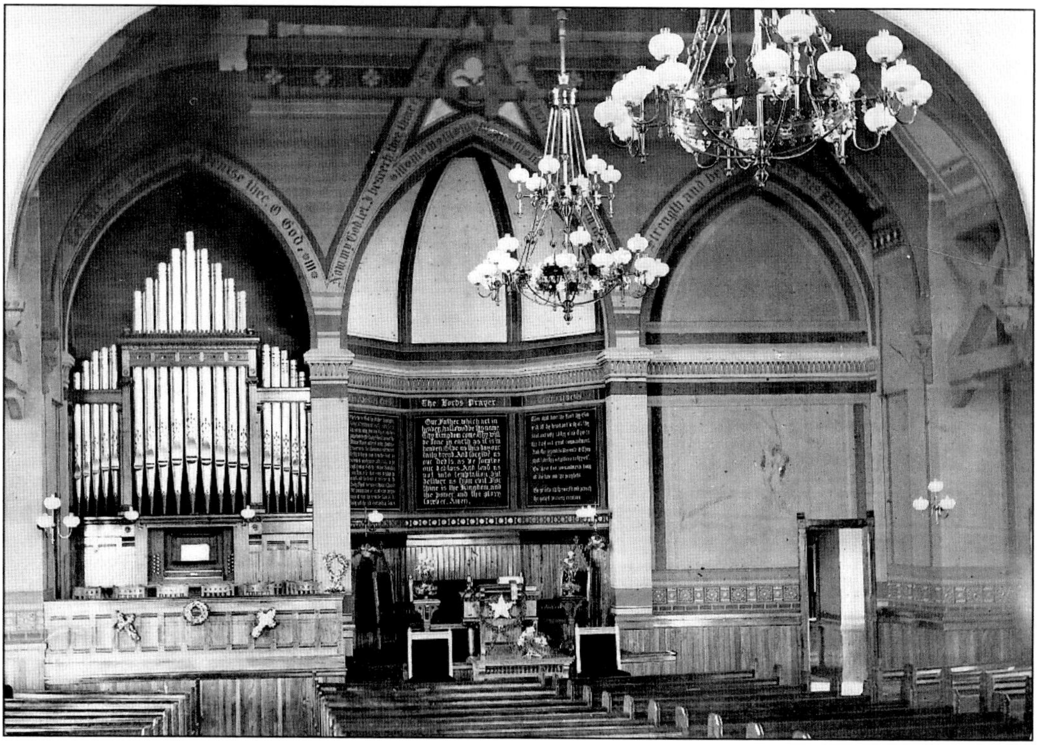

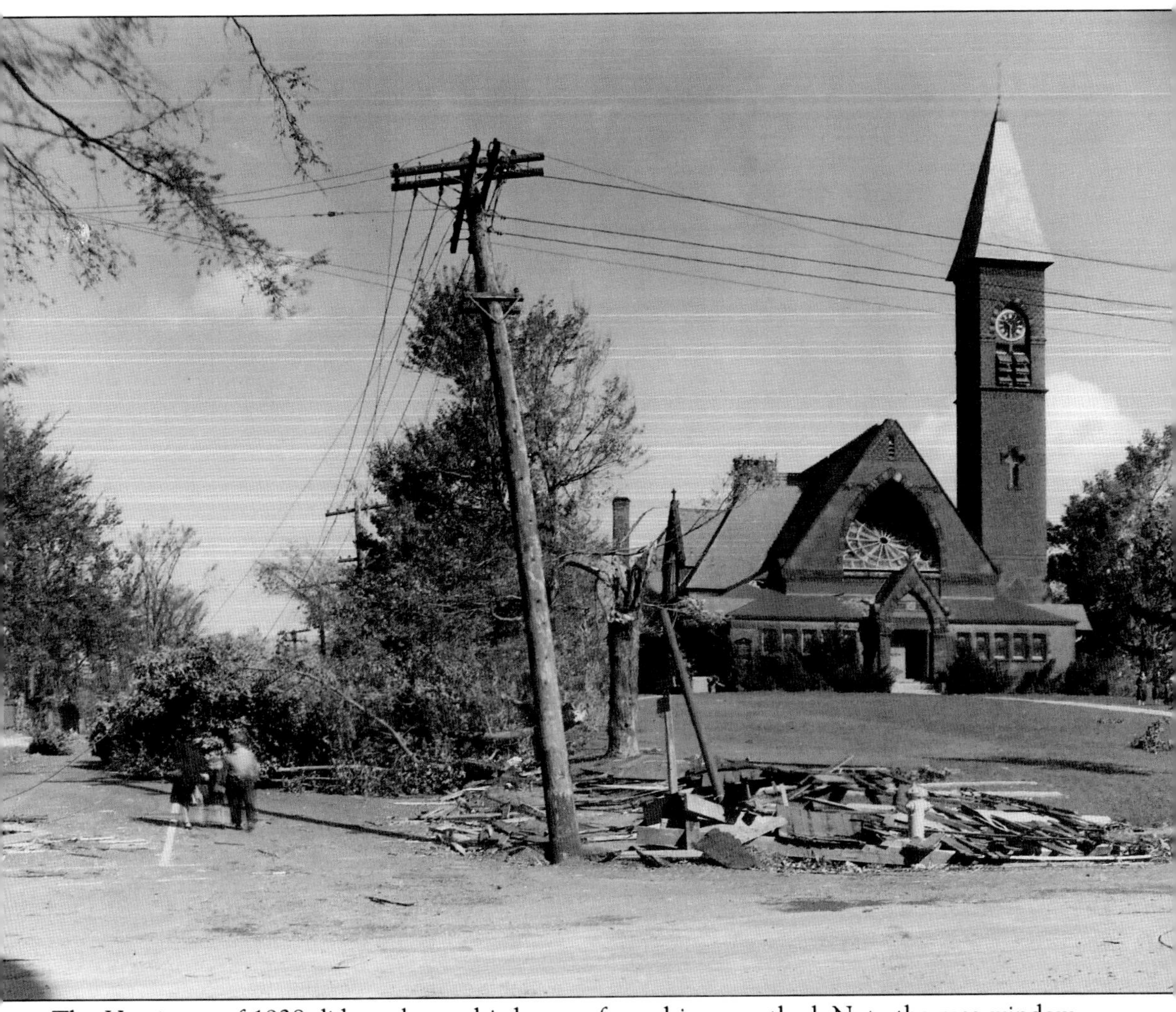

The Hurricane of 1938 did not leave this house of worship unscathed. Note the rose window of the First Congregational Church blown in. In the foreground lies part of the Syndicate Block's roof.

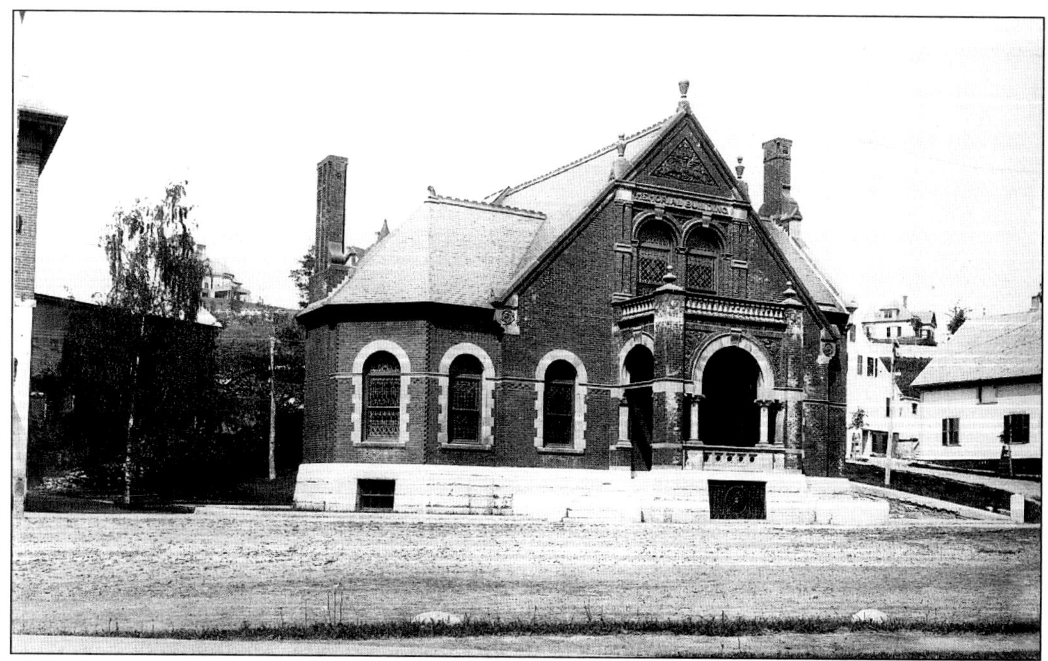

The Levi Heywood Memorial Library was built in 1885–86. It served as a library for approximately one hundred years. The Gardner Museum now occupies the building. The windows on the first floor were made of cathedral stained glass and two in the Trustee's Room represented Arts and Sciences.

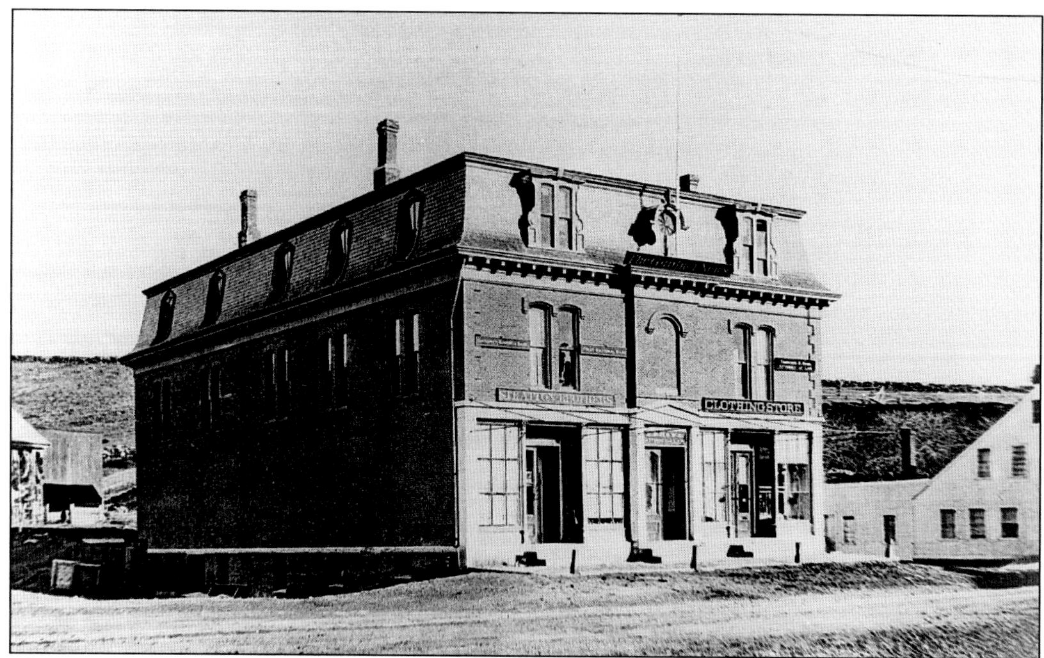

The Bank Building, located on Pearl Street next to the Gardner Museum. The building housed, at various times, the First National Bank, the Gardner Savings Bank, the Gardner Water Company, the *Gardner News*, G.R. Godfrey Harness Maker, and upstairs, Malta Hall. Henry R. Godfrey was the last tenant, and about a year after he left the building was torn down in 1939.

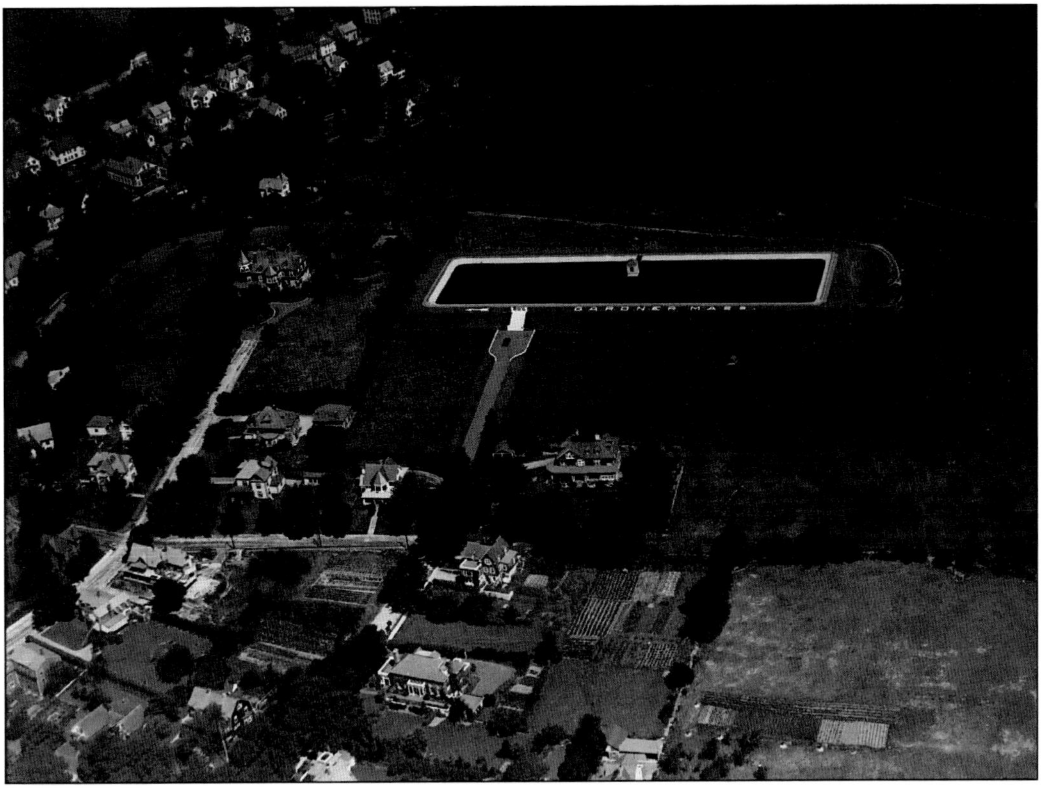

The reservoir was built by the privately held Gardner Water Works in 1881. Many construction workers at this site were early Finnish and Swedish settlers. Note the arrow next to Gardner in the picture—this denotes the direction to the Gardner Airport. The town bought out the Gardner Water Works in 1902. In place of the reservoir two holding tanks were installed in August and November 1989.

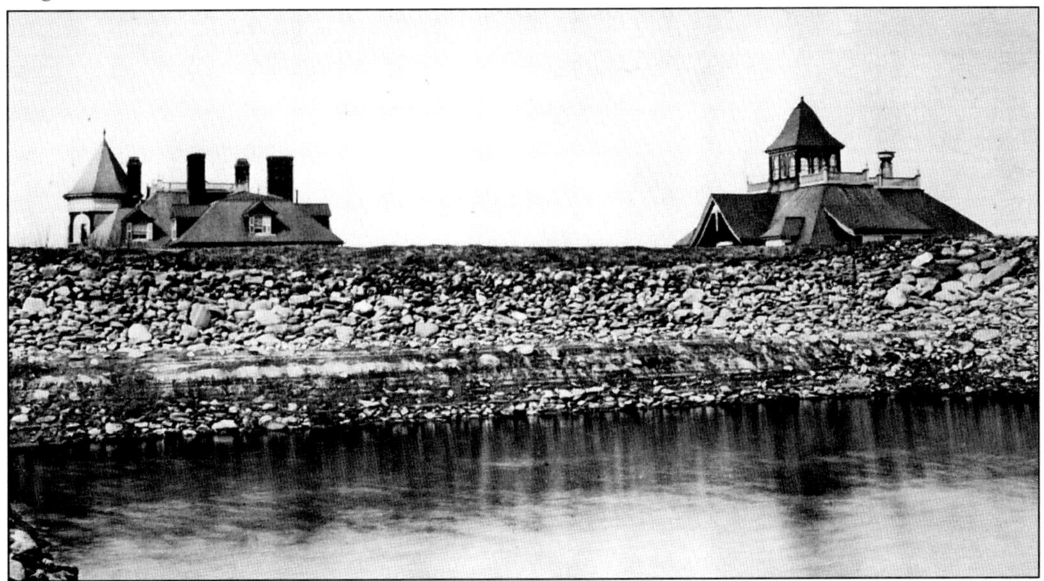

When maintenance had to be done the reservoir was drawn down.

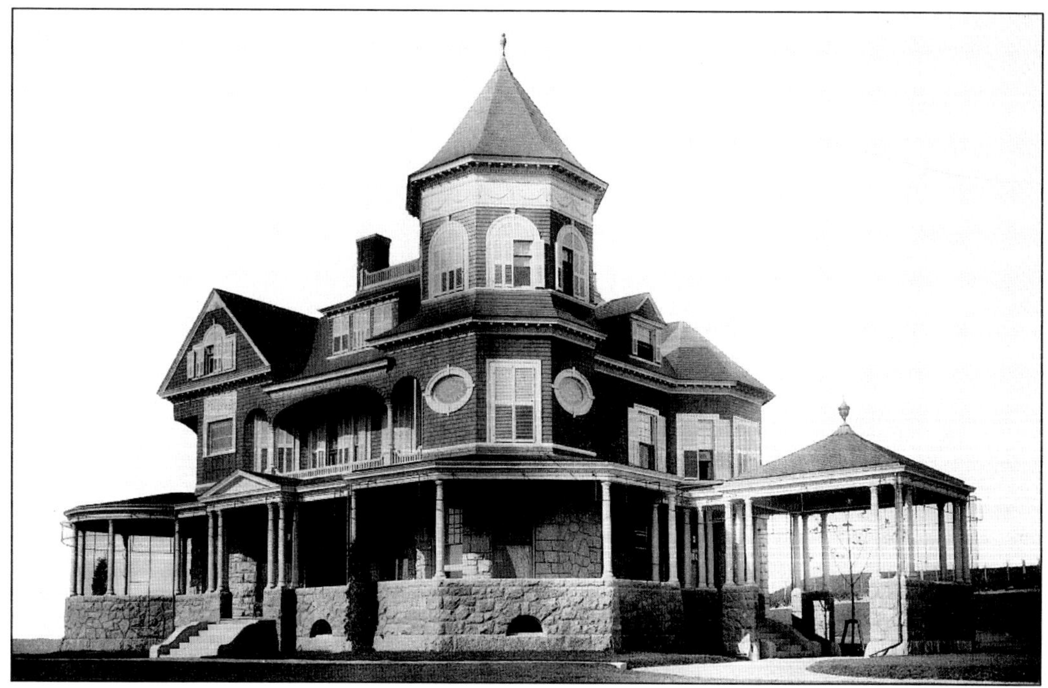

The George H. Heywood house built on Reservoir Hill in 1895 by Barker and Nourse architects from Worcester. This is typical of the homes that the factory owners were building at the turn of the century. Several hundred guests danced under chinese lanterns at the "At Home" celebration on September 14, 1895.

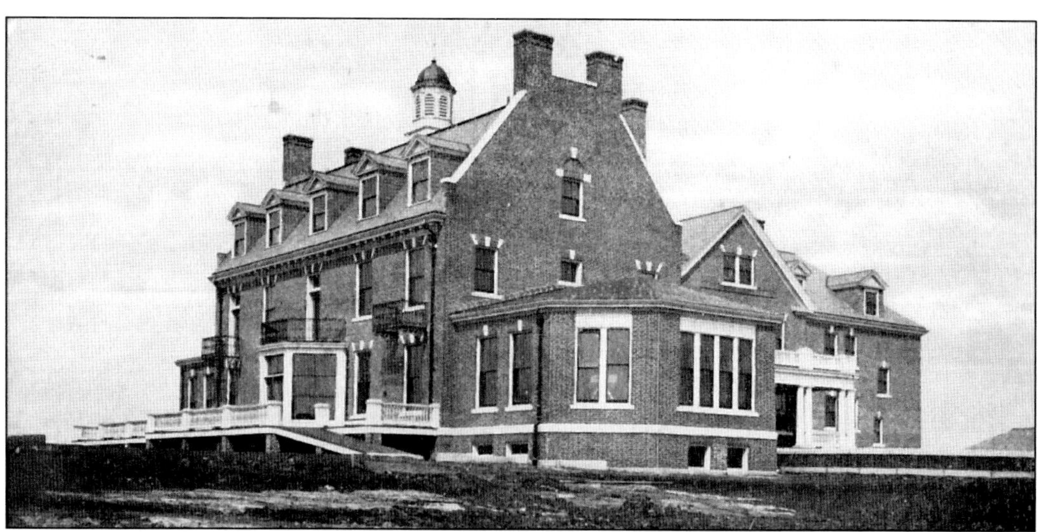

The Henry Heywood Memorial Hospital, now called the Heywood Hospital, was built between 1906 and 1907. The hospital has changed in many ways since 1907 but the basic structure from that time is still visible.

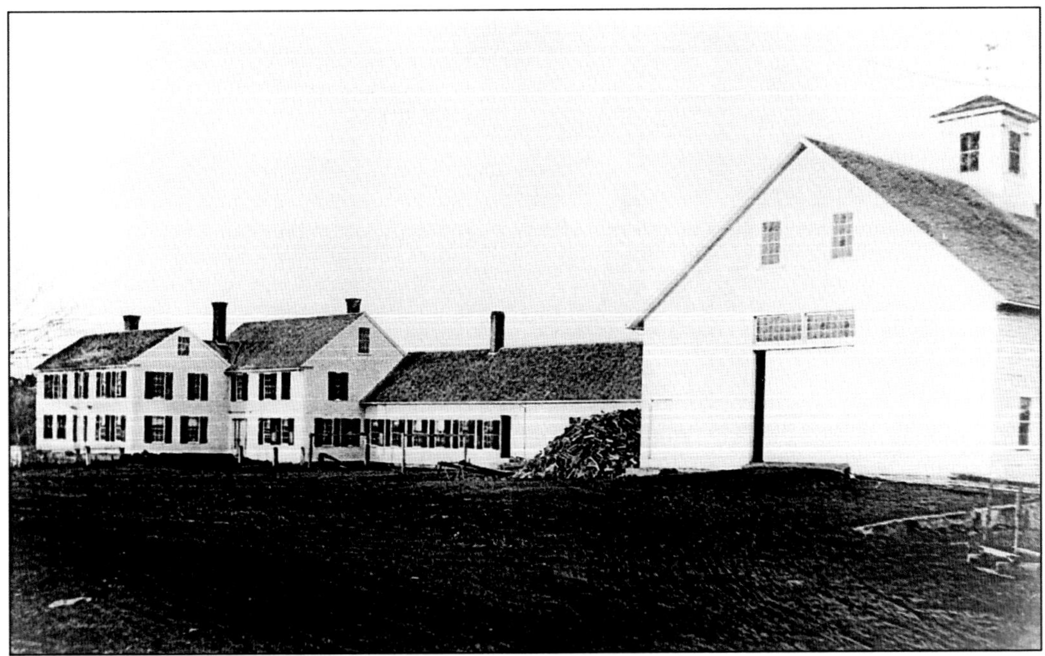

The Town Farm was located where Perreault's farm presently stands on Green Street (Route 140). It was built by Abram Stone and was purchased by the Town of Gardner in 1848 to care for its indigent citizens. This building was destroyed by fire in 1892.

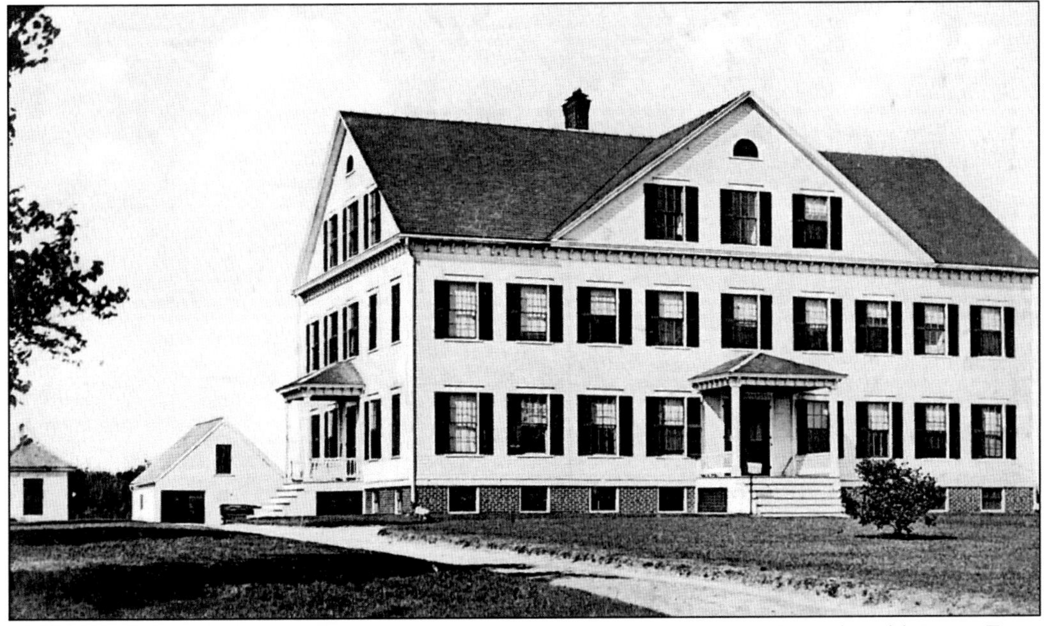

The "new" Town Farm was located across Green Street (Route 140) from the old Town Farm site. It was built in 1892 and served in this capacity until the 1930s when the state and federal authorities began assuming responsibilities. The building no longer exists but stood by the present entrance to the Gardner City Forest.

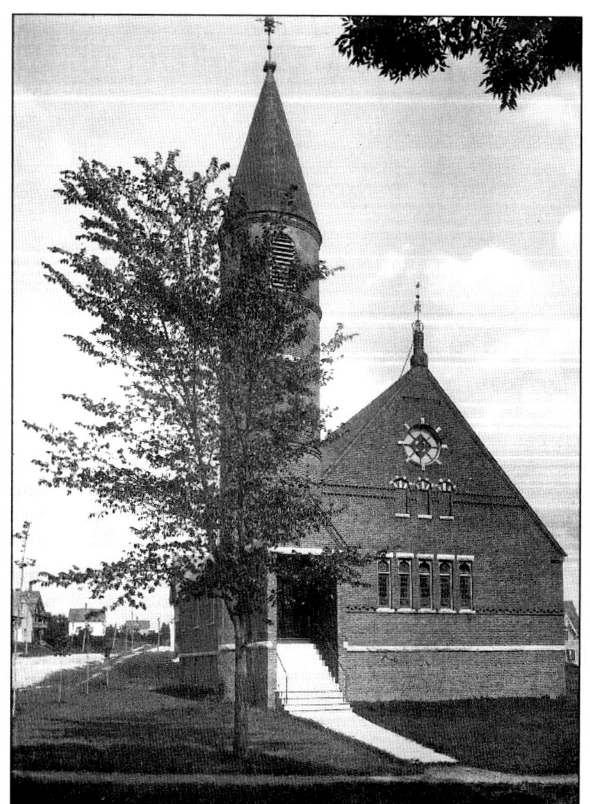

The First Unitarian Church was built in 1887–88. An addition of a wing on the south side basement level was made in 1962. A silver dollar traced at one corner of the original plans marked the site of the tower.

Heywood Block was originally known as the Market Block and was built by Charles Heywood about 1879. It consisted of two building connected by an addition. A fire in 1890 caused some damage but the building was repaired and continues to exist at 53-57 Chestnut Street.

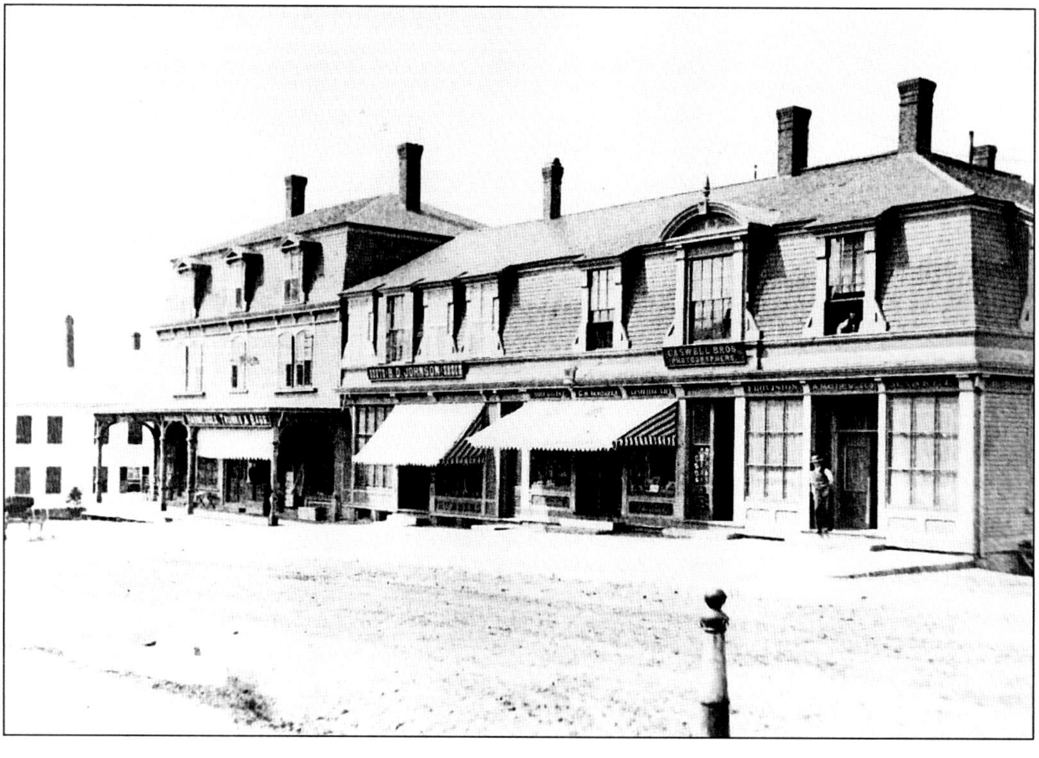

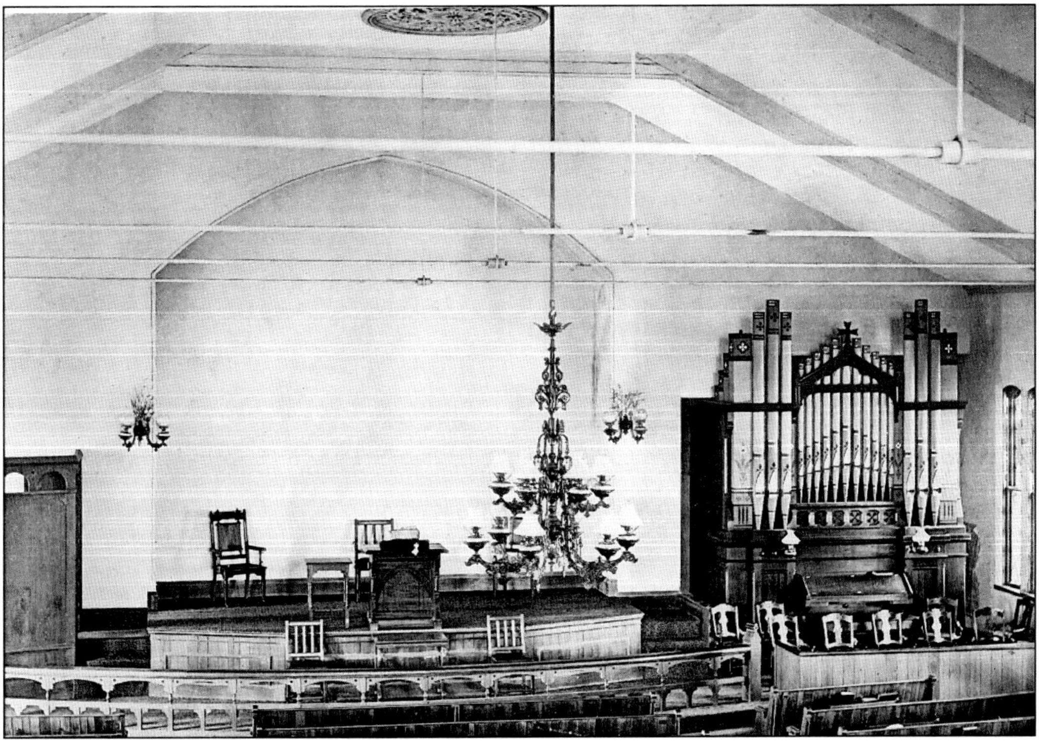

The interior of the Chestnut Street United Methodist Church before the fire.

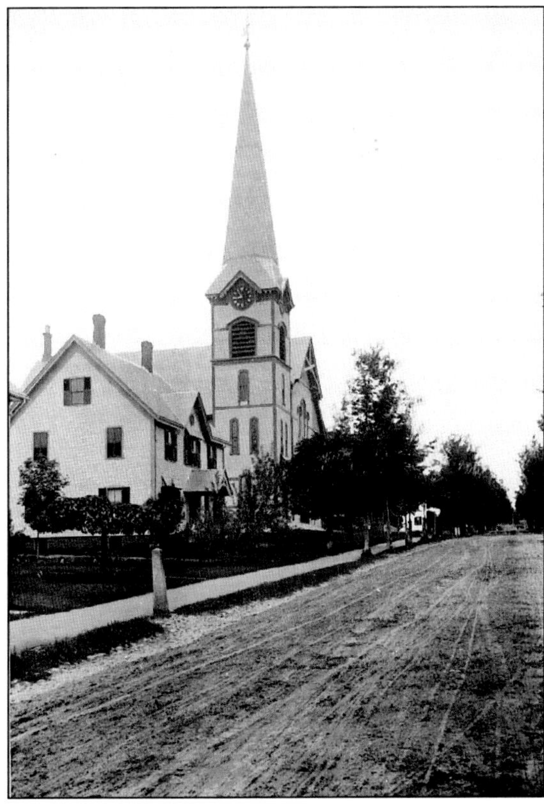

The Chestnut Street United Methodist Church, or the Methodist Episcopal Church, was built in 1876 on the site of the current Methodist church. The building had an addition, with a gymnasium used for sports such as basketball on the second floor and a bowling alley in the basement, for use at the rate of 10¢ an hour. The church was destroyed by a spectacular fire on February 25, 1959.

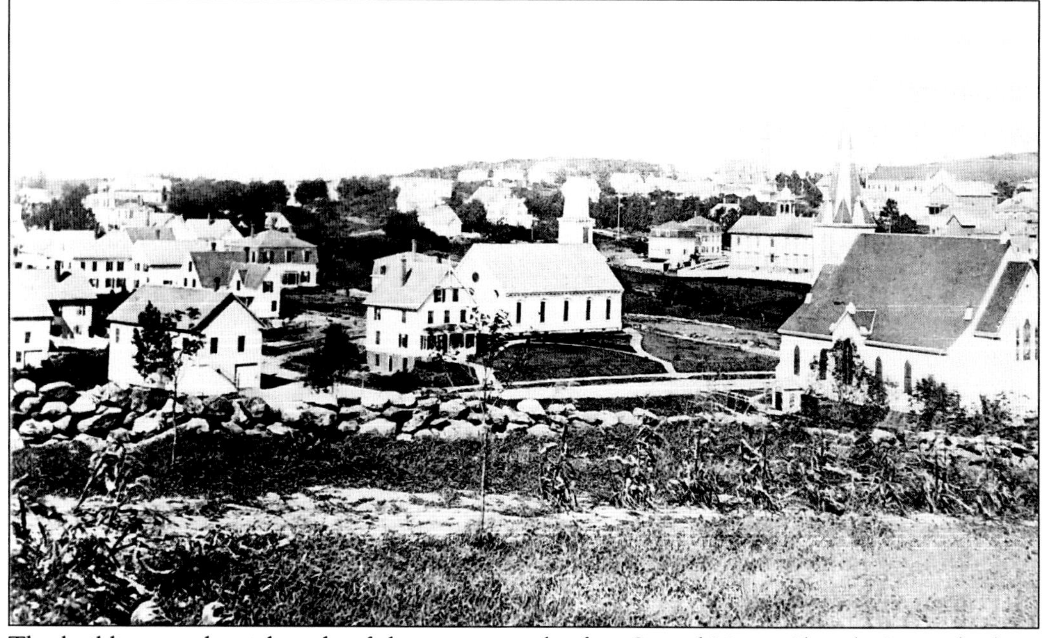

The building on the right side of the picture is the first Sacred Heart Church. It was built in 1874 and served the parishioners until May 28, 1887, when fire demolished the building. Also visible are the Universalist Church (center) and the Centre School (in the background).

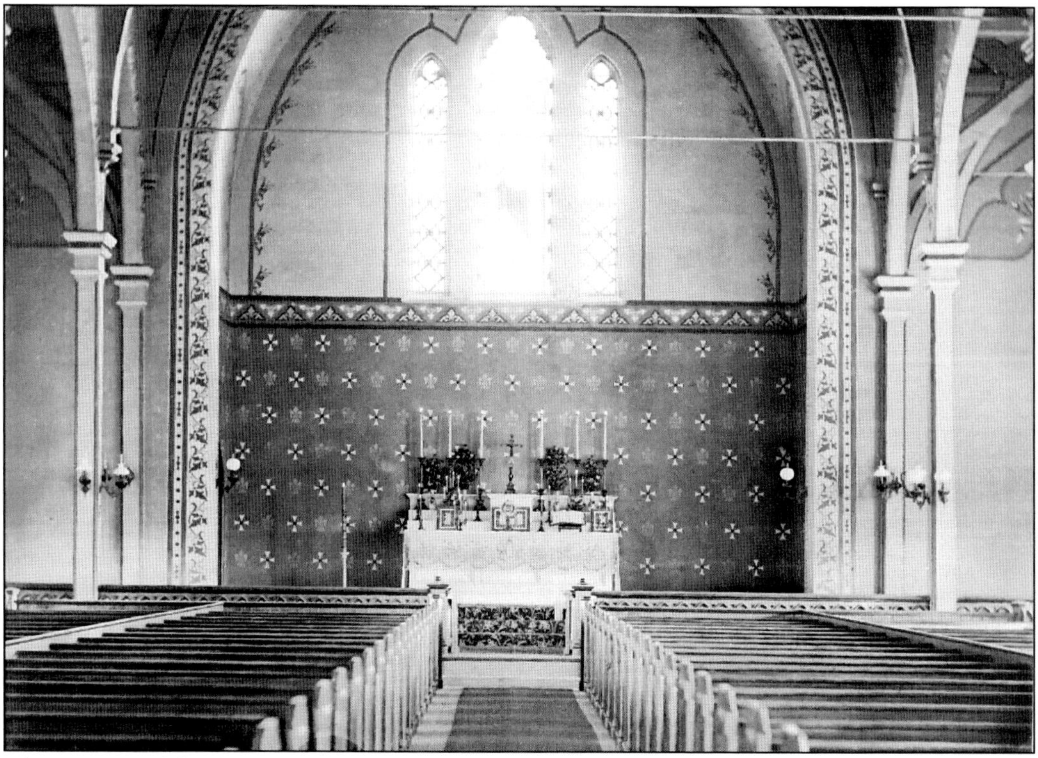

The interior of the first Sacred Heart Church about 1880.

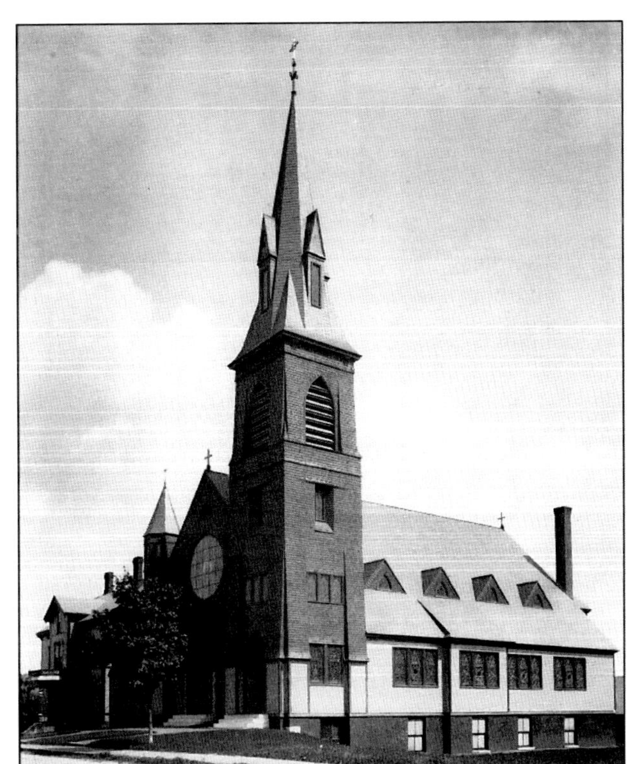

The second Sacred Heart Church, completed in 1893.

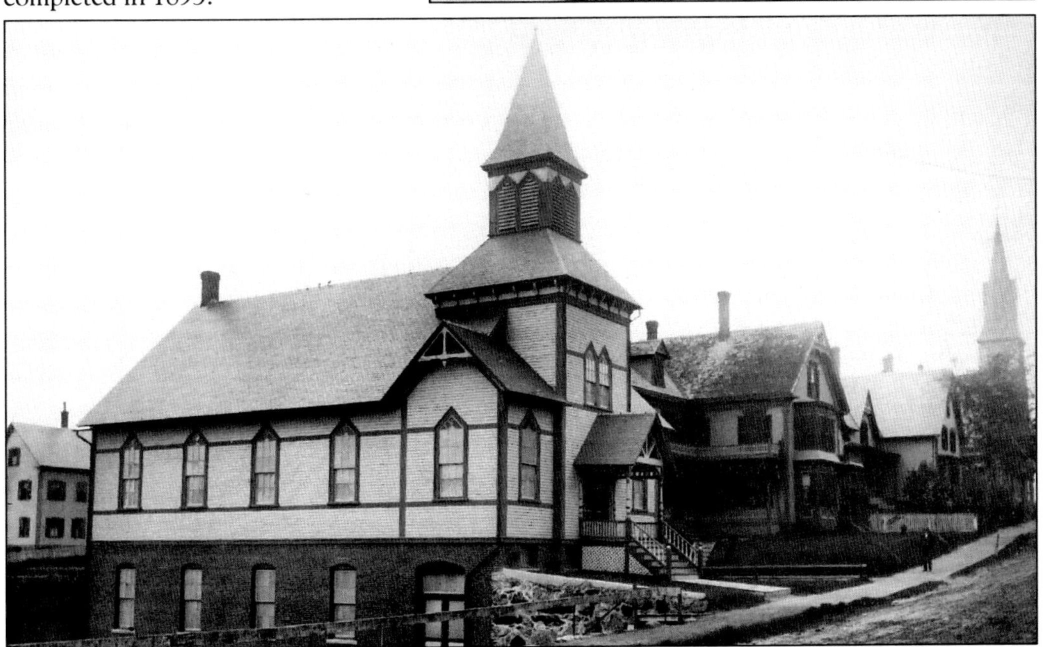

The Scandinavian Evangelical Lutheran Church was located on Cross Street a short distance east of South Lincoln Street. The church was dedicated in 1897. It served the parish until 1946. The church is presently known as the First Lutheran Church and is located at the corner of Elm and Lawrence Streets. The building was then owned by the Thayer Co. and later by the Simplex Time Recorder Company. In 1962 it was torn down.

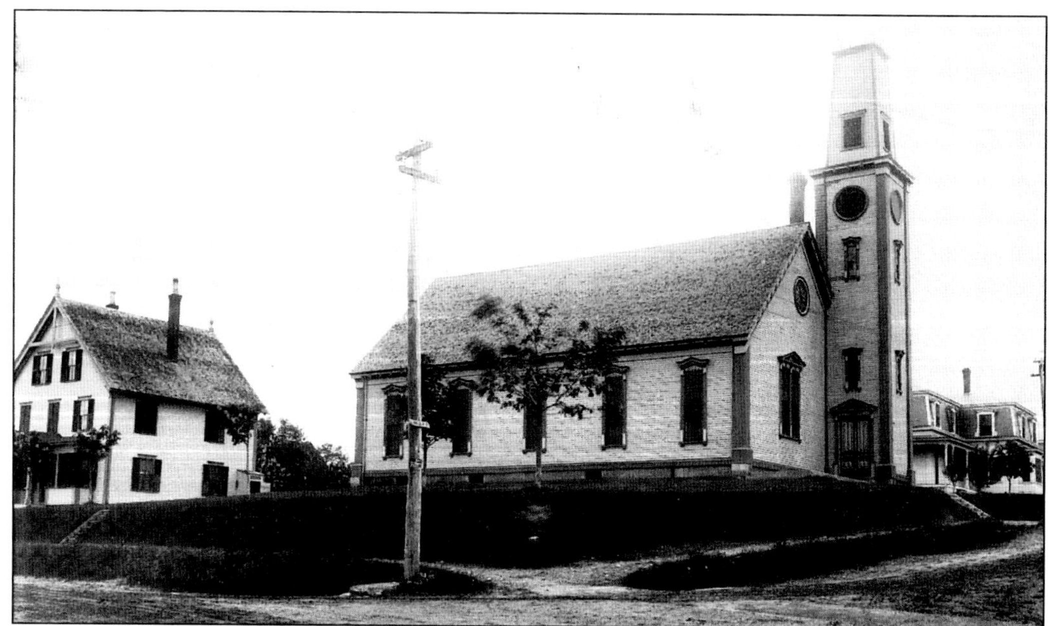

The Universalist Church, located on the corner of Lincoln and Cross Streets. The Universalist society, after meeting in the original meeting house for a number of years, built this structure in 1874. The church lasted for the next seventy-six years before closing in 1950. The building still exists but without the steeple.

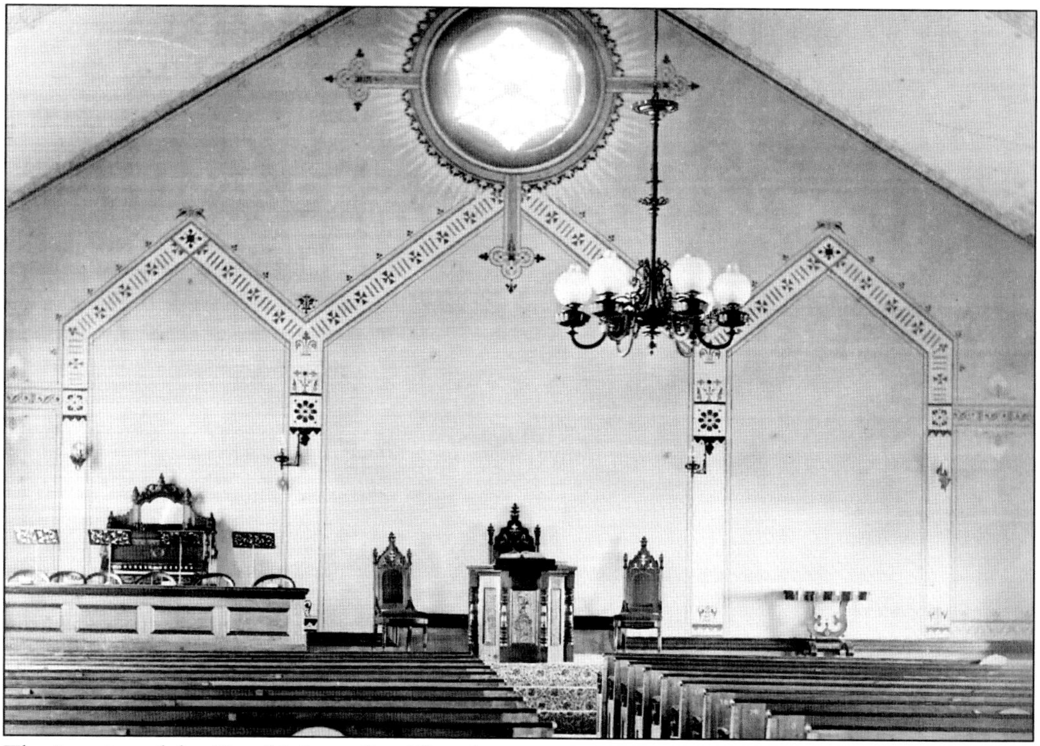

The interior of the First Universalist Church.

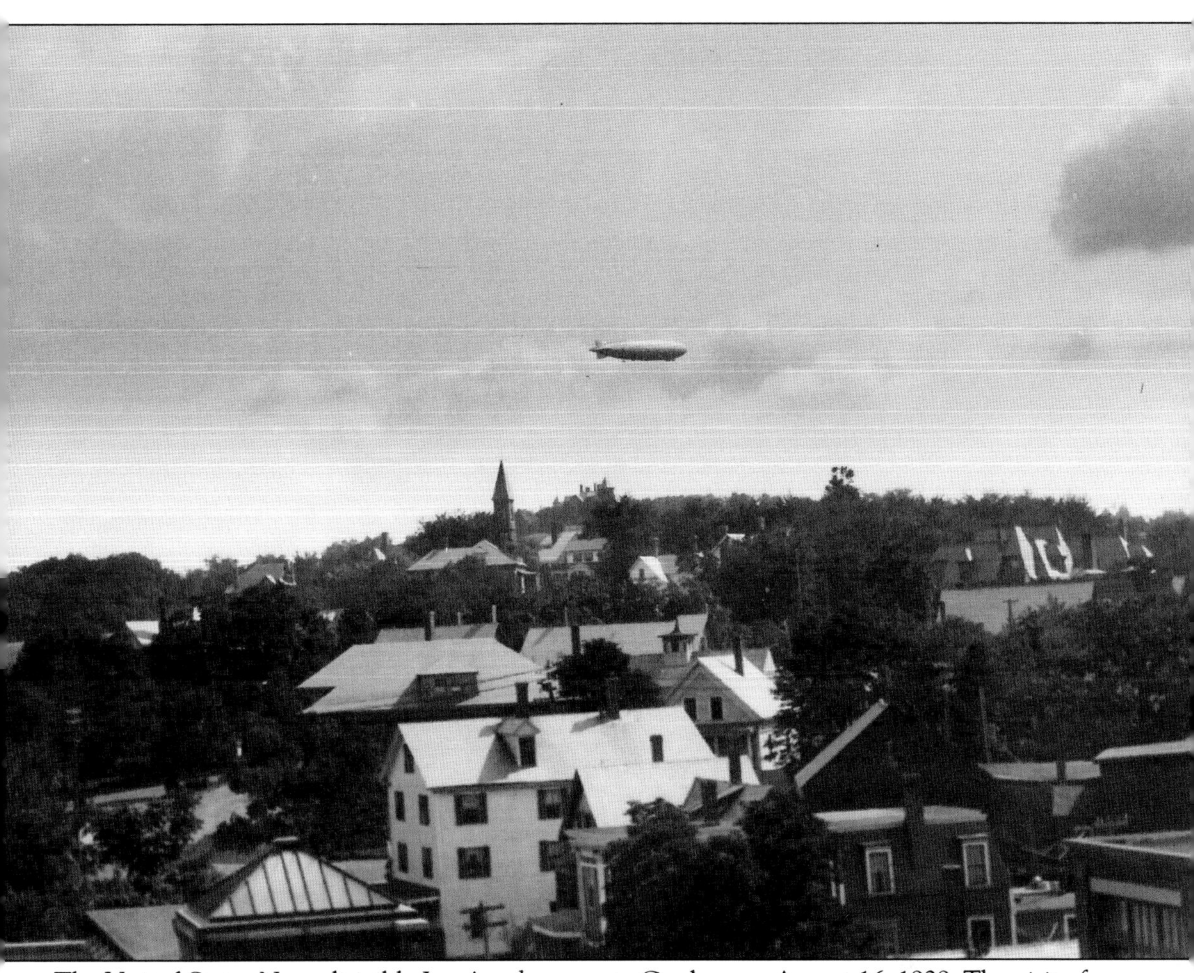

The United States Navy dirigible *Los Angeles* came to Gardner on August 16, 1929. The visit of the giant 658-foot airship was part of a tour of the New England states.

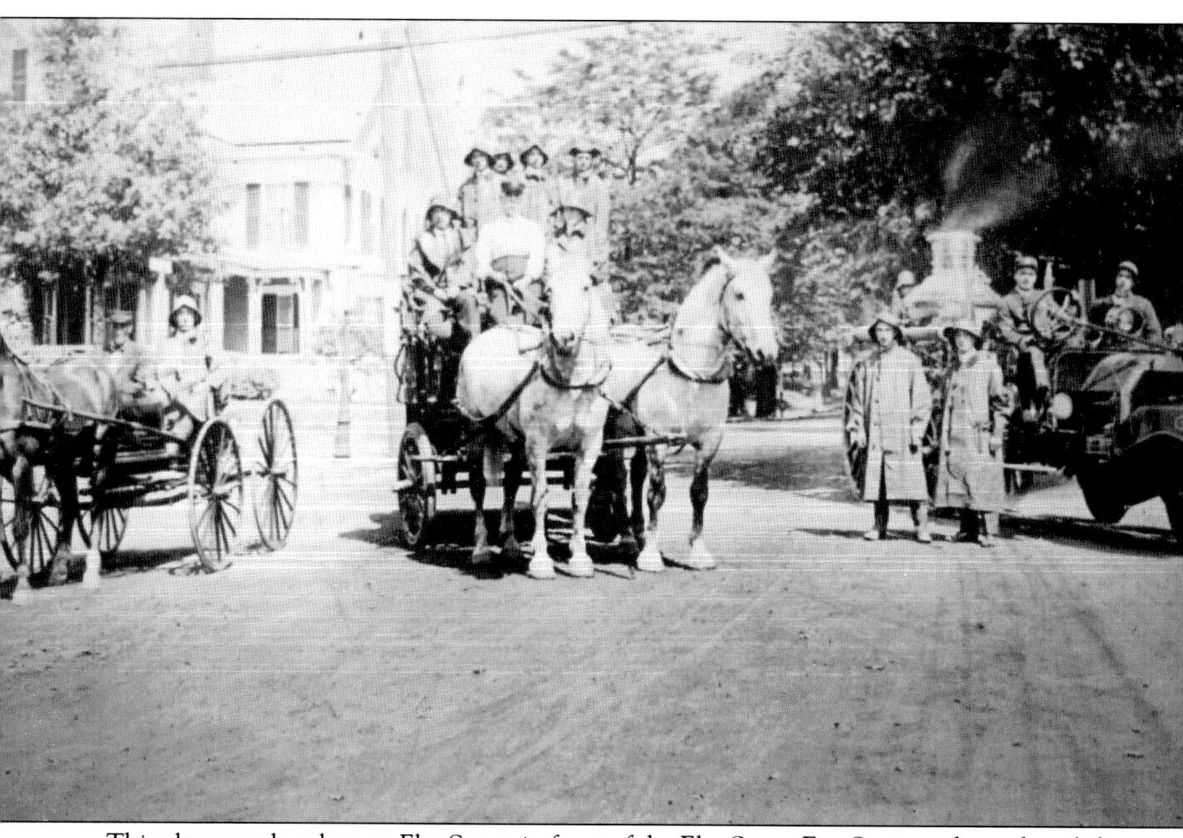

This photograph, taken on Elm Street in front of the Elm Street Fire Station, shows from left to right: Chief Hodgman's wagon; Hose No. 3, with Tom and Jerry (the two white horses); and the Knox Martin Tractor, purchased in 1913 to pull Steamer No. 1.

Three

West Gardner: The Square

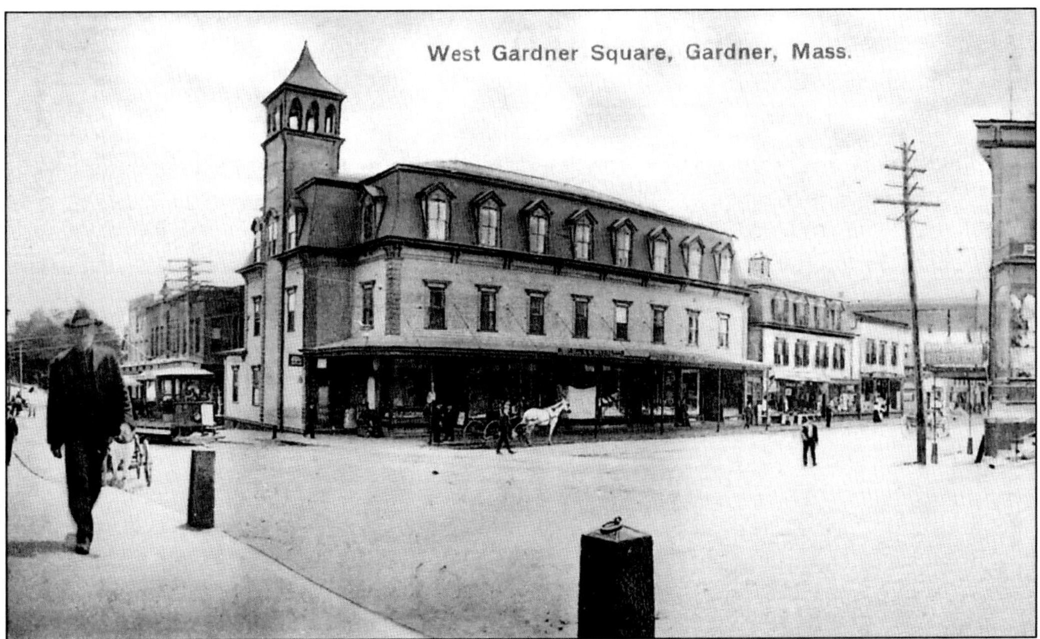

The Garland Block. Dr. Guy W. Garland built his block on Jackson's Corner, named for Josiah A. Jackson, whose house occupied the site at the corner of Main and Parker Streets in 1886. Later the building was known as the Garbose Block and then the Liggett Block.

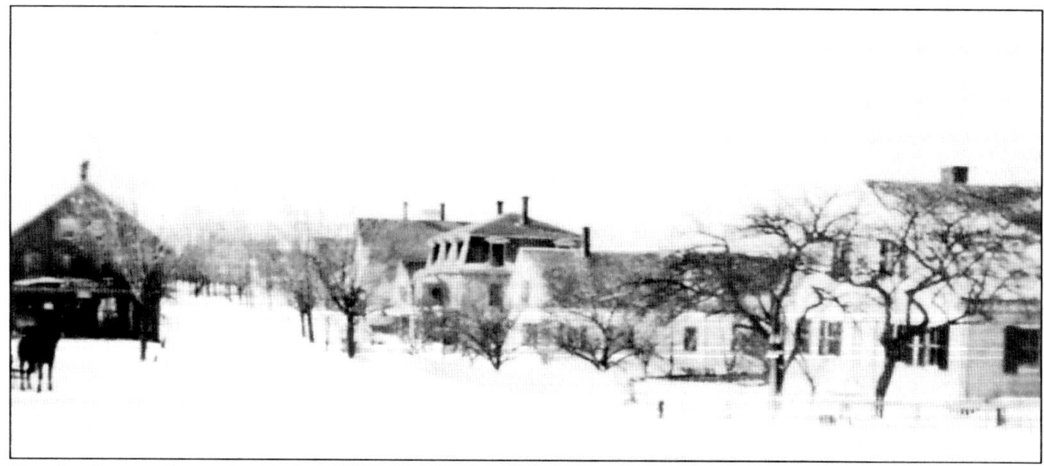

Frank Conant's store is partially visible on the left while the houses lining Pleasant Street are clearly visible on the right, ending at the corner of Pleasant and Parker Streets where Josiah A. Jackson lived.

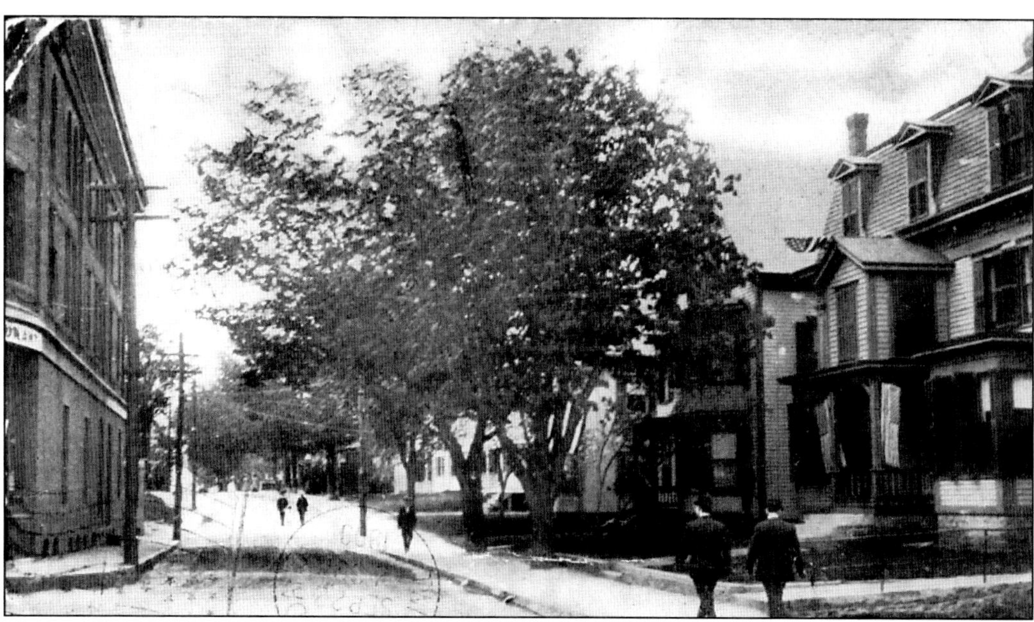

Pleasant Street about 1900 with Rosenberg's Block (the late Shawmut Bank building) on the left. On the right are the houses of, perhaps, Ezra Osgood, N.M. Prehore, and Mrs. M.E. Priest.

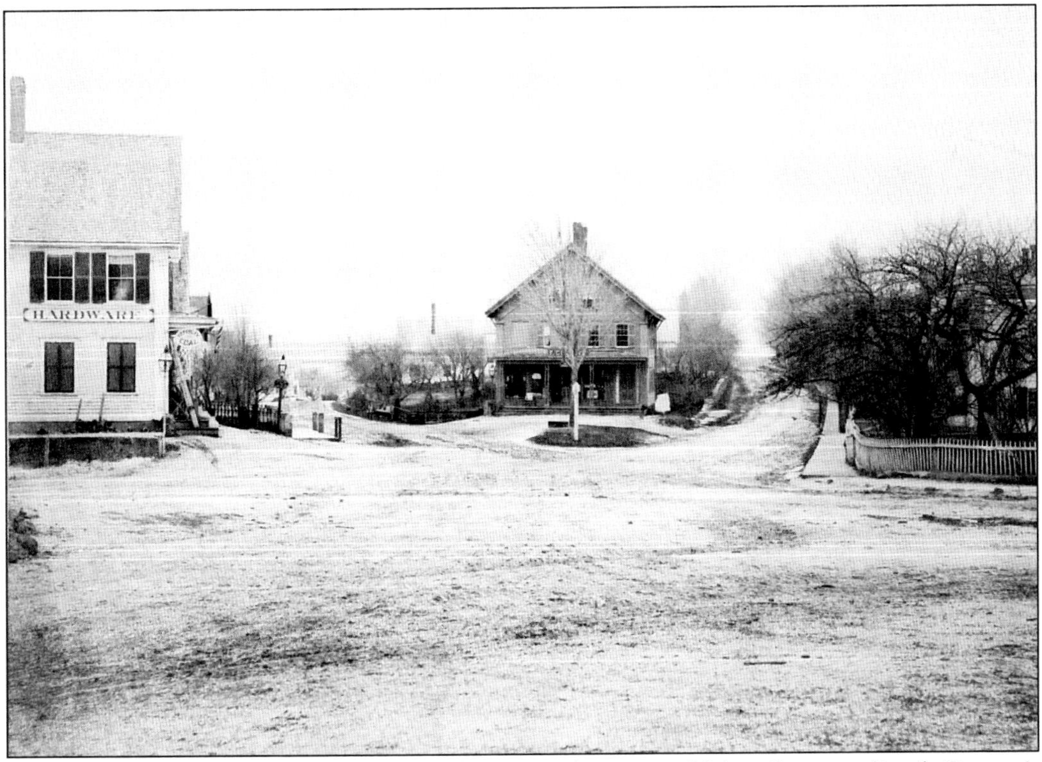

West Gardner about 1880. In the center, between Pleasant and Main Street, is Frank Conant's dry goods store; on the right is the first Davis Hardware Store in which T.P. Perley began his grain business.

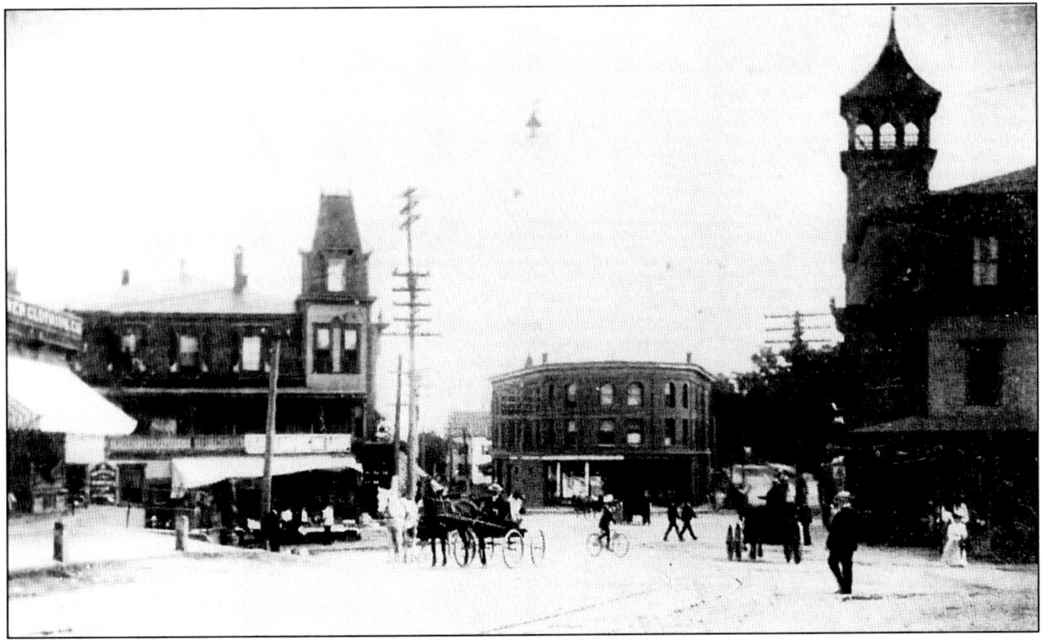

West Gardner Square about 1900. From left to right are Hager's Block, Rosenberg's Block, and the Garland Block.

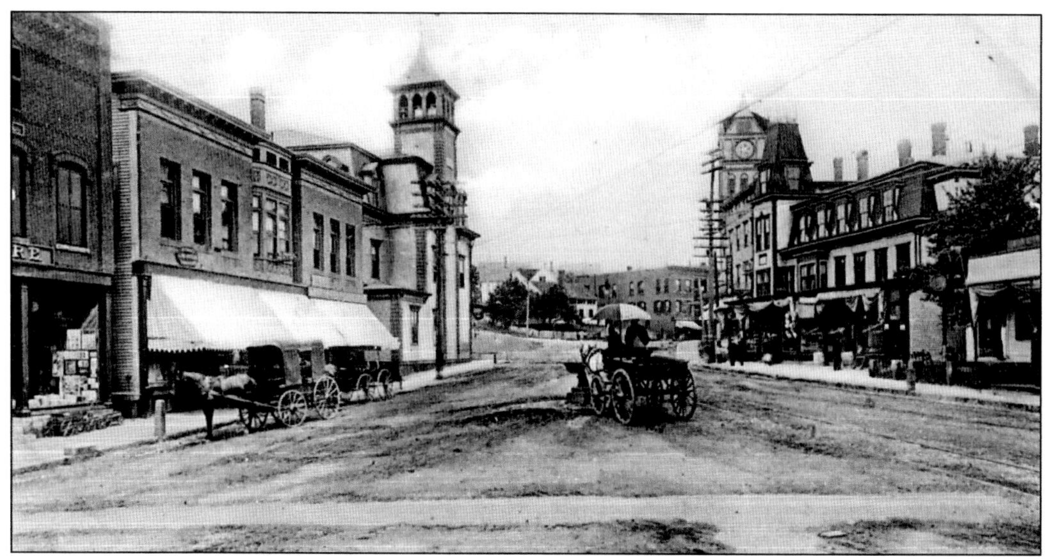

West Gardner Square, from Main and Pleasant Streets around 1900. The Walter Davis Hardware Block is at the extreme left of the picture, followed by the Riordan Block and the Garland Block. Across the street are the Stevens Block and Hagar Block.

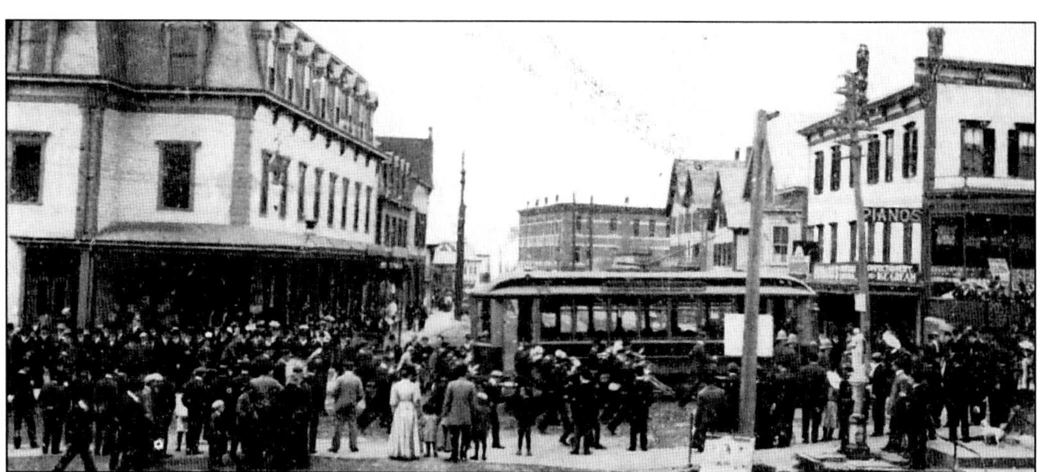

The West Gardner Square on Memorial Day, 1907. A trolley of the Gardner, Westminster, and Fitchburg Street railway is stopped on Central Street at the entrance to Parker Street. On the right is Alger's Block; on the left is the Garland Block.

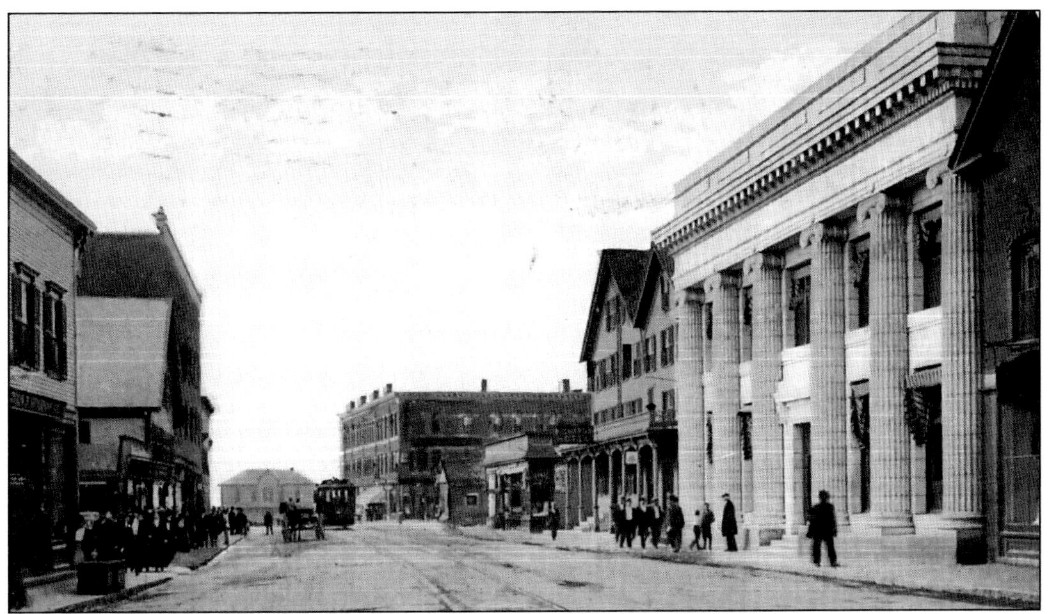

Parker Street with the Gardner Savings Bank and Richards Hotel on the right. In the distance the Commercial House is barely visible.

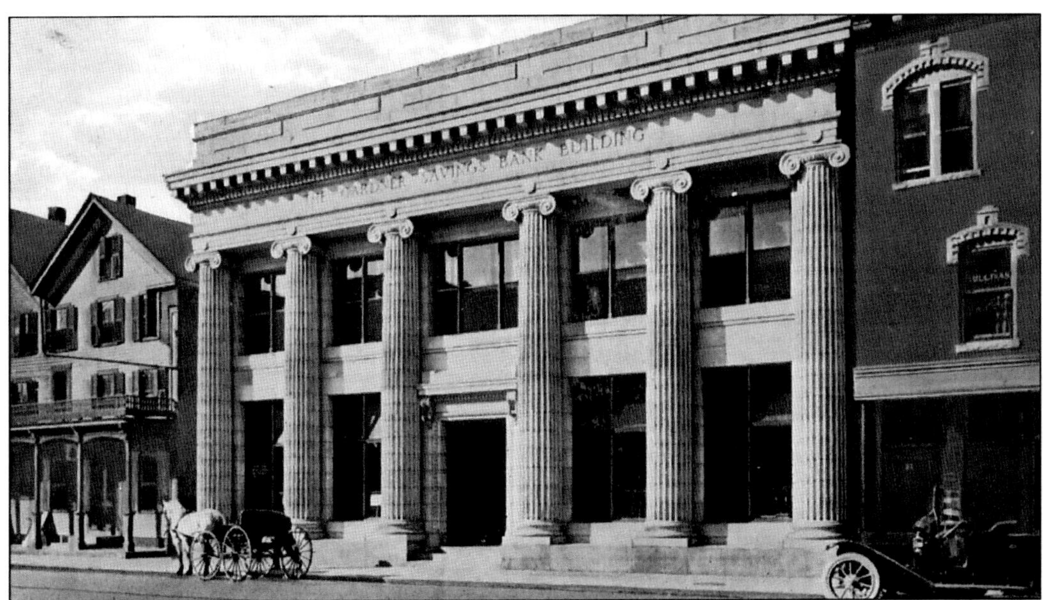

The Gardner Savings Bank. Chartered in 1868, it occupied quarters in the Bank Building on Pearl Street and the Syndicate Block. In 1909 it moved into its new quarters on Parker Street. The bank is today a branch of the Bank of Boston.

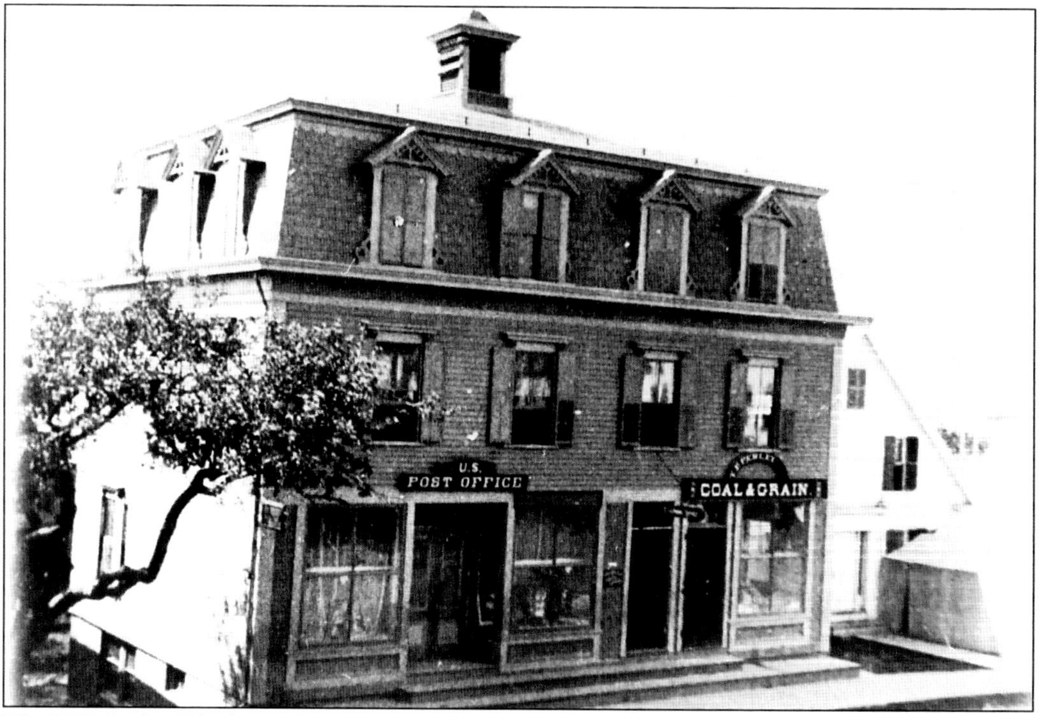

The T.P. Perley Block was located on Parker Street where the Music Forum store stands today. T.P. Perley operated a coal and grain business. The building, built in 1883, was torn down to make way for the Michelman Block in the early 1910s.

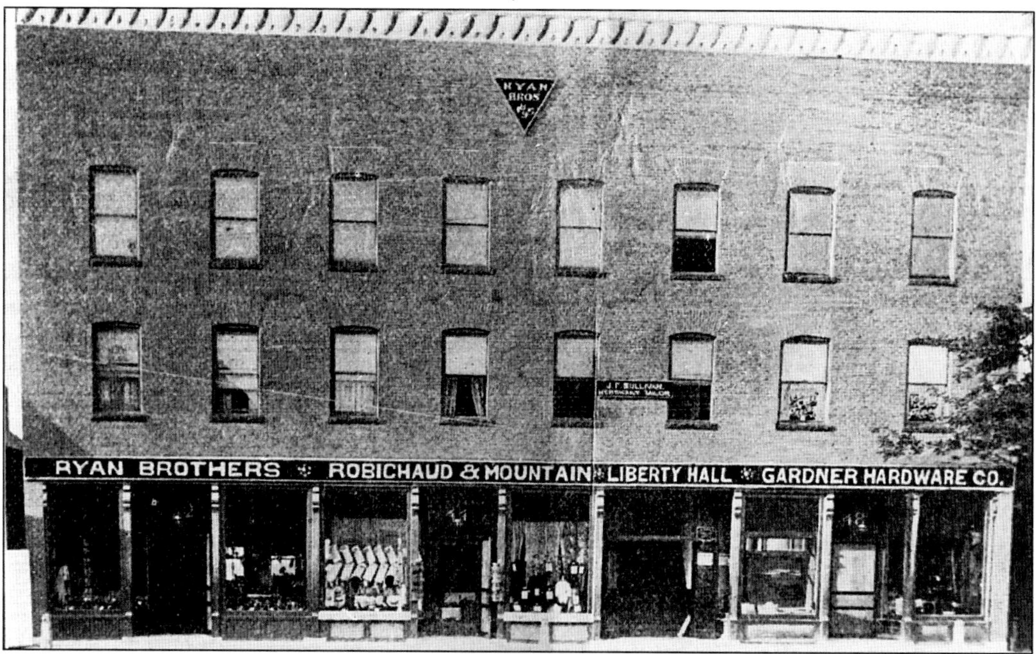

The Ryan Brothers Block, built in 1895 on Parker Street, also housed Robichaud and Mountain clothier's and the Gardner Hardware Company. The upper floors were lodge halls. The building still stands today.

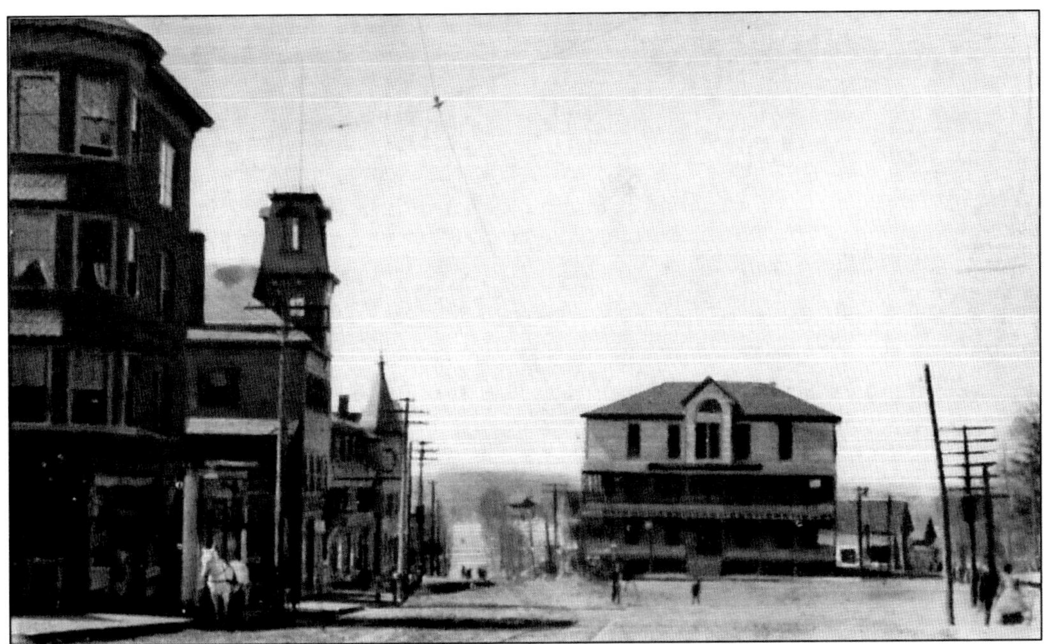

Looking down Parker and West Streets where the Commercial House dominates the junction of the roads. Parker Street was laid out at the insistence of Dr. David Parker and his son Horace, thus its name.

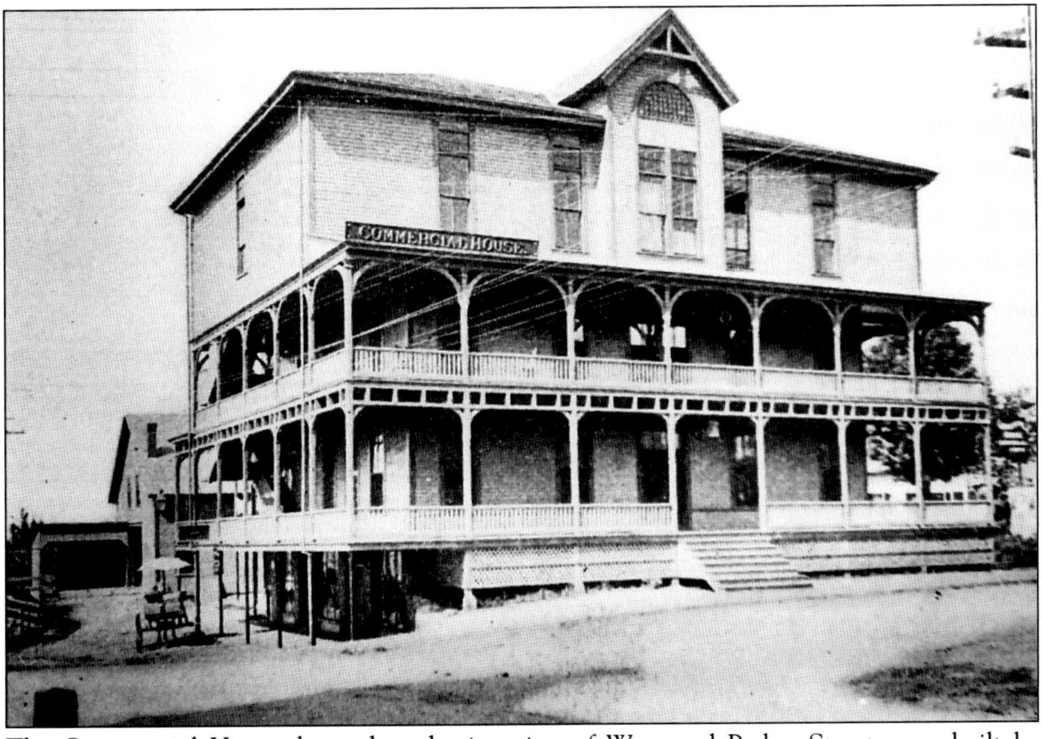

The Commercial House, located at the junction of West and Parker Streets, was built by Milton M. Favor in 1884. The building was also known as Barthel Hotel and the FOE Hall. The structure was razed in 1953.

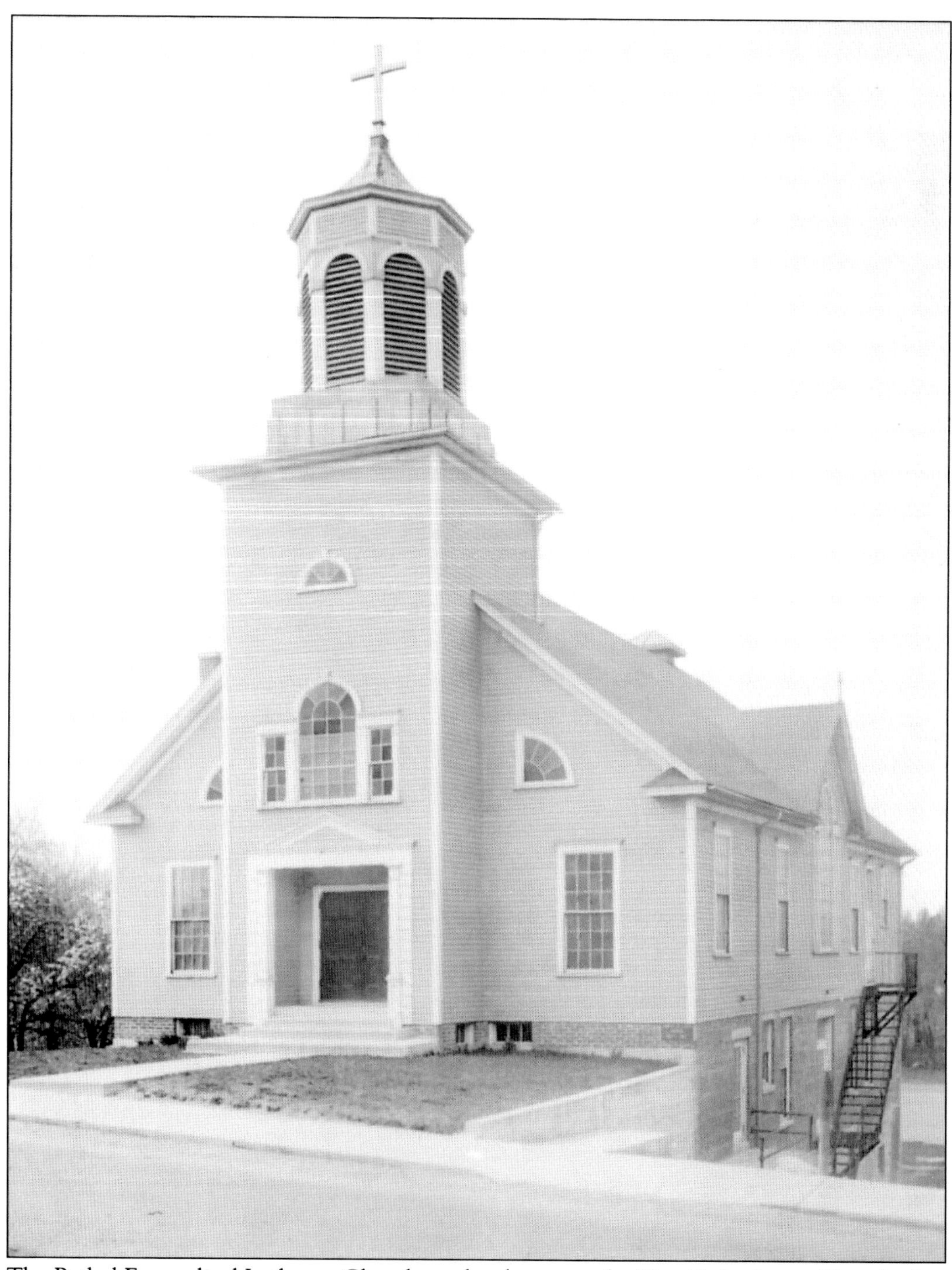

The Bethel Evangelical Lutheran Church, under the name the Finnish Lutheran Church, first met at 175 Nichols Street in the National House, and later in the old St. Paul's Episcopal Church on Main Street. In 1926 they bought this property on West Street. It was just a short distance from picnic grounds they had purchased on Parker's Pond in 1908 called Suomi Park. The building was finished in 1927. The Immanuel Lutheran Church and Bethel Evangelical Lutheran Churches joined to become the Covenant Lutheran Church.

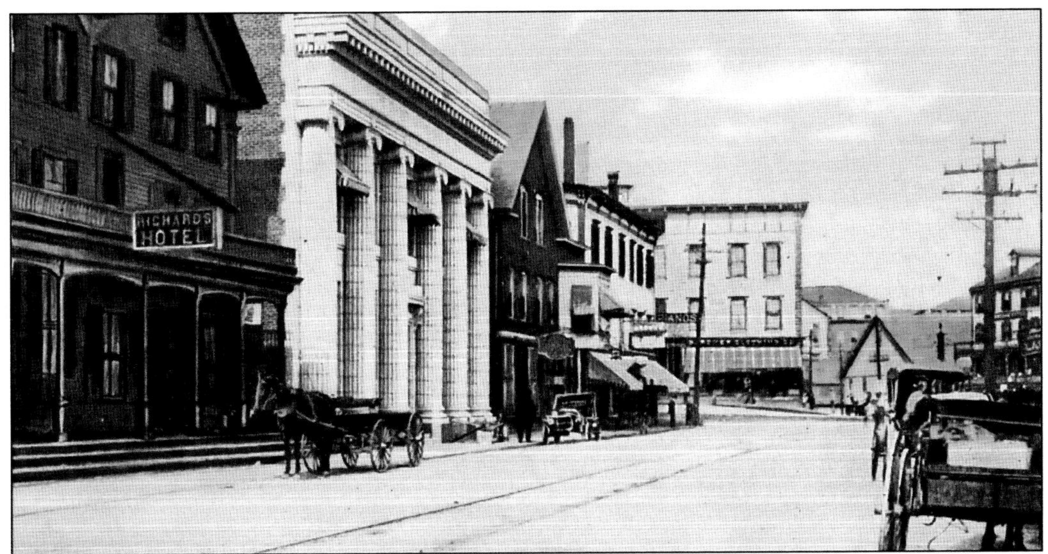

Looking east on Parker Street is Richards Hotel, run for many years as Mechanic's Hotel, just before the Gardner Savings Bank. The Methodist Church built the original structure for their use before building their church on Chestnut Street. A.M. Richard's took over the hotel in 1880 and greatly enlarged the premises.

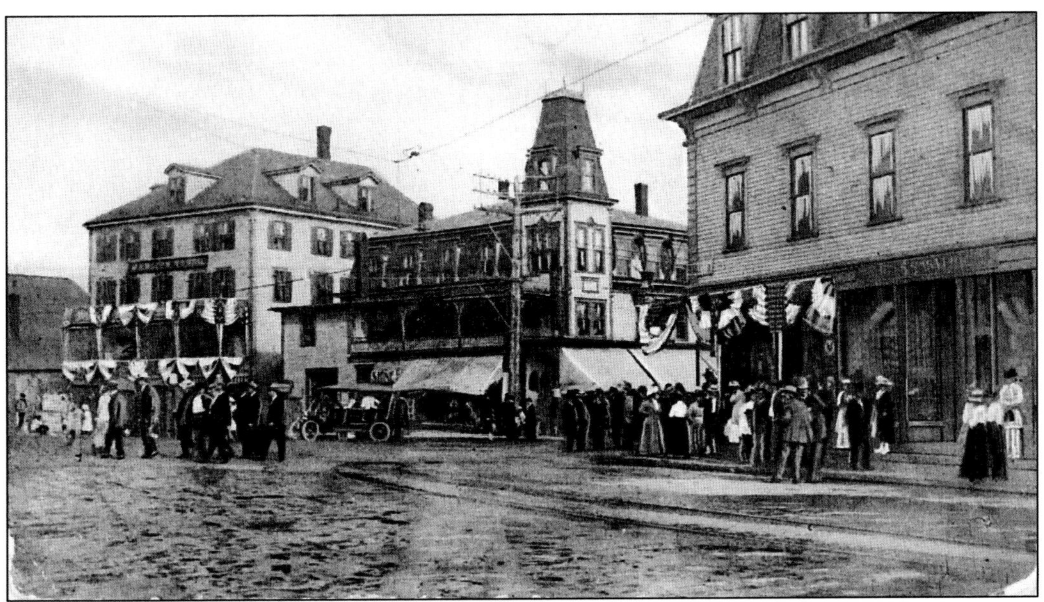

The Mansion House was another hotel in the square, on what is today West Lynde Street. A public parking lot presently occupies this location. In 1902 this house saw, as one of its guests, Carrie Nation, renowned crusader against alcohol, from where she was ejected.

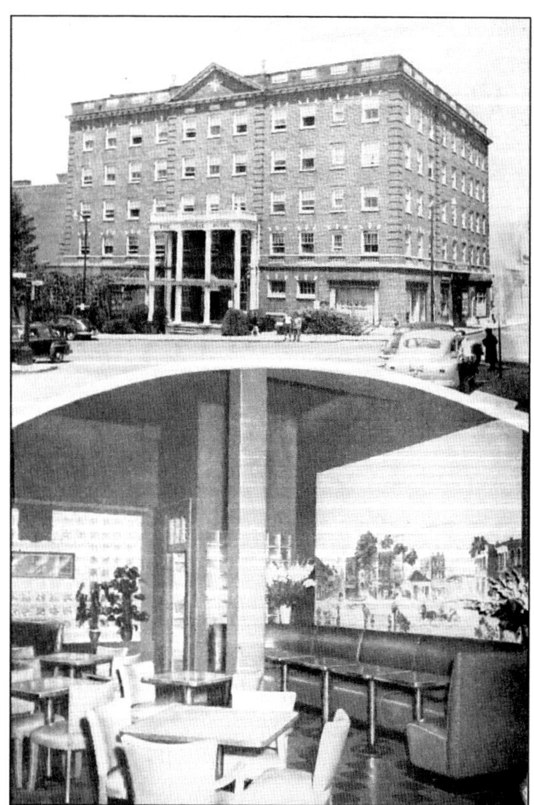

The Colonial Hotel Project was a joint venture between the chamber of commerce and the American Hotels Corporation. The citizens of Gardner subscribed for stock in the hotel to finance its construction, which took place in 1923–24. The 100-room hotel is today an apartment complex called Colonial Apartments, located on 19 City Hall Avenue.

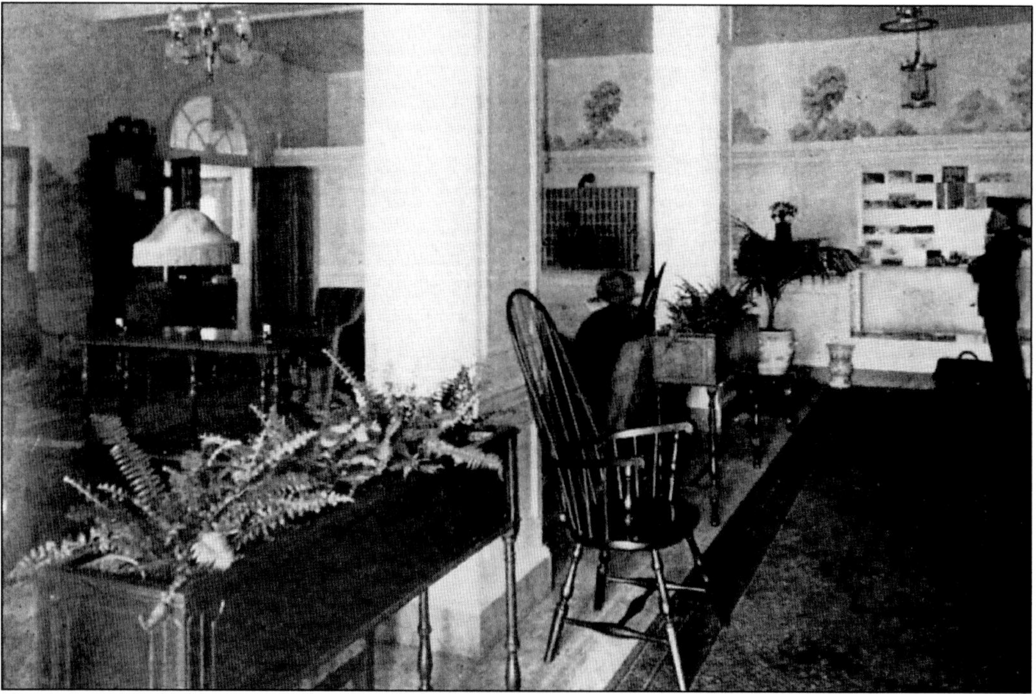

The lobby of the Colonial Hotel from the mid-1950s.

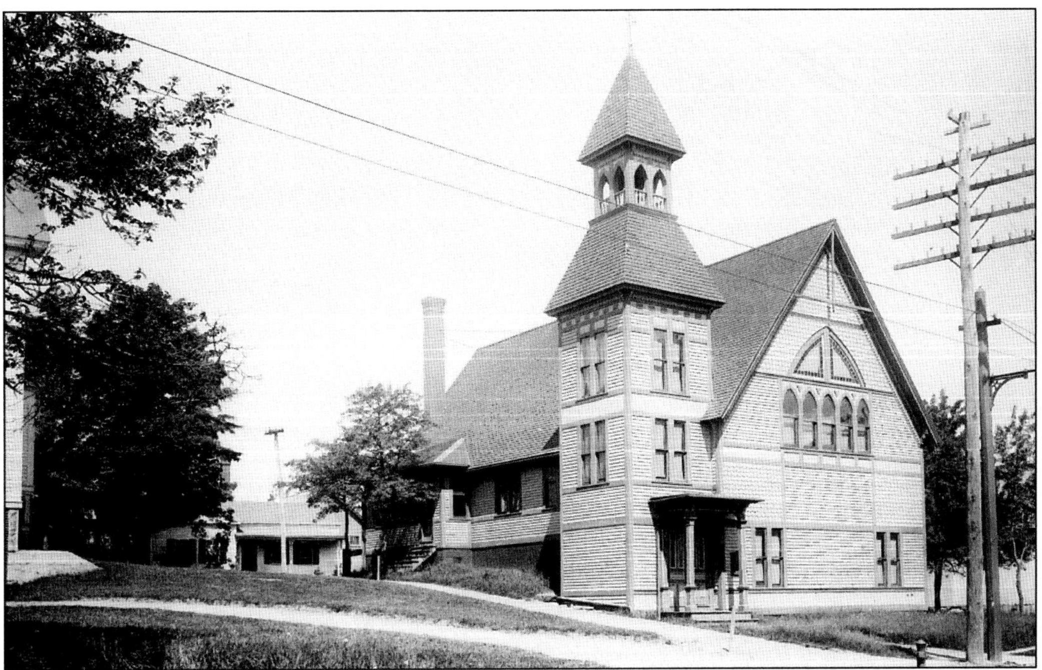

St. Paul's Episcopal Church was located on Main Street, then called North Main, about where City Hall Avenue intersects. The building was built in 1883–84. The Episcopalians used the church until 1907, when they moved into their new church. The Finnish Lutheran Church purchased the property and occupied it until 1923, when the city took the building and land for City Hall Avenue.

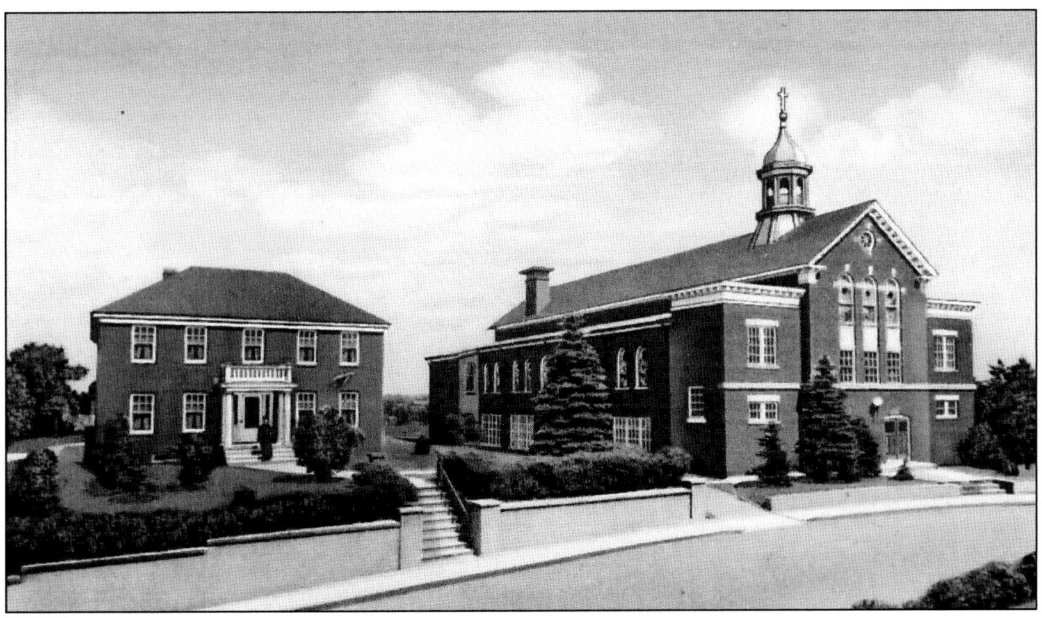

St. Joseph's Church was built at 358 Pleasant Street in 1912–13 to serve the Polish-speaking citizens of Gardner.

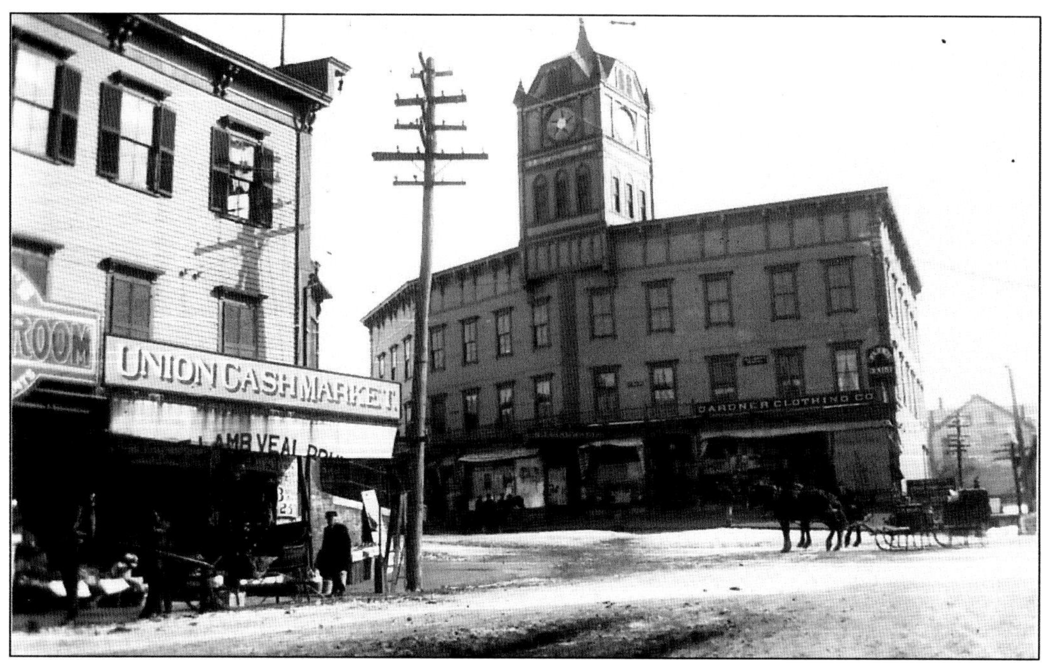

The Union Cash Market was located in the Alger Block on the corner of Parker and Vernon Streets. It was operated a short time in 1904 and 1905 by Sydney Atwood. In the background is the C.B. Steven's Block.

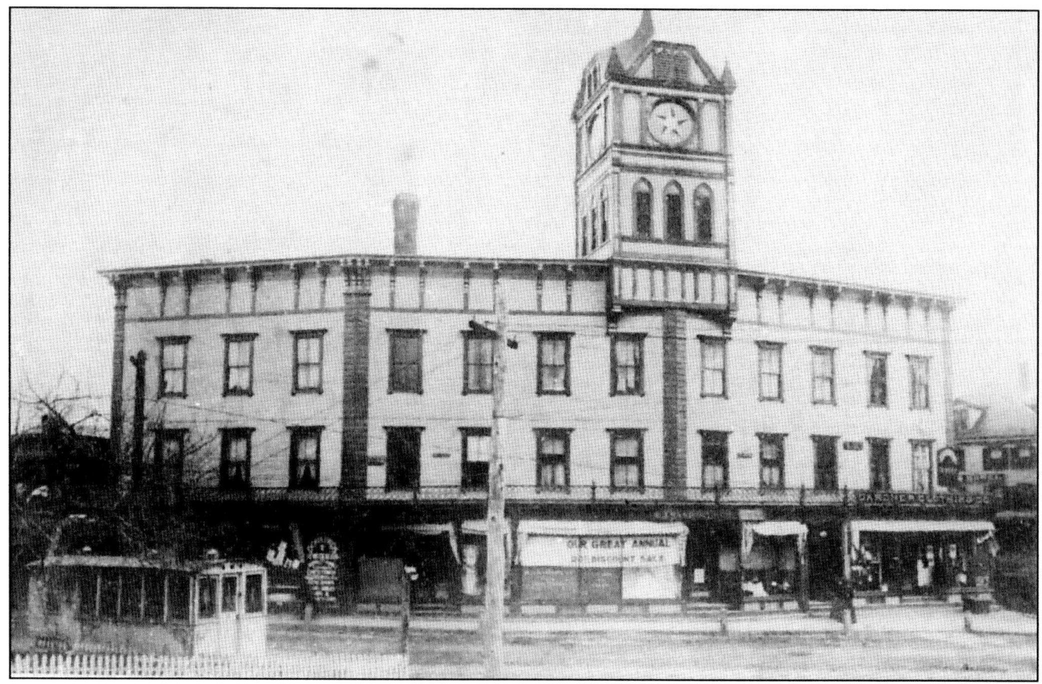

C.B. Steven's built his first block in 1880 on the corner of Central and Lynde (later West Lynde) Streets. A fire damaged the structure in 1890 but Stevens rebuilt and added the unique tower. The tower was removed for safety and structural reasons in 1909 but the building remains substantially as it was from that time.

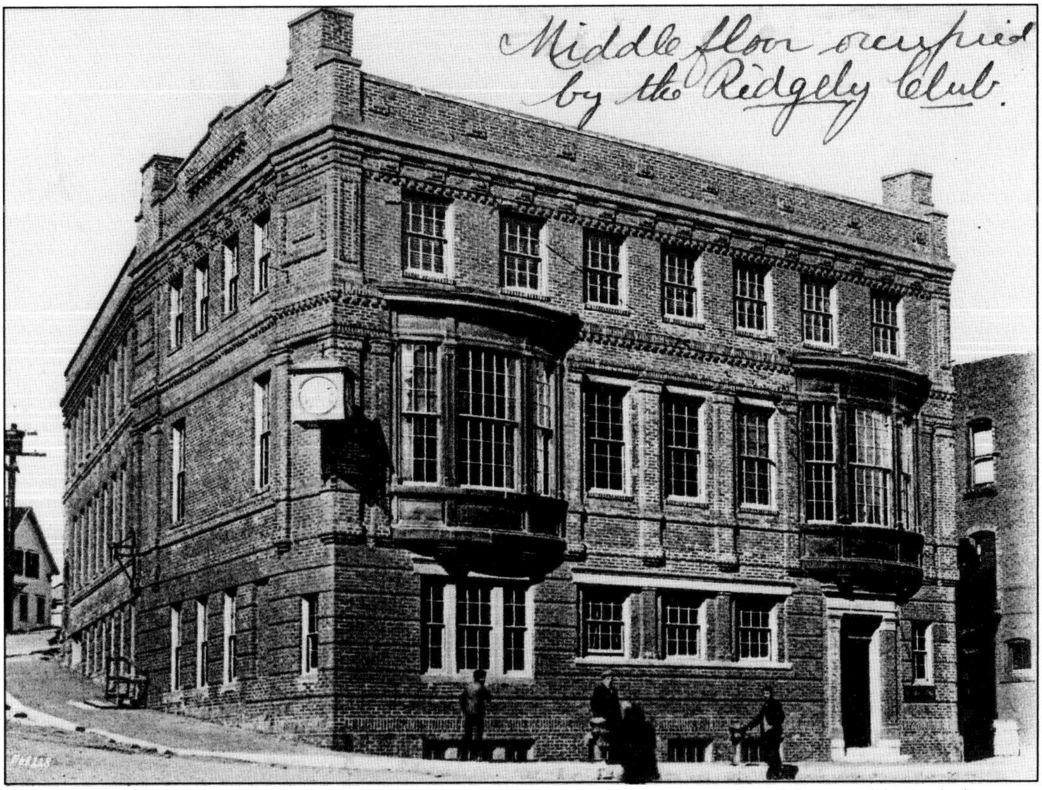

The *Gardner News* building was built in 1906. It was planned to resemble an old English print shop. The paper price was 1¢ a copy then, with a yearly subscription costing $1.

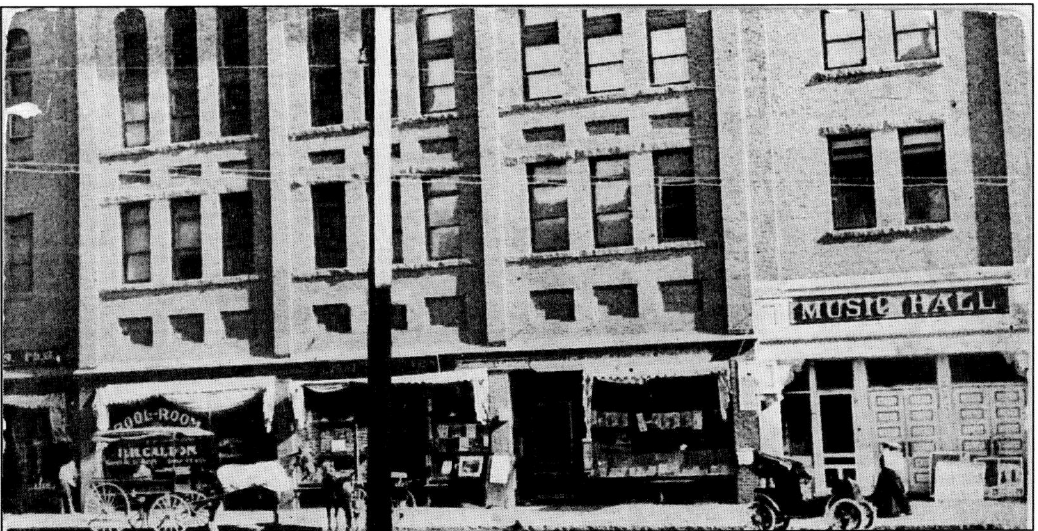

The Uptown Theatre's (Music Hall) grand opening was on March 5, 1897. It also housed a number of stores. The opening play was *The Girl I Left Behind.*

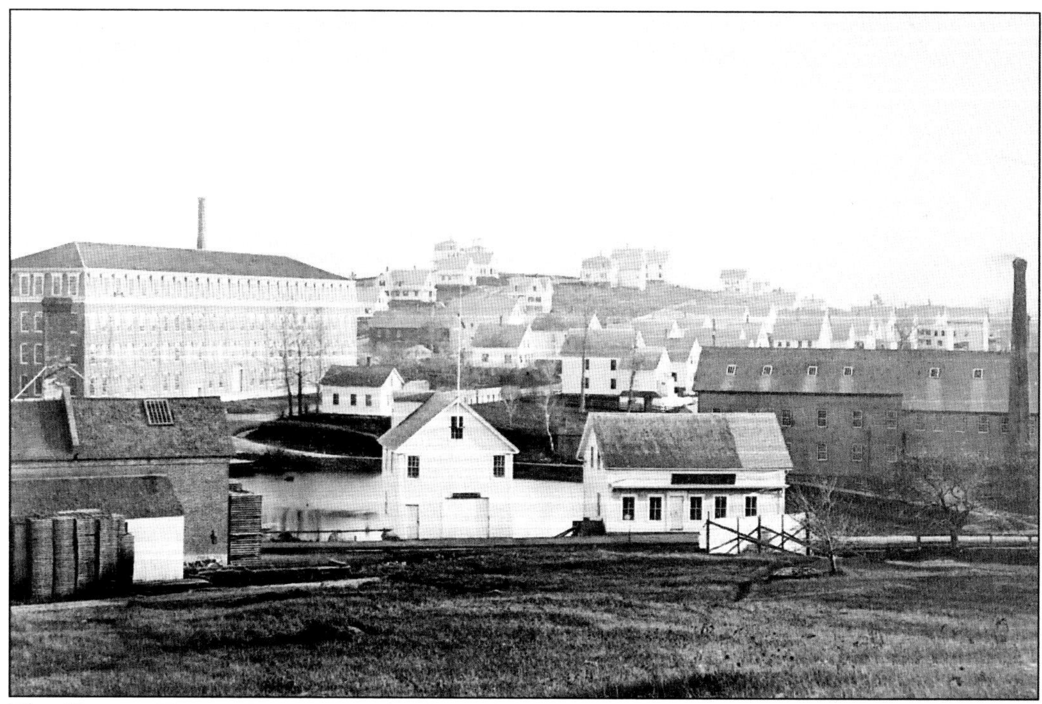

The Torrent Engine House was the first "fire station" in West Gardner. The building was located on Central Street near number 270. Behind the station is the mill pond of the L.H. Sawin Company; to the right is a tin smith shop; and to the left is part of the Heywood Brothers and Company factory.

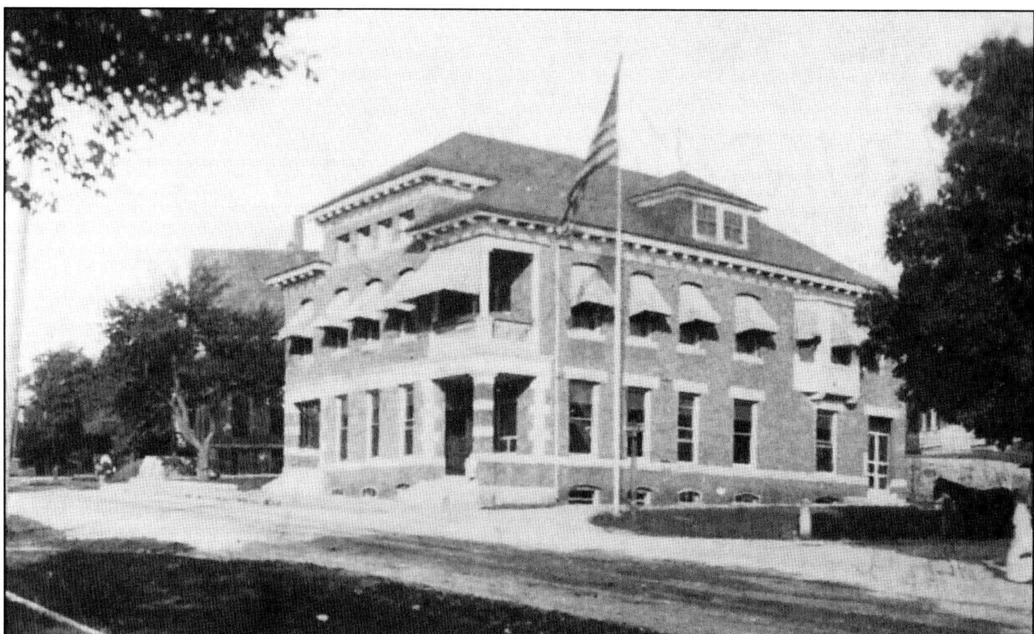

The first building built for use as a post office in 1899–1900, was located on the corner of Central and Maple Streets. George L. Minott was the first postmaster here and initiated Gardner's first free mail delivery.

"It is by all odds the best Band in New England."
—The Boston Journal.

REEVES'

American Band!

AND

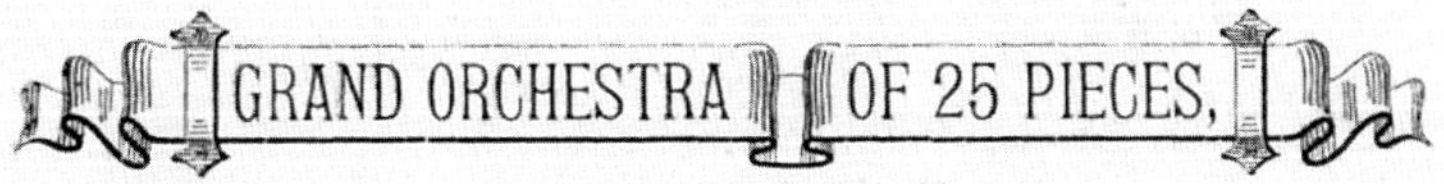

OF PROVIDENCE, R. I.,

Under the Leadership of Mr. D. W. REEVES,

WILL GIVE A GRAND

CONCERT & BALL!

—AT—

ELLSWORTH'S SKATING RINK,

GARDNER, MASS.,

WEDNESDAY EV'G, NOV. 28, 1883,

assisted by

Bowen R. Church, Fred Padley, Nichols, Schell, Frank Krall, Fischer, Scott, Fookes, Lafricain, Bosworth,

and a corps of other most distinguished Soloists and Musicians.

It is rarely indeed that this renowned Band appears in full strength outside the largest cities. Their music is universally admitted to surpass anything heard in this country.

FLOOR TICKETS TO CONCERT AND BALL, $1 00. CONCERT, reserved seats, 50c—on sale at Garland's Drug Store on Monday, Nov. 26, at 9 A. M. TURKEY SUPPER in the Basement of Rink, by A. M. Richards, $1 00 per plate.

Doors open at 7; Concert 7.45 to 9.30; Dancing to 3 A. M.

"A Band whose music is perfection itself."
—The Washington Star.

Ellsworth's skating rink was located on Pine Street where Miller's Opera House is located today, between West Lynde Street and 87 Pine Street. The skating rink lasted a short time and was turned into store and the first Miller's Opera House. This broadside indicates just one of the activities that took place at the rink. The building burned on January 11, 1892.

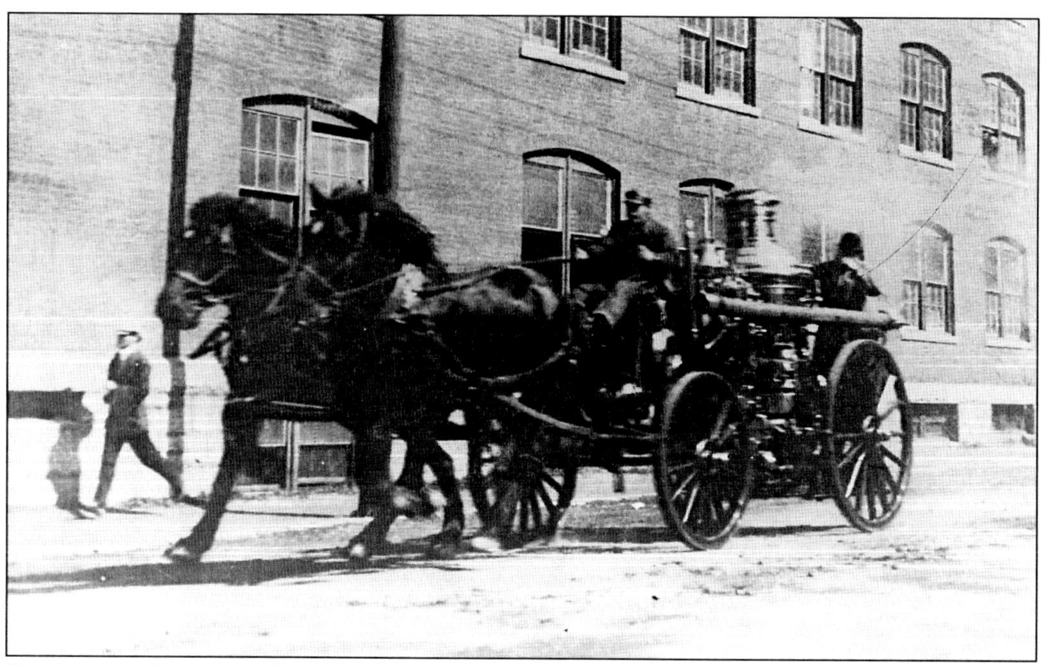

Steamer No. 2, an Amoskeag machine, races down Central Street past the factory of Heywood Brothers and Wakefield, *c*. 1905.

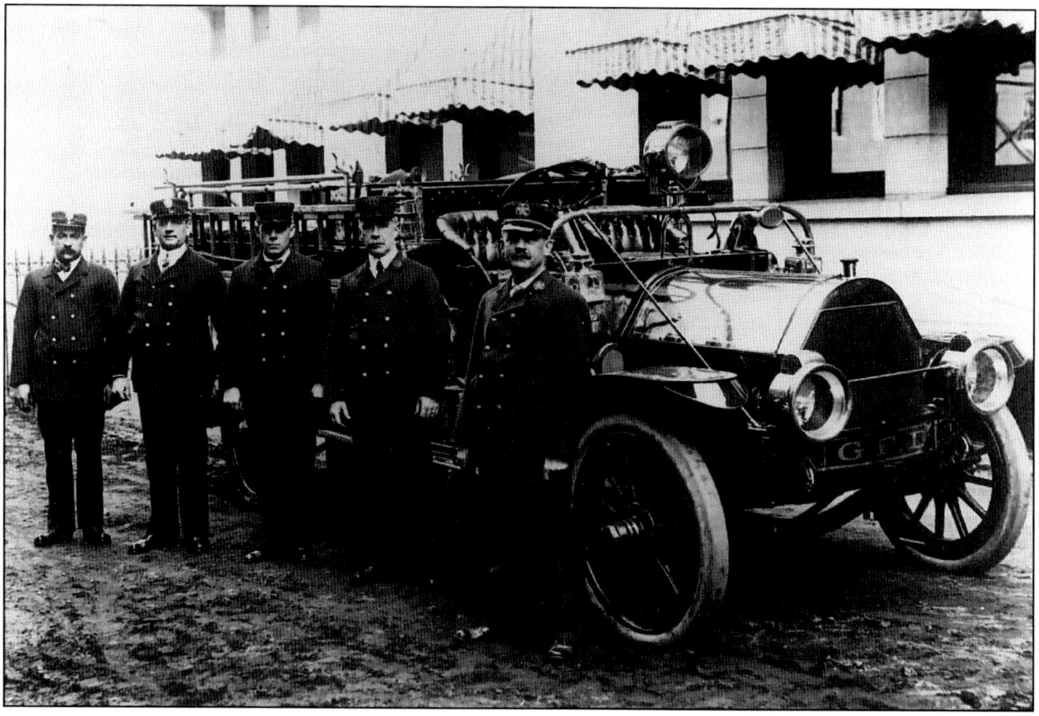

One of the two Knox Combination Hose and Chemical Wagons purchased by Gardner in 1912. Standing by the machine are, from left to right, Henry Thibodeau, William Biron, John Hurley, Addison Walker, and Chief George S. Hodgman. Charles Greenwood was agent for the Knox Motor Company of Springfield, Massachusetts.

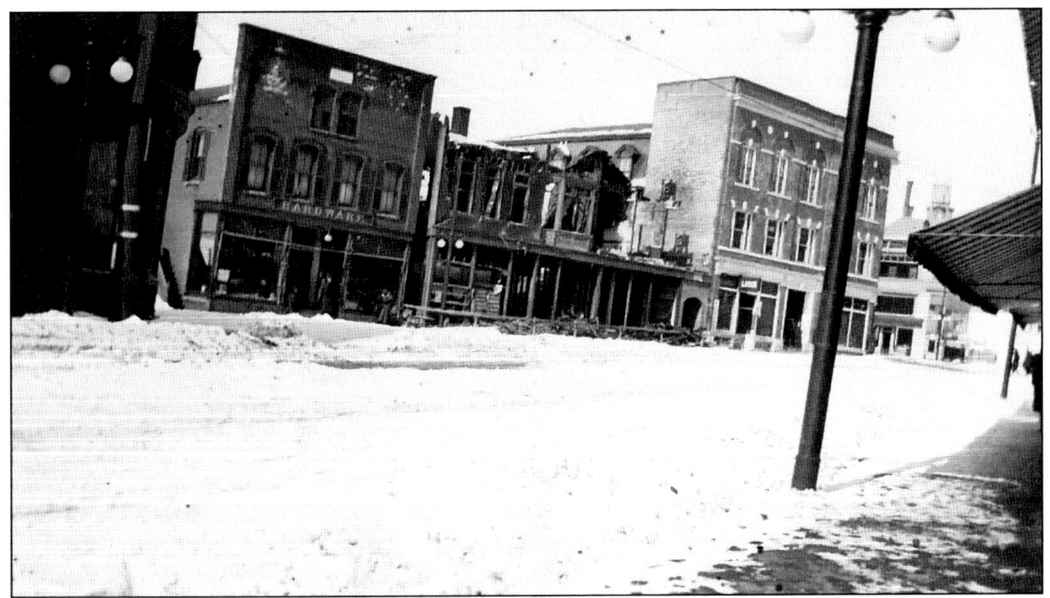

The Riordan fire, which took place in February 1916.

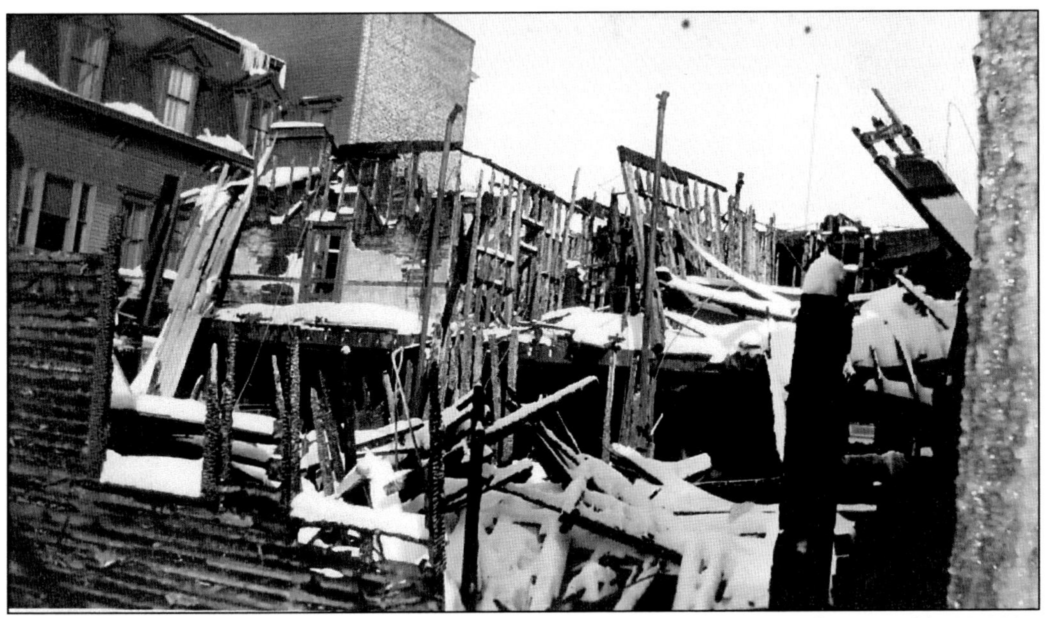

Riordan and Michaelman's store was completely destroyed with property damage of $100,000.

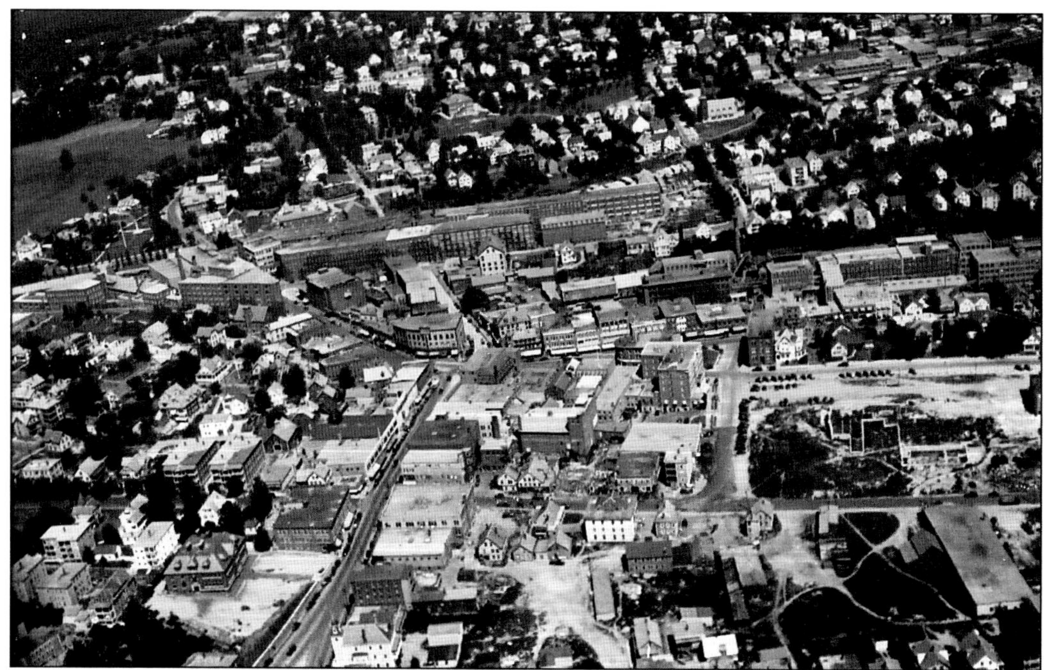

Looking east over West Gardner. Note there is no city hall, post office, or police station, and that City Hall Avenue reached only to Connors Street.

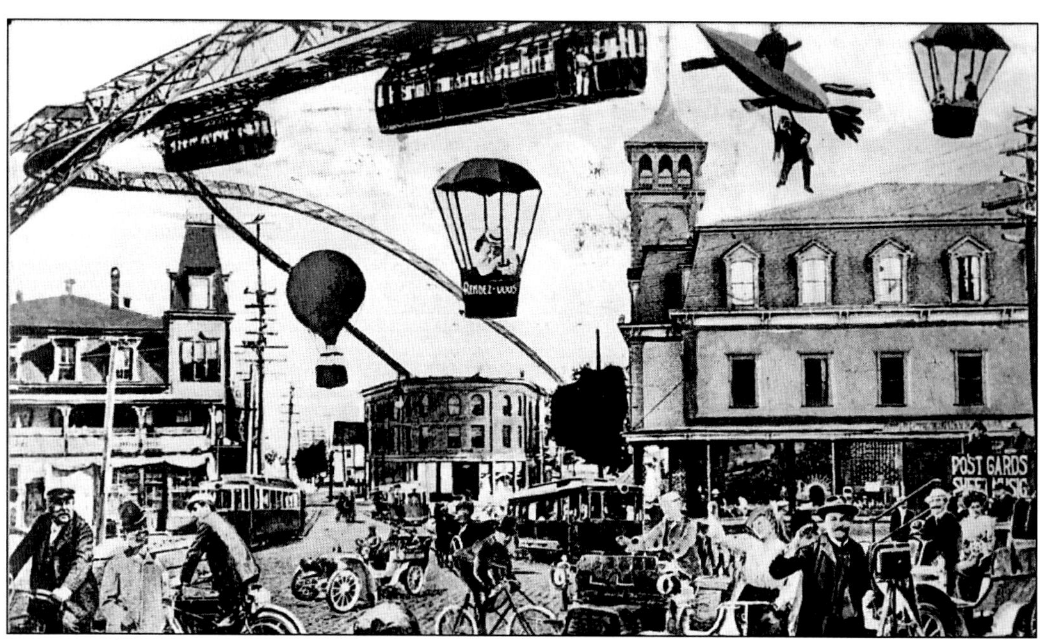

How Gardner was going to look in the future to someone in the early twentieth century.

Four

The Depot: Union Square

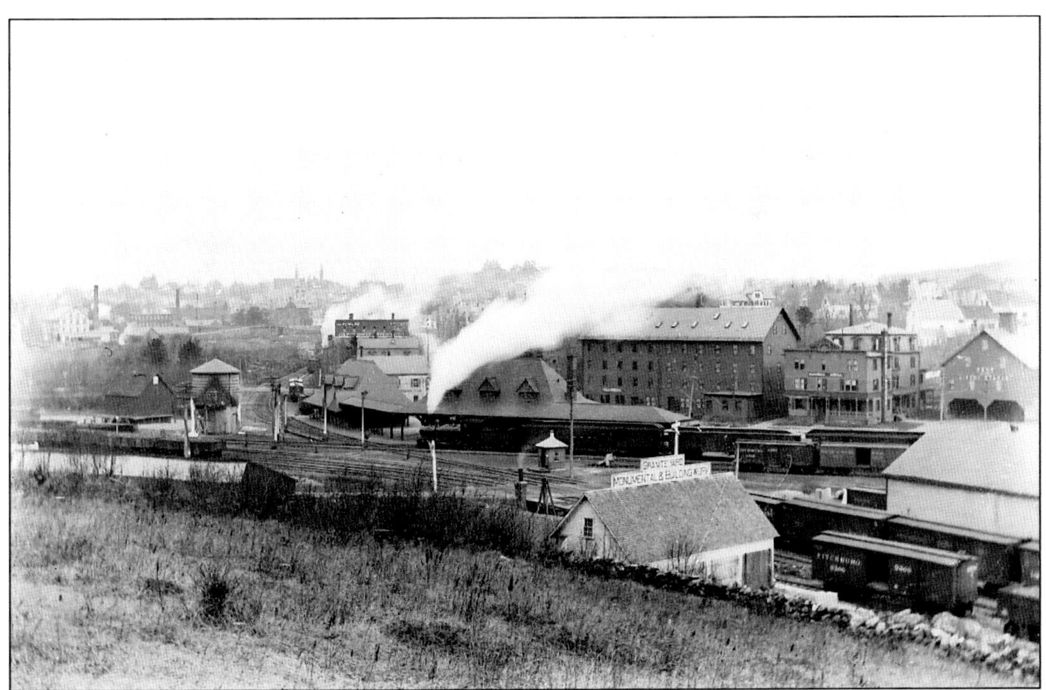

Gardner Depot was built in 1895–96 near the site of the original Vermont and Massachusetts Railroad Station. The Vermont and Massachusetts Railroad came into Gardner in 1847. This was the site for many years of the famous first large chair manufactured by P. Derby Company. In the background can be seen the old W.W. Alley Chair Plant (later Howe and Spaulding), the Gardner House Hotel, and its livery stable. Union Station was torn down in 1959.

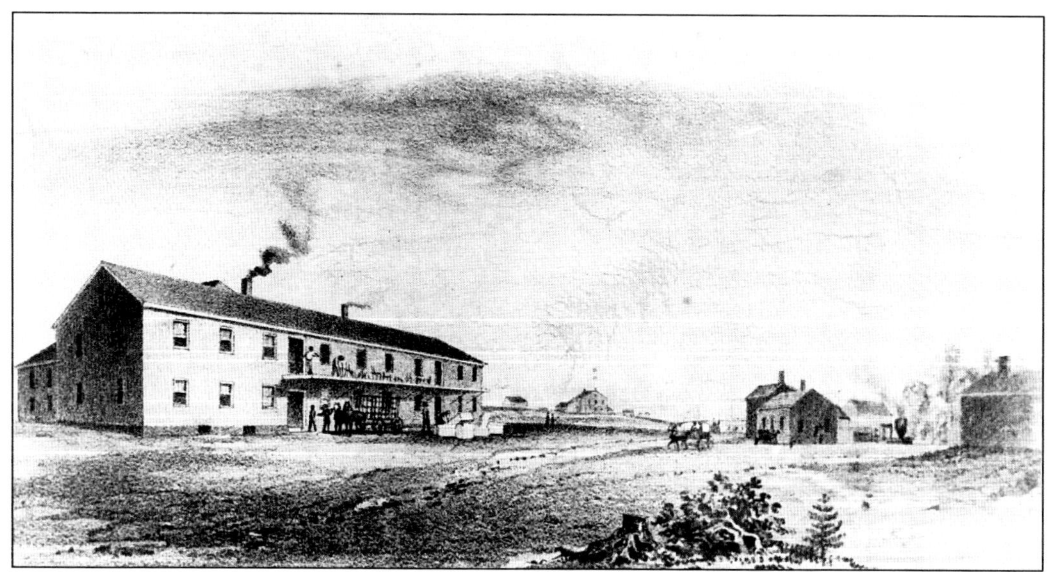

A.H. Brick's shop at the depot. A depot is visible on the right side of the picture. Later A.H. Brick's shop was bought by Greenwood and Wright. The shop was eventually torn down.

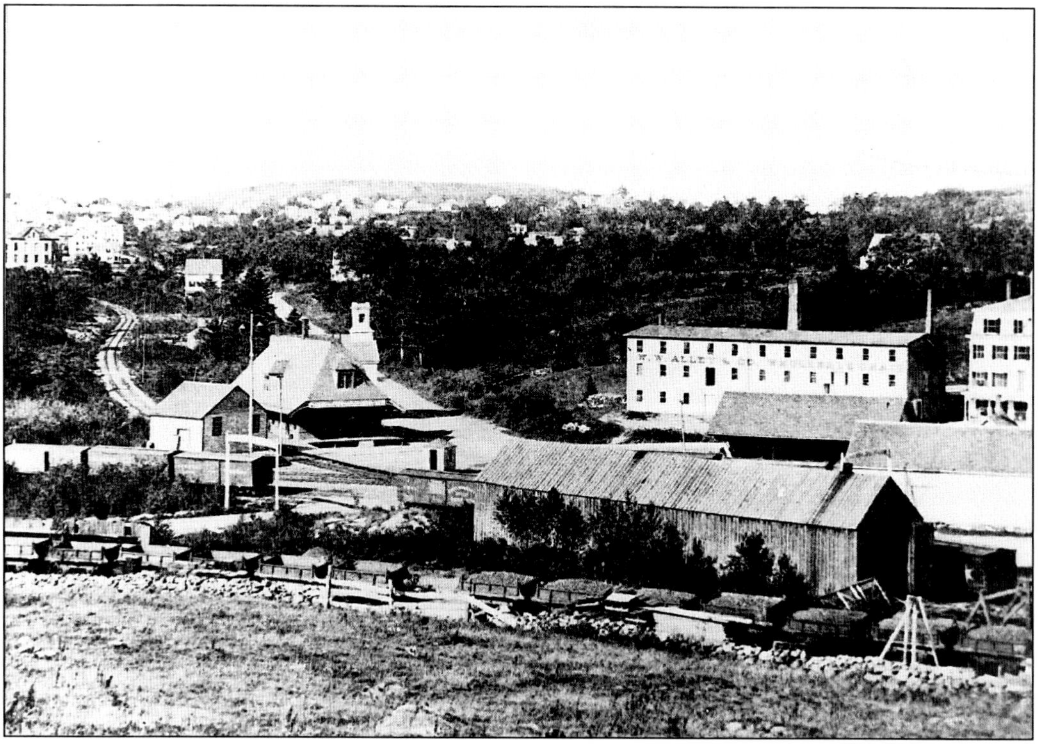

Mr. William W. Alley of Boston operated a paint shop at the depot from 1870 to about 1875. It was originally owned by S.W.A. Stevens, C.S. Greenwood, and Wright and Moore. By 1878 the plant was owned by S.K. Pierce and Philander Derby. In 1882 C. Webster Bush of the firm of Conant and Bush purchased the property, located near the site of the Salvation Army Store.

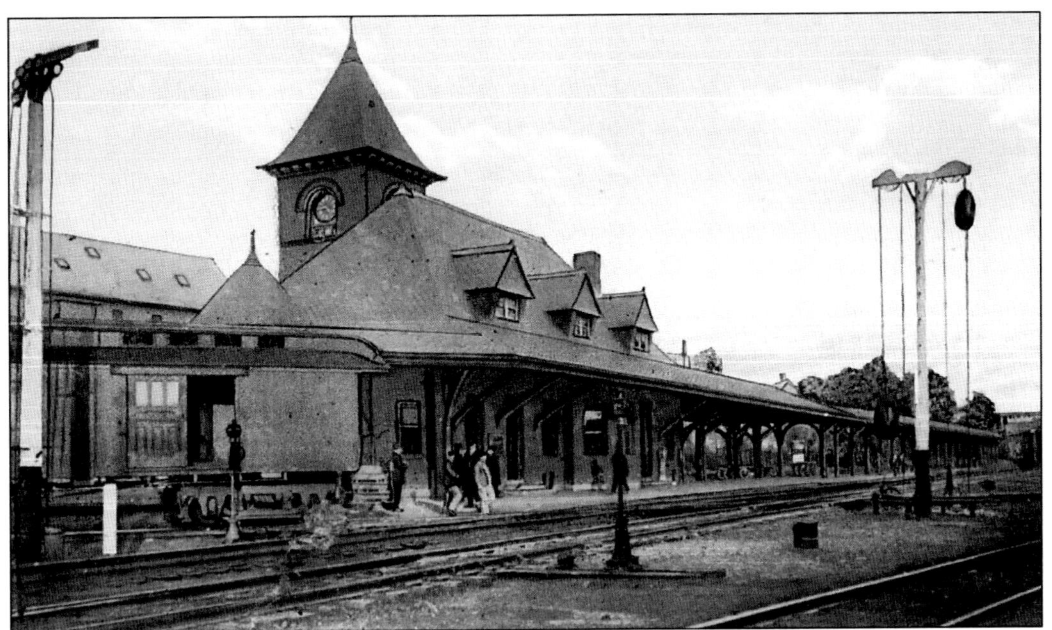

The baggage platform area where passengers awaited the arrival of the trains.

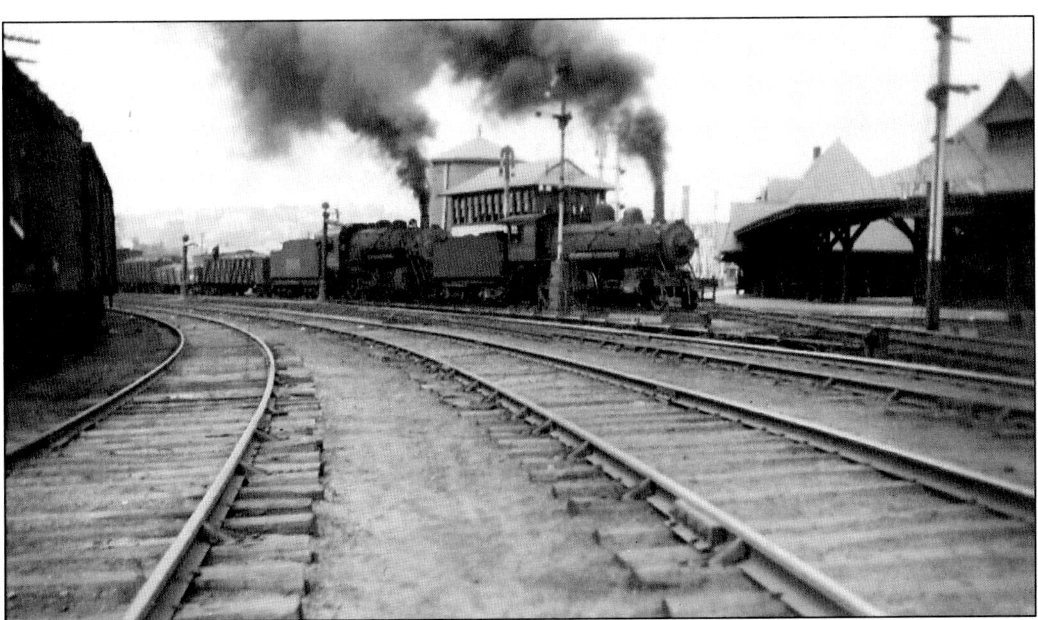

One of the large trains passing through the depot, with two steam locomotives at its head. Pusher engines were sometimes needed at the rear of the train to make the grade into Gardner.

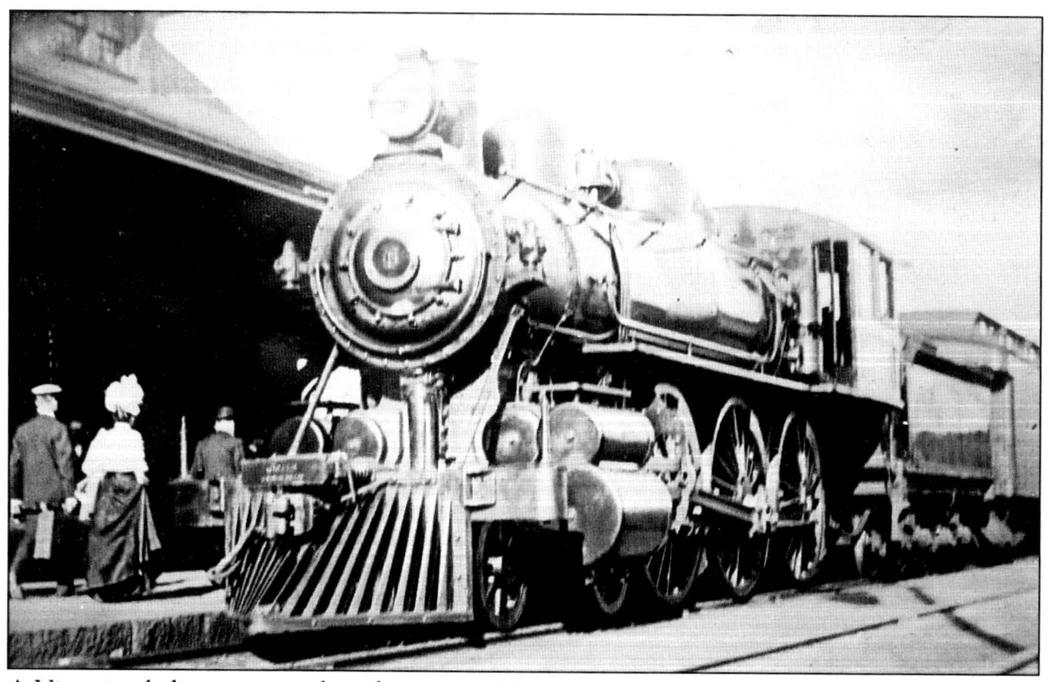

A Victorian lady prepares to board a train at Union Station.

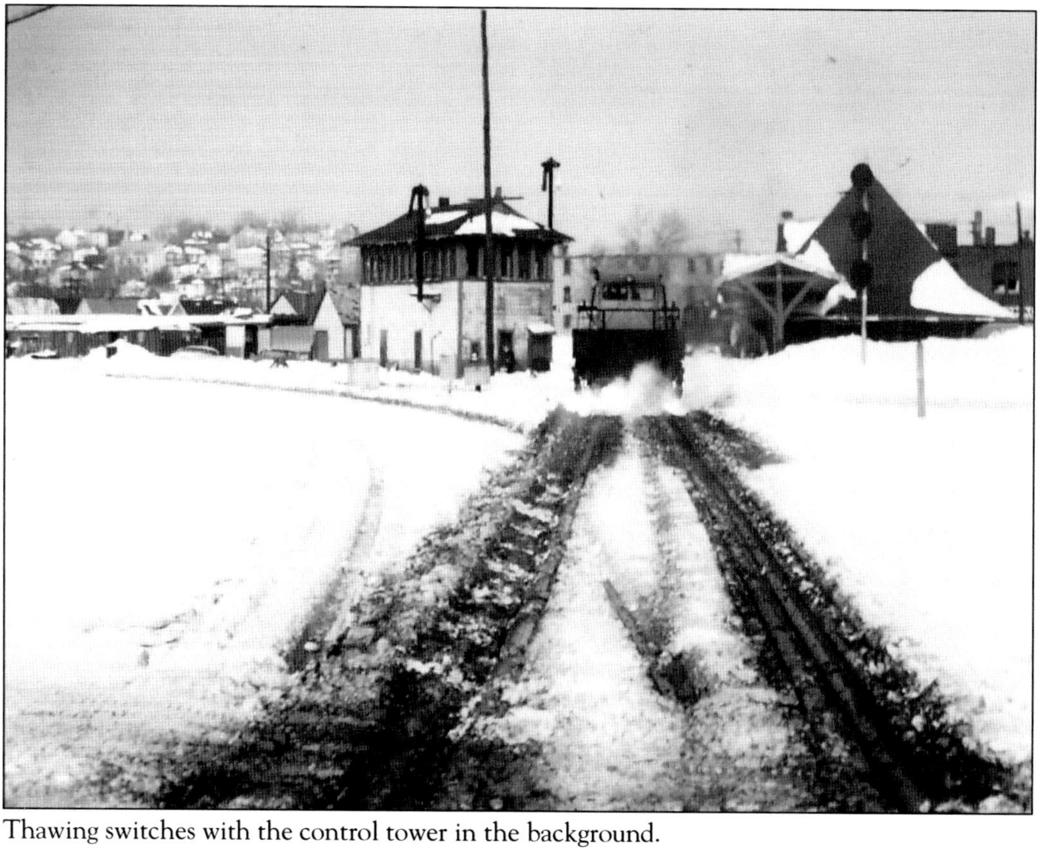

Thawing switches with the control tower in the background.

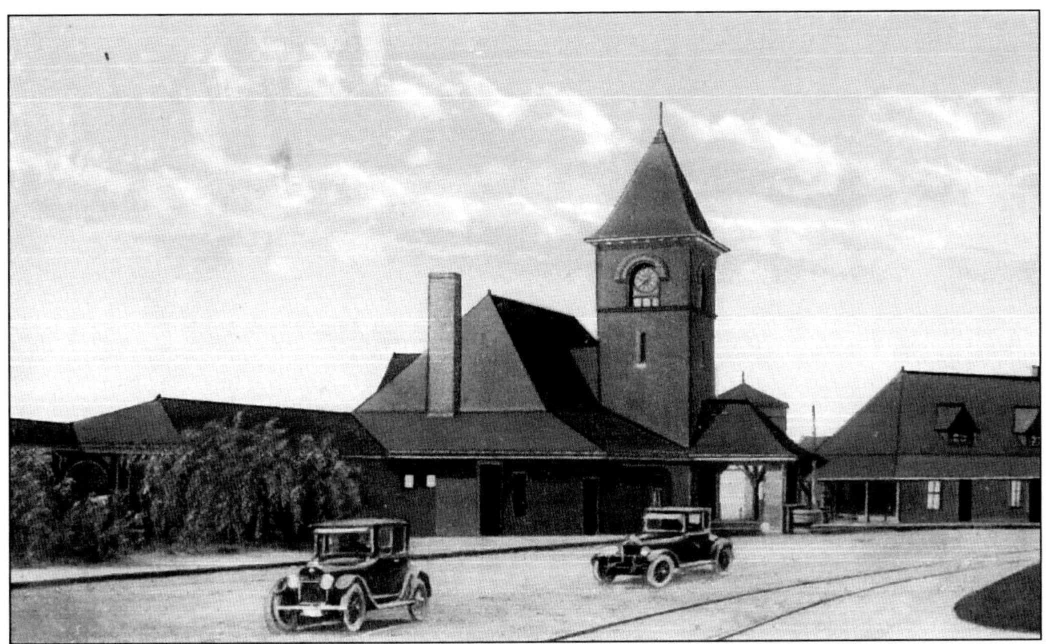

Union Station, built in 1895–96, stood in Union Square where the Music Forum is now situated. In 1902 President Theodore Roosevelt spoke at the station. A short distance east of the depot sat the first large Gardner chair, the Derby Chair.

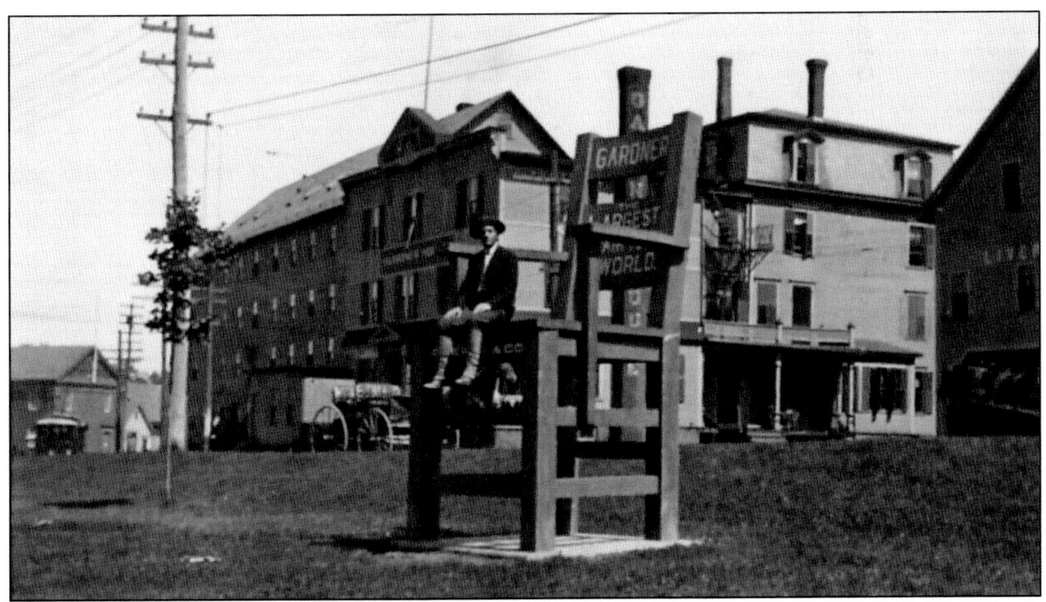

The Derby Chair with the Gardner House in the background.

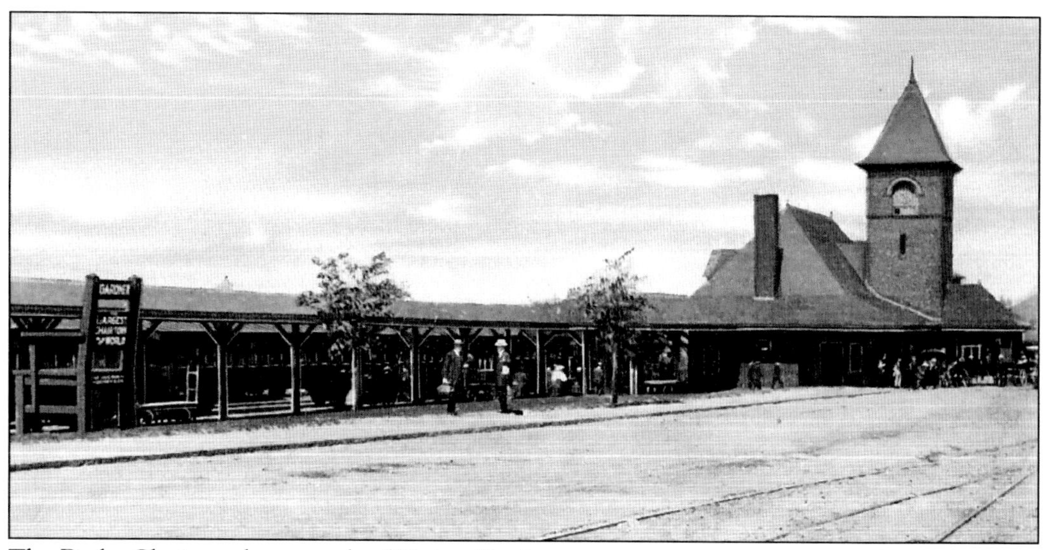

The Derby Chair on the grounds of Union Station.

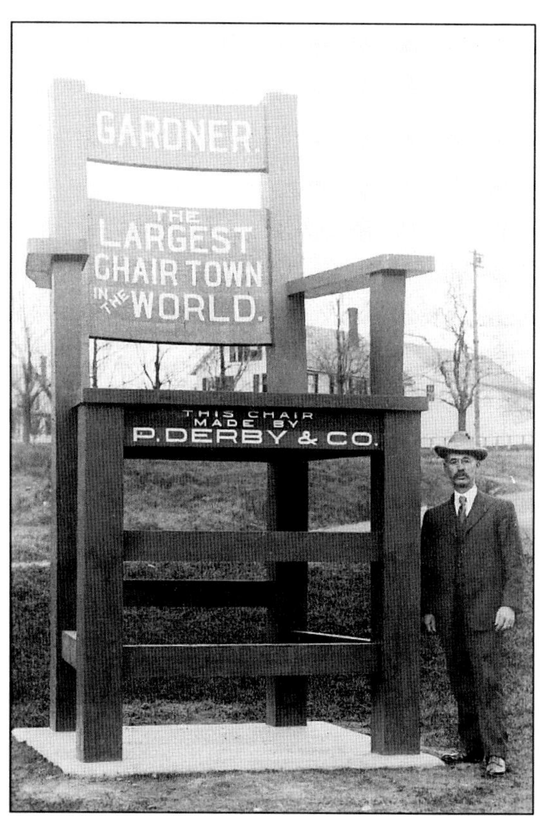

George C. Goodale stands beside the large Mission Chair he built for P. Derby and Company.

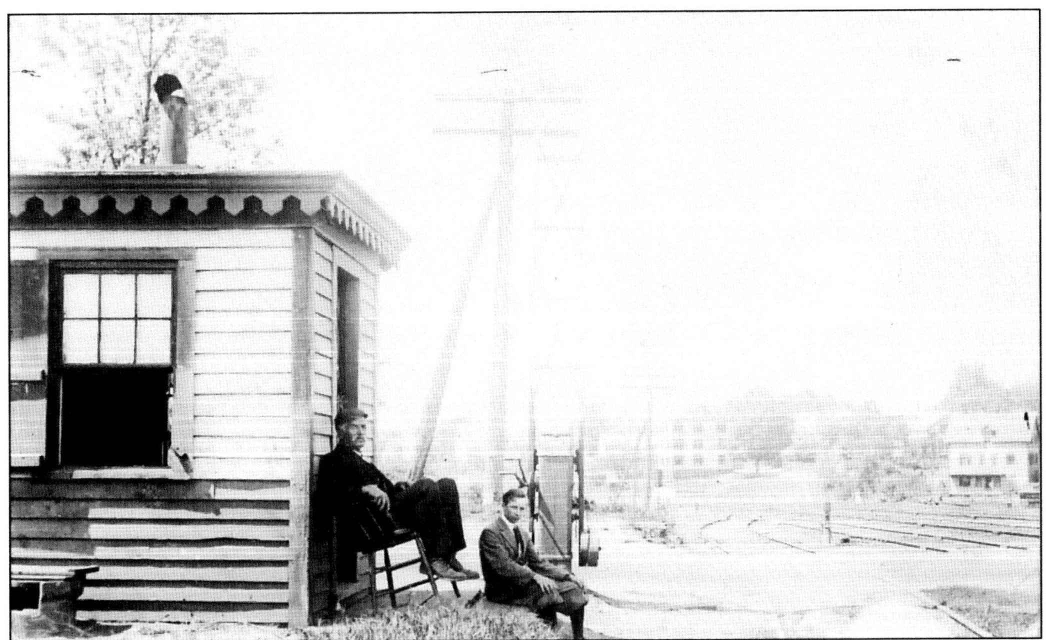

Bull Run Crossing was one of Gardner's many railroad crossings, including: Osgood Crossing at the depot on Conant Street, Kendall Crossing on South Main Street near the R. Smith Company, Sawin's Crossing on South Main Street near Travers Street, Gate's Crossing on West Broadway, Union Street Crossing before the bridge, Hale's Crossing on Whitney Street, and Heywood Crossing on Central Street.

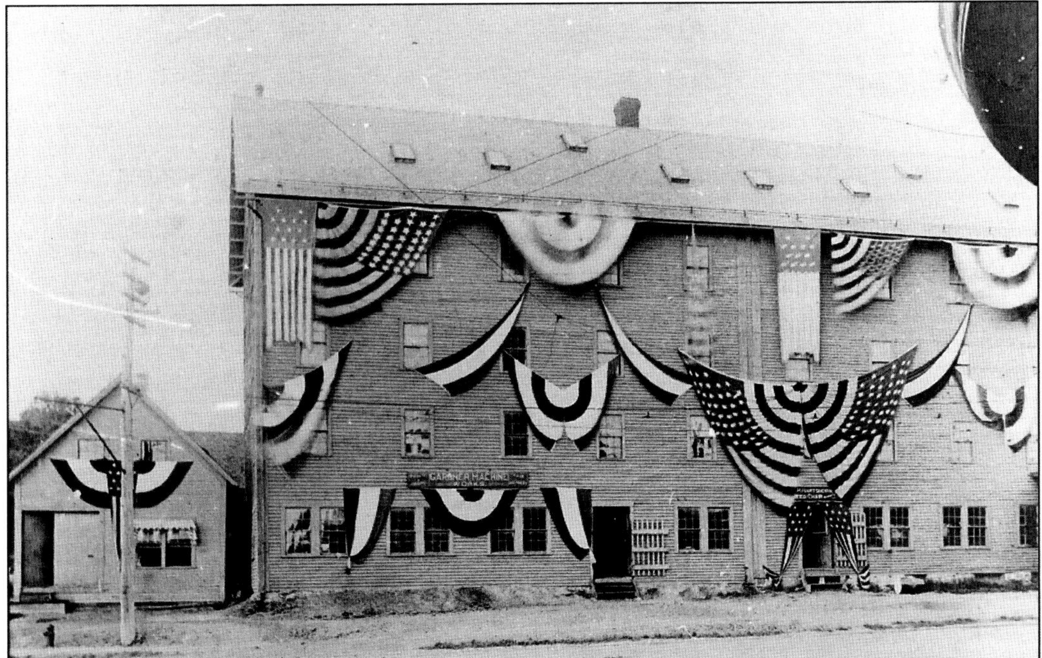

Gardner Machine Works, built by William H. Hobby, manufactured woodworking machinery. It is presently the site of the Salvation Army Store. The C.H. Hartshorn Company occupied a portion of the building.

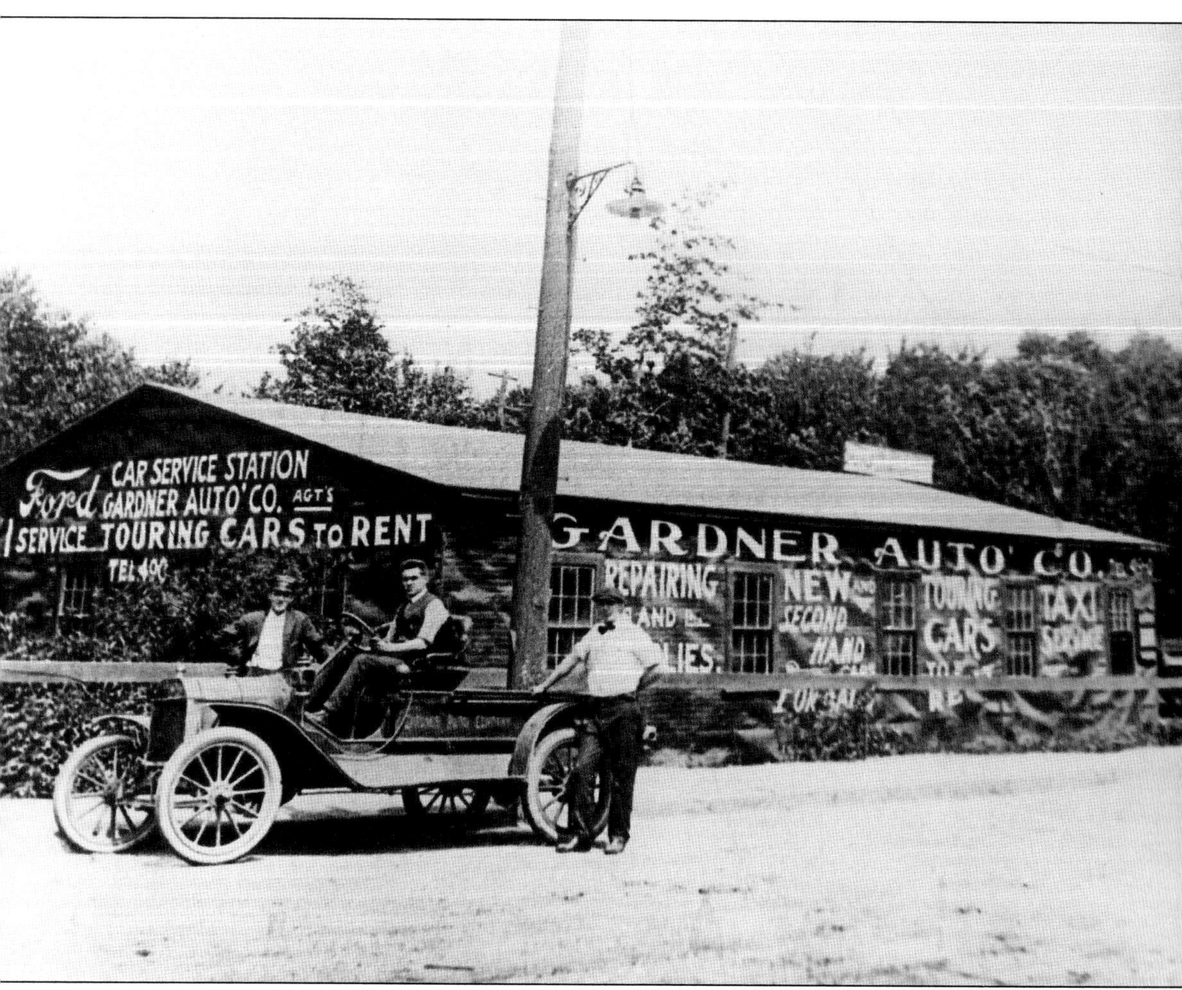

The Gardner Auto Company was incorporated in 1907, with John R. Conant as its first president. About 1910 the officers of the company were, from left to right: Clifton J. Parker (treasurer), driver Joseph Parker (secretary), and William W. Fitzsimmons (president). Located originally on the north corner of Main and Chestnut Streets, the company later moved to the present site of General Automotive across the street.

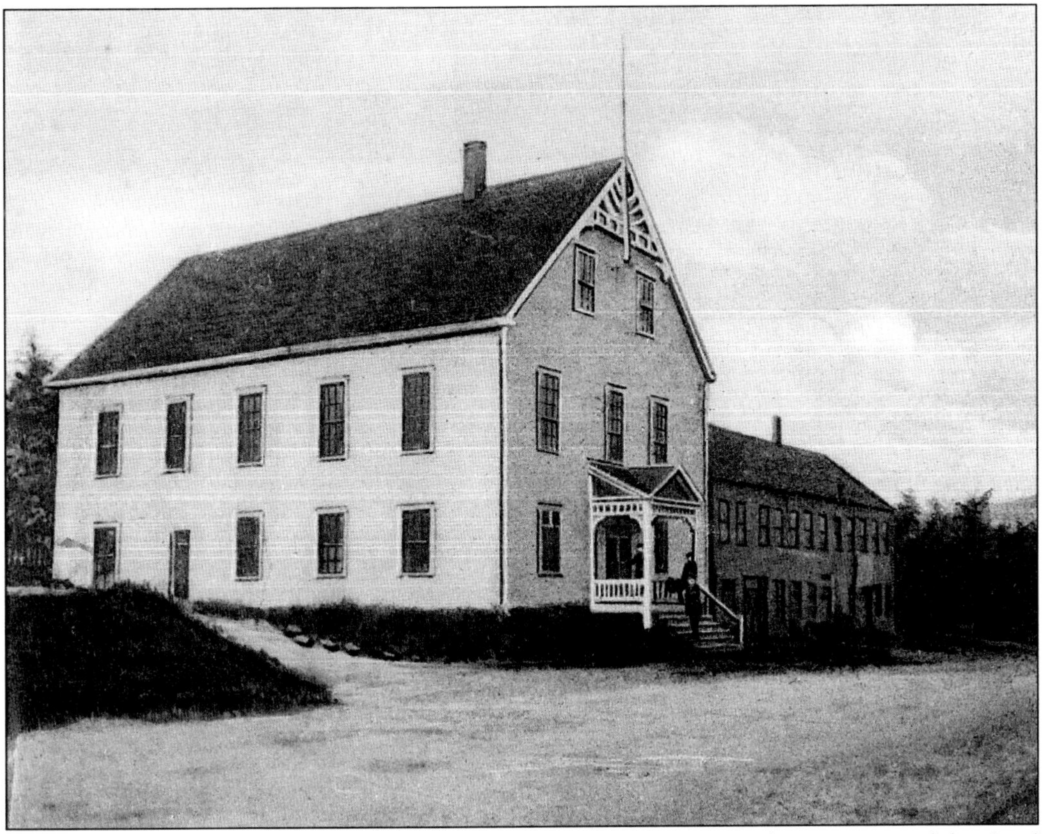

The Grand Army of the Republic (GAR) Hall was built to memorialize veterans of the Civil War. The hall was located near 450 Chestnut Street.

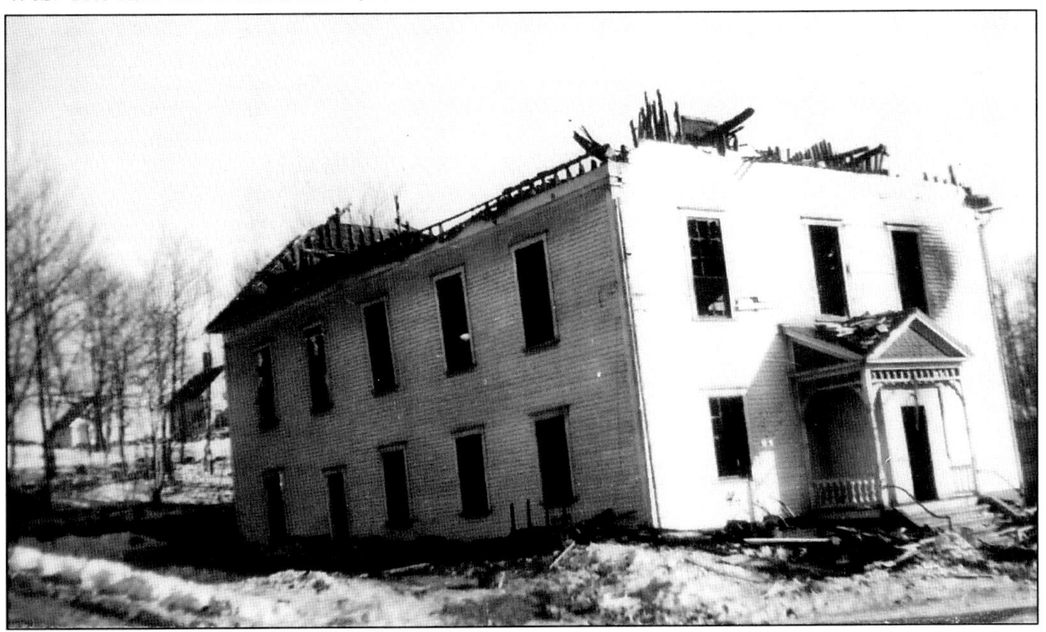

The GAR Hall burned shortly after World War II on January 31, 1946.

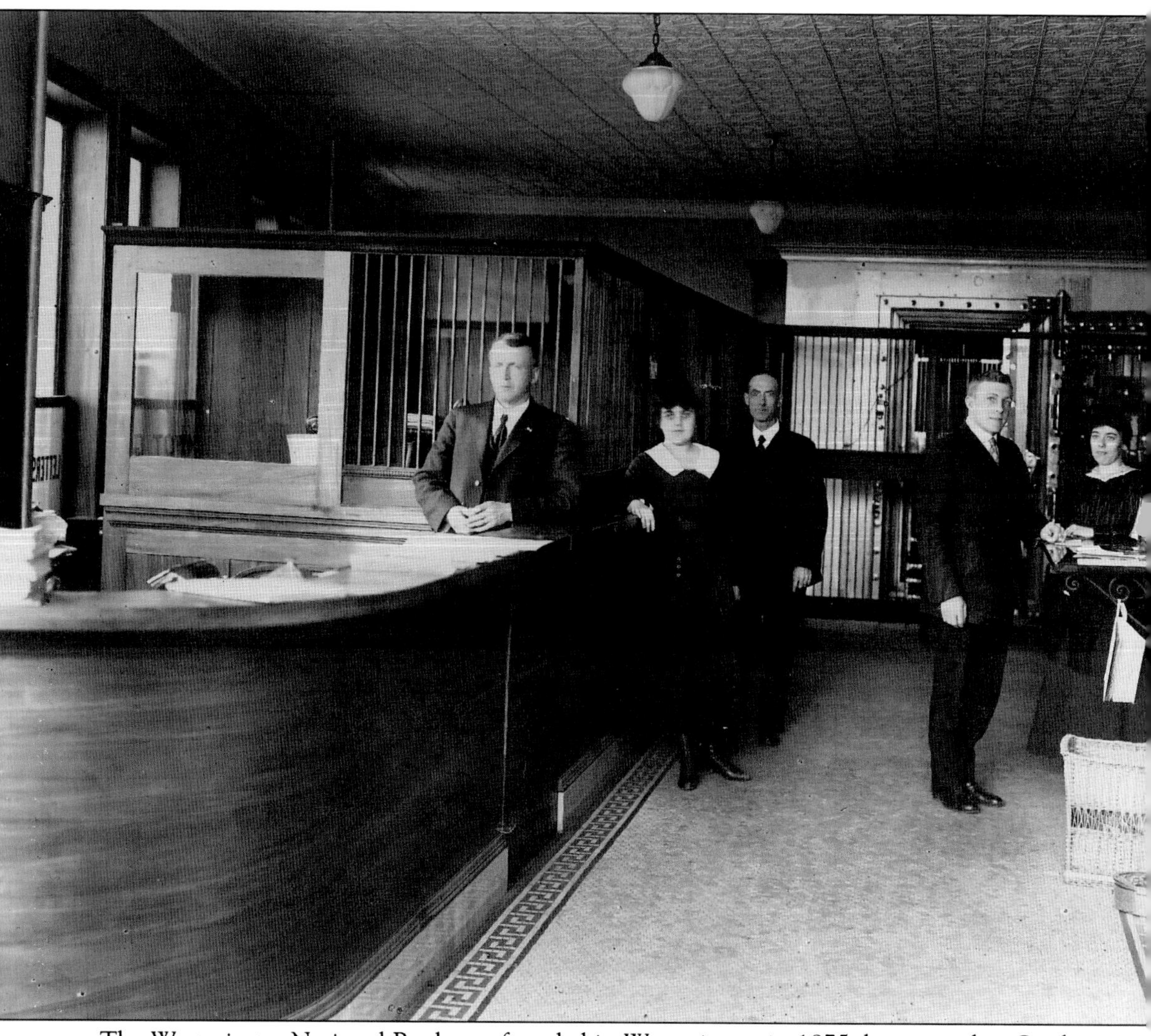

The Westminster National Bank was founded in Westminster in 1875, but moved to Gardner in 1894, and was located on Chestnut Street near Parker Glass. In 1916 it moved to West Gardner and the name was changed to the Gardner Trust Company. From the left to right are Frank Fenno, unknown, Frank Lavallee, Everett Black and Belle Murray.

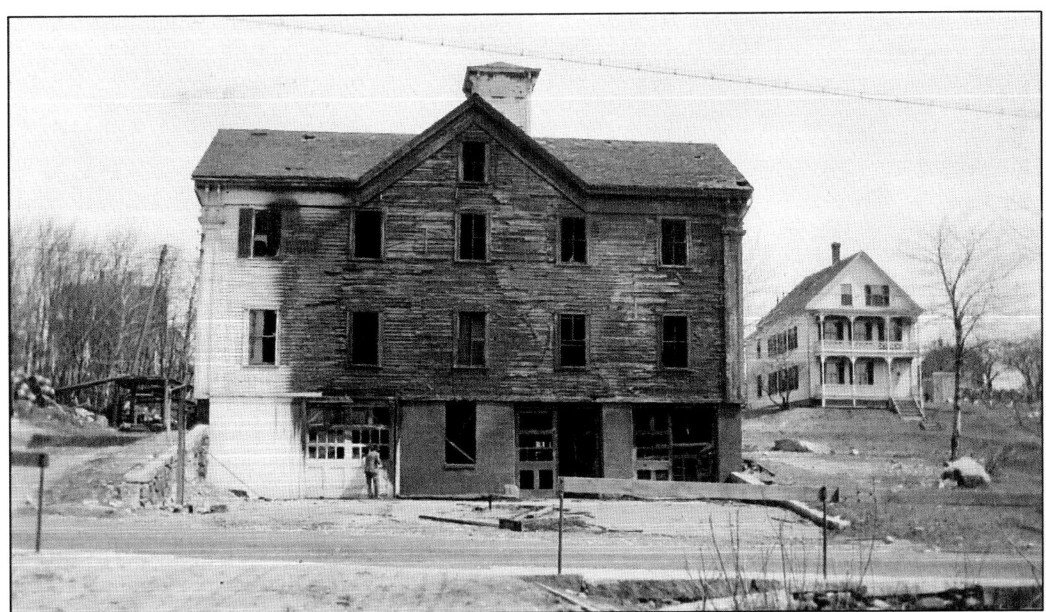

The Chestnut Street Fire Station burned March 28, 1916. The former Bell Schoolhouse in South Gardner, it was built in 1845 and located on East Broadway. In 1890 it was moved to Chestnut Street near the L.H. Sawin Factory.

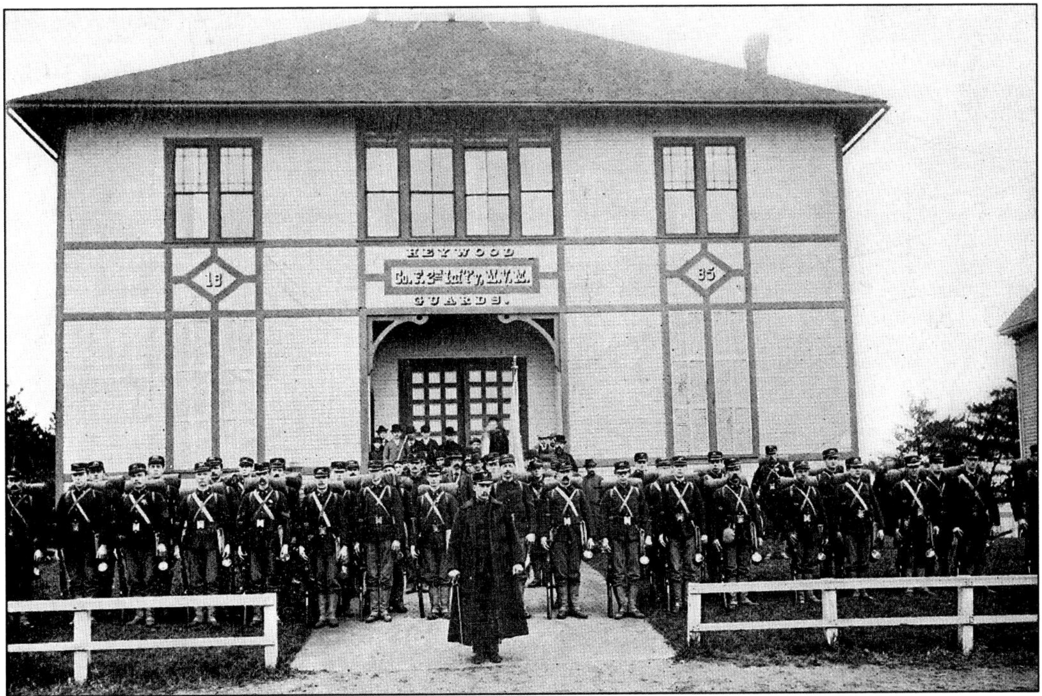

The Heywood Guards Armory building, erected in 1885, located on Elm Street near the junction of Elm Street and Fairlawn Avenue. In 1902 the building was moved to a spot behind the "new" high school building, now the Helen Mae Sauter School. Here it was used by the high school cadets for drill practice. About 1912 the building became a gymnasium for the high school. Here such sports as basketball were played. The building was torn down in 1930.

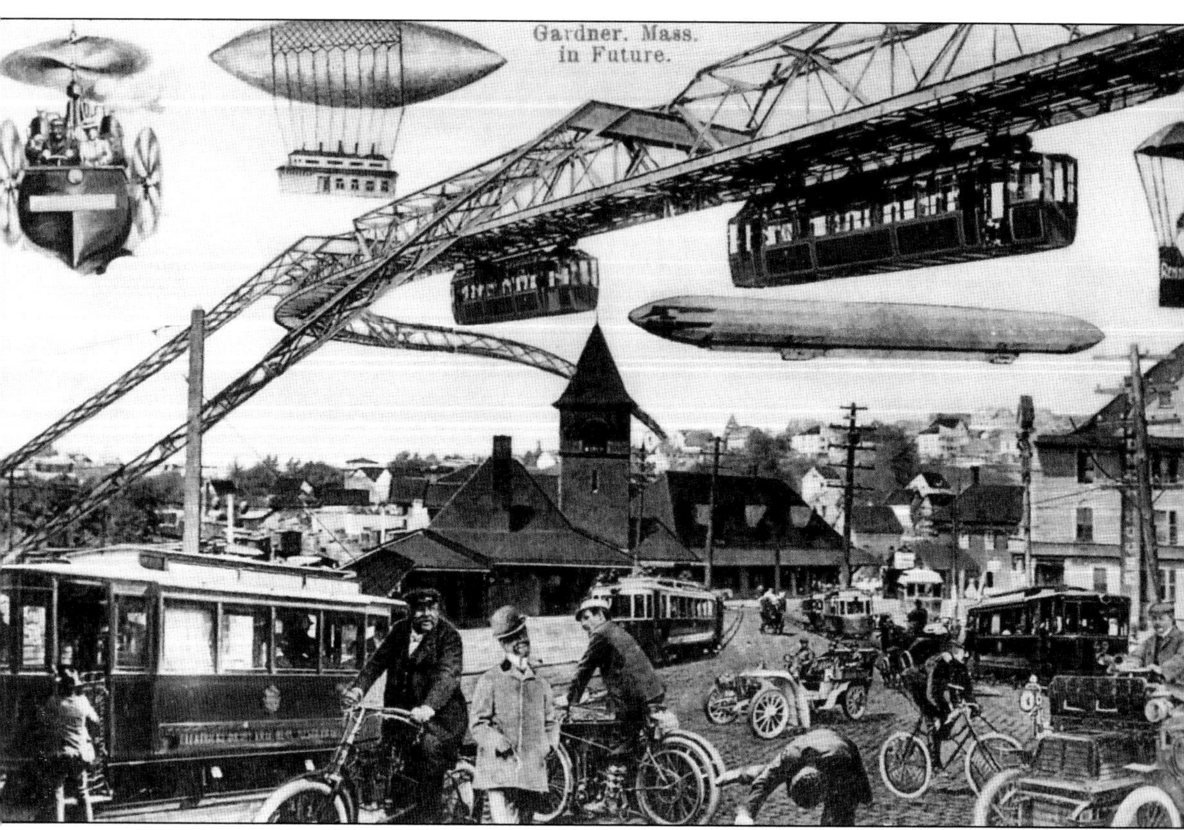

An artist's conception of the depot as it might have looked in the future.

Five

Recreation, School, and Sports

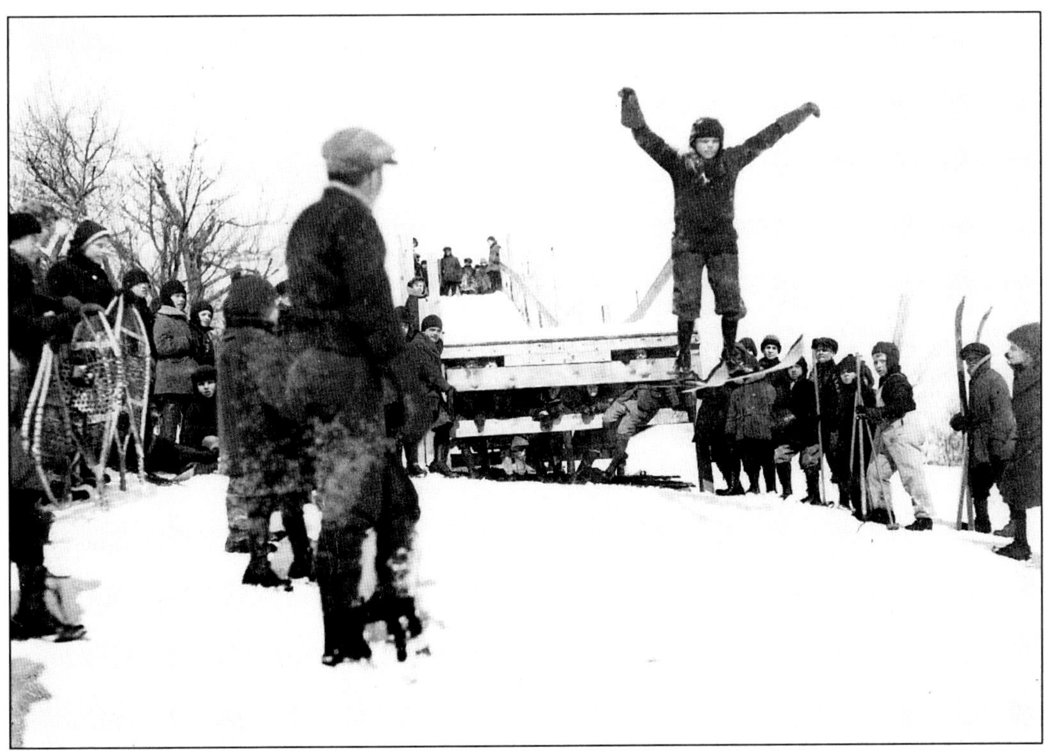

The idea for a ski jump on the south side of Kendall Hill started with a winter carnival in 1923. It was not until 1924 that the jump was ready. It lasted only a few of years.

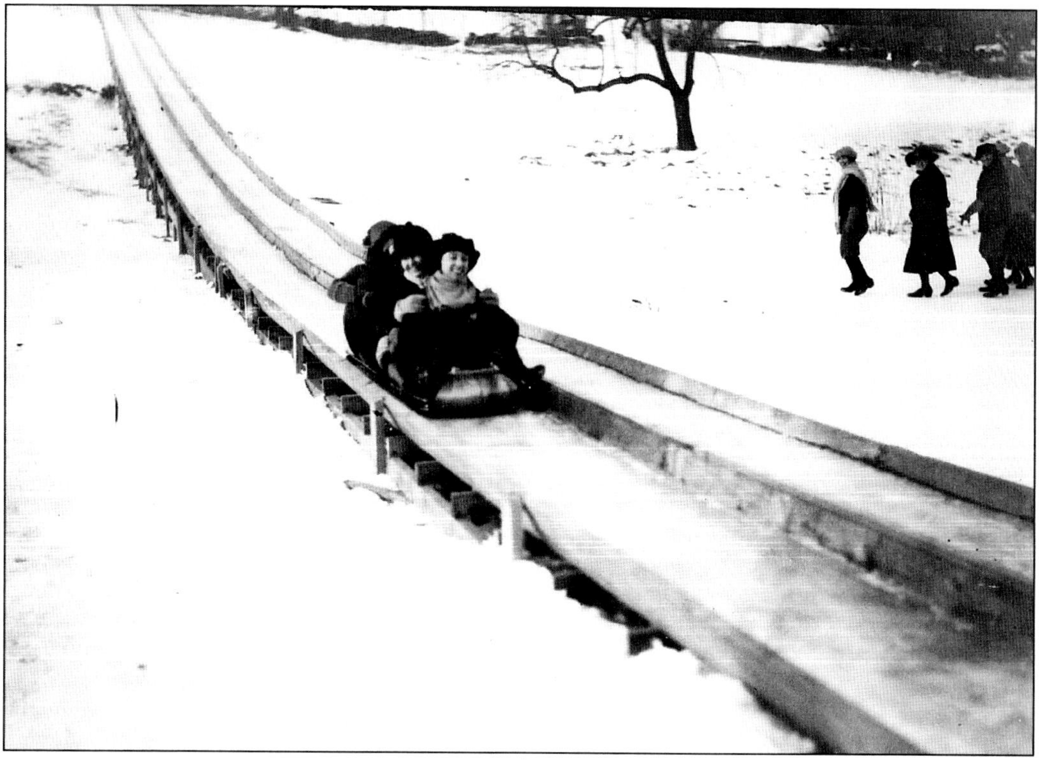

A toboggan slide or shute was also built on Kendall Hill in 1923. It, too, lasted only a short time.

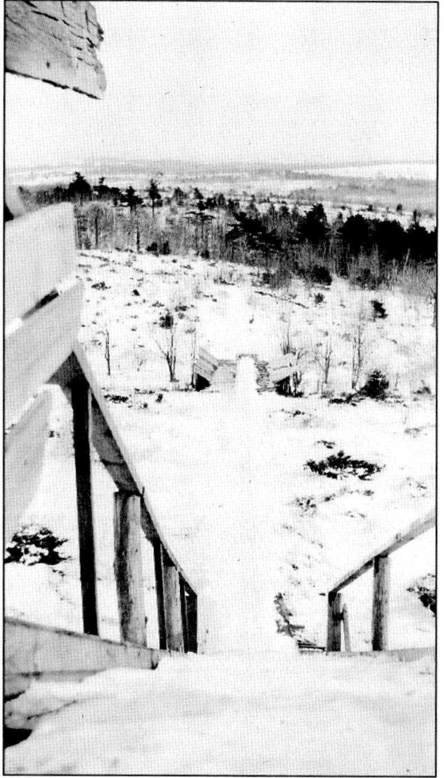

In 1930 the second ski jump in Gardner was built on the south side of Parker Hill. Like the slide and jump in the previous two photographs, it lasted only a few years.

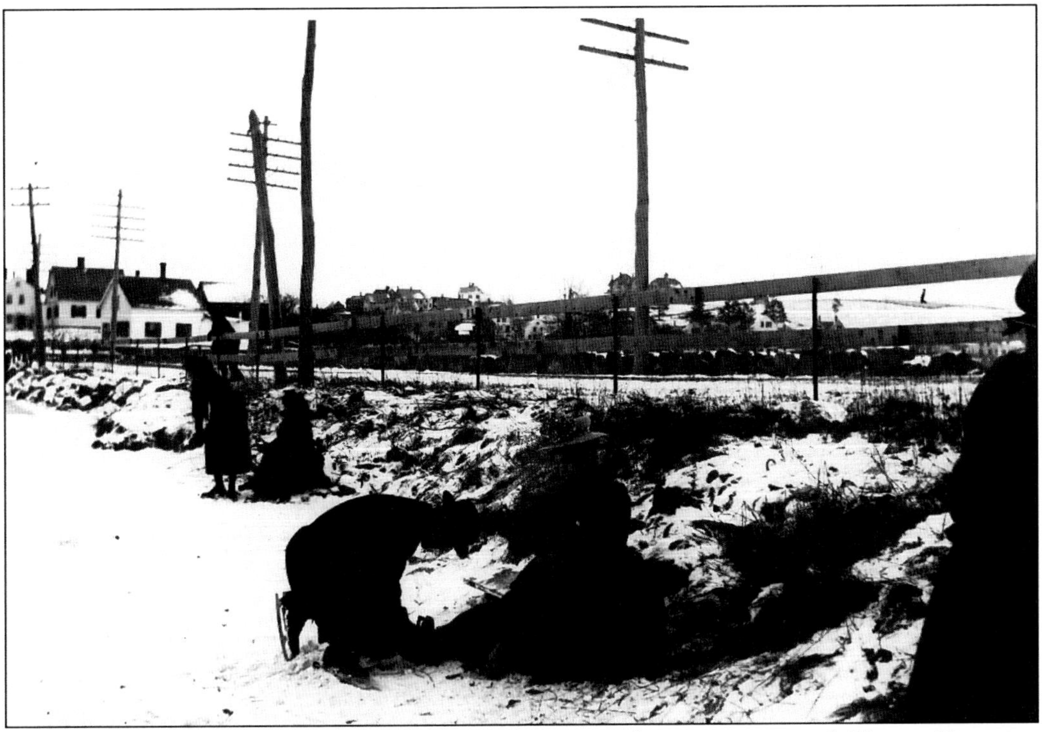

Skating was one of the earliest winter activities our predecessors practiced. Here a Victorian gentleman helps a Victorian lady into her skates on the shore of upper Bent's Pond.

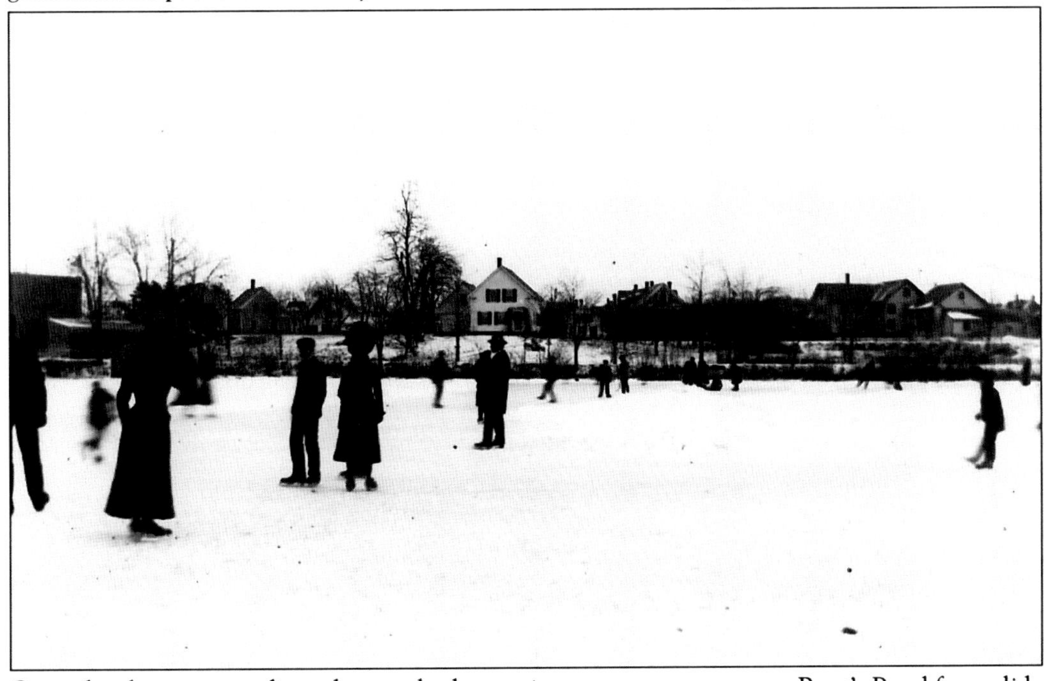

Once the skates were adjusted properly the parties went out onto upper Bent's Pond for a glide over the ice. This is an example of recreation provided by the mill ponds the mills created. Among other recreational activities were fishing, bathing, and boating.

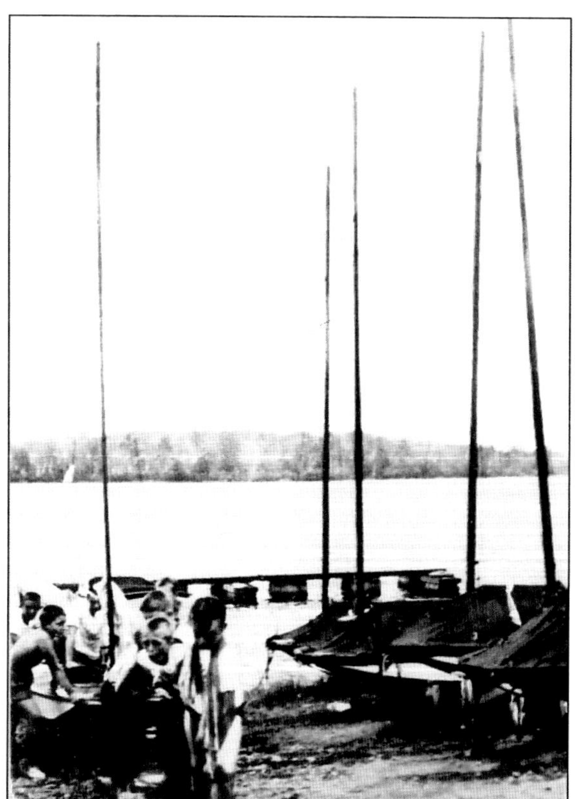

The Monadnock Moth fleet at Camp Collier was originally designed by Henry W. Sheldrick for his son William L. Sheldrick. The first regatta at Camp Collier took place in 1939. The craft became so successful that an article appeared in *Boys Life Magazine* in 1951. While the fleet lasted, each year the Underwood trophy, presented by Clinton J. Underwood, was inscribed with the winner's names.

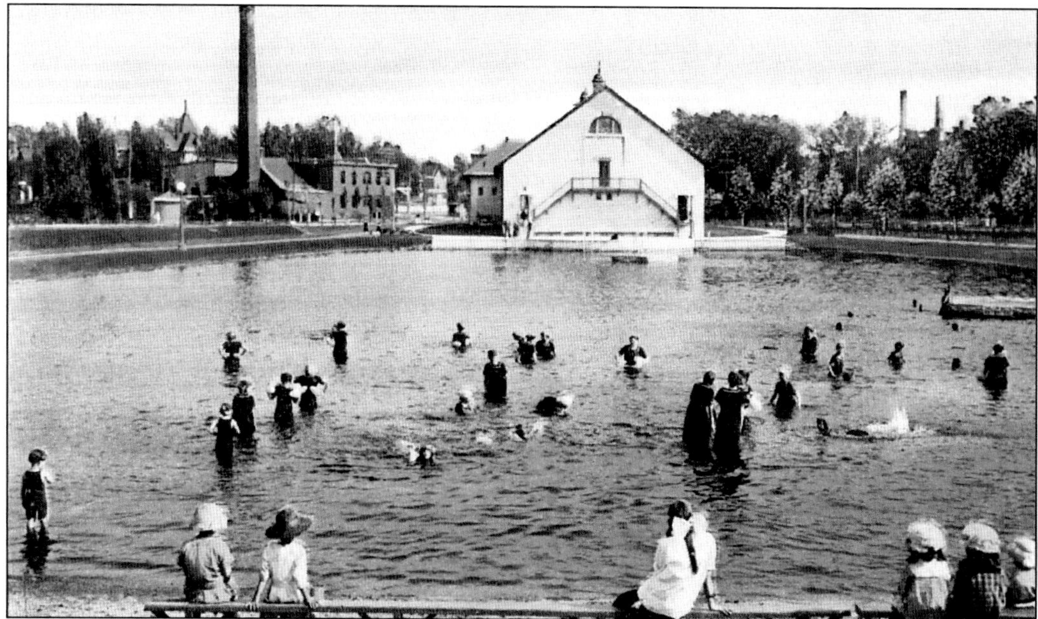

The outdoor Greenwood Memorial Pool as it looked for many years. The Bath House was presented to the town of Gardner by Levi Heywood Greenwood in memory of his parents in 1915. The indoor pool building is also present. At one time heating was provided by Heywood Wakefield, when steam was piped from their power plant, now destroyed, to the pool.

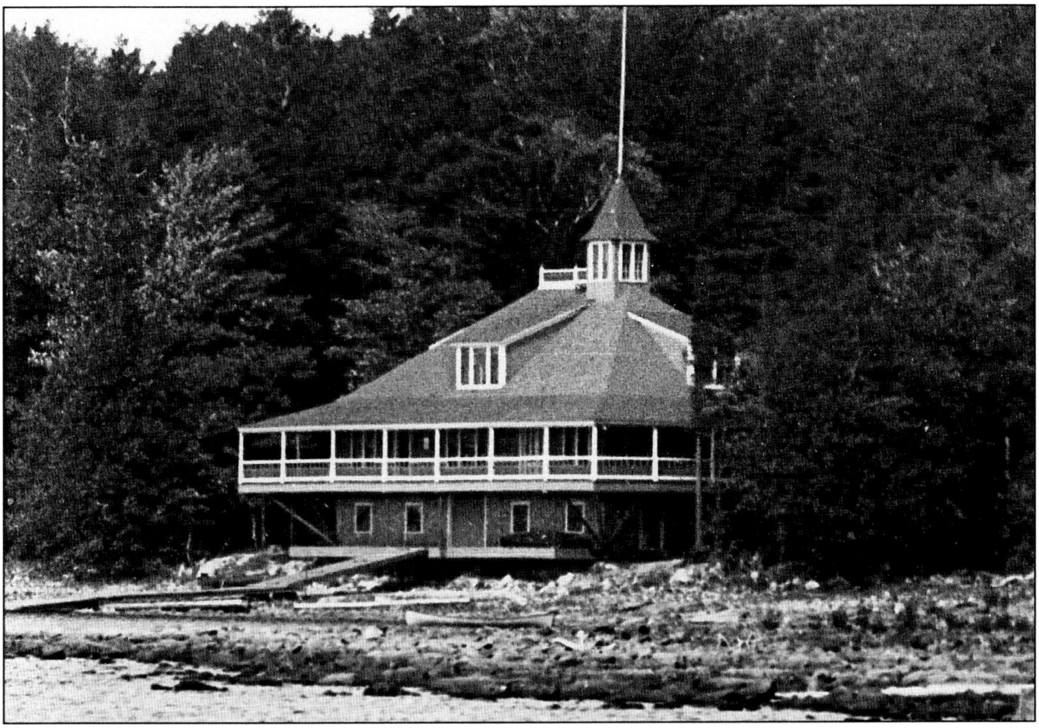

The Gardner Boat Club house on Crystal Lake. The club house, built in 1890, was located several hundred feet north of the pumping station. Here the Boat Club held parties and took boats out onto the lake. At times the club house was decorated with chinese lanterns. Lanterns were also placed on boats which cruised the lake, creating a myriad of lights floating over the lake. The club house was torn down in 1923.

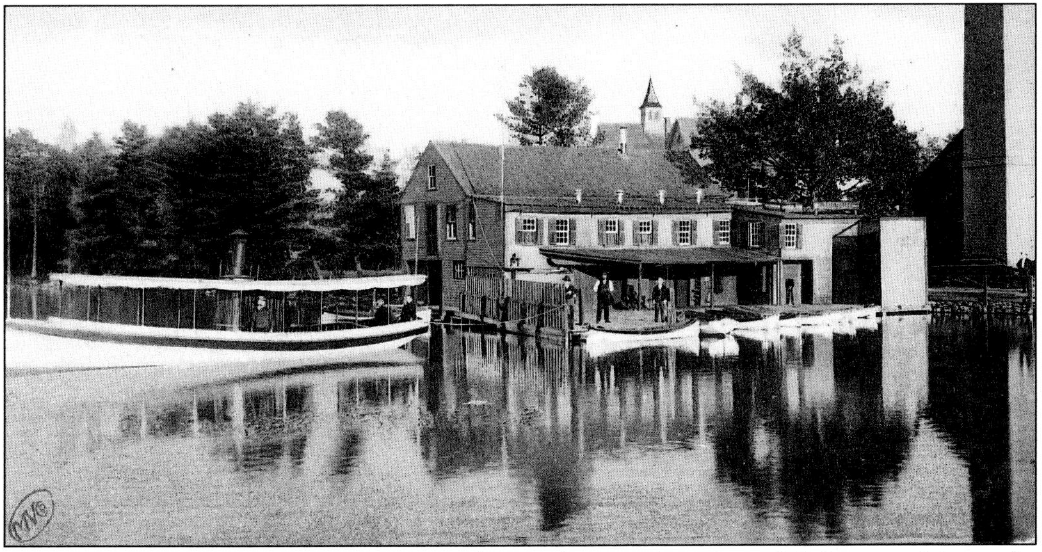

Foster's, originally Hill's, Boat House at the southern end of Crystal Lake rented boats for excursions onto the lake. It was also the southern terminus for the steam boats which plied the waters of Crystal Lake between the boat house and Crystal Lake Park at the northwest end of the lake.

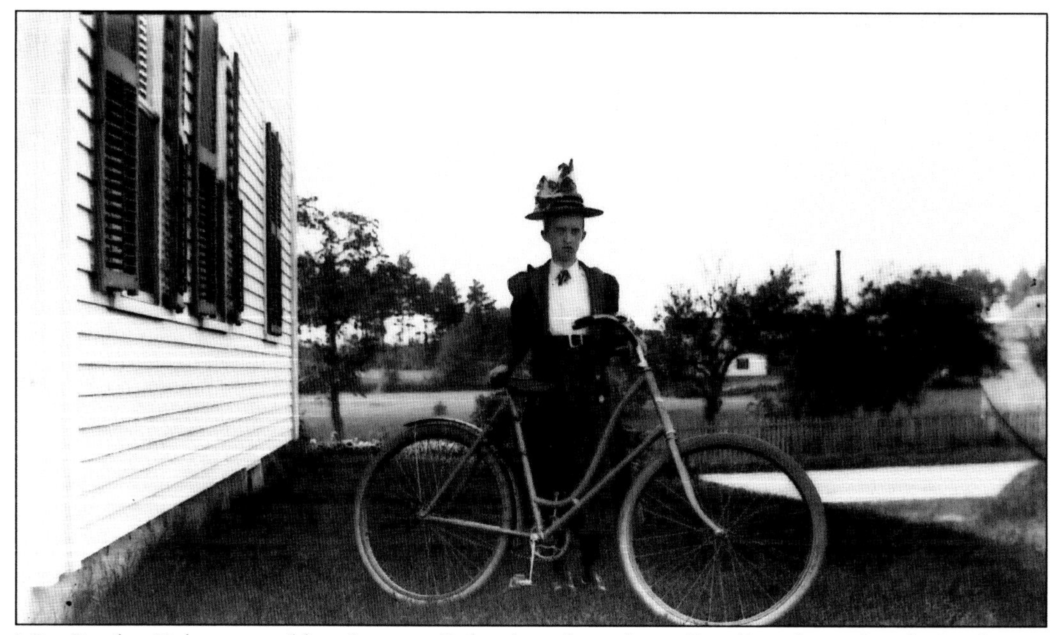

Miss Bertha Coleman and her favorite Columbian bicycle on East Broadway, South Gardner.

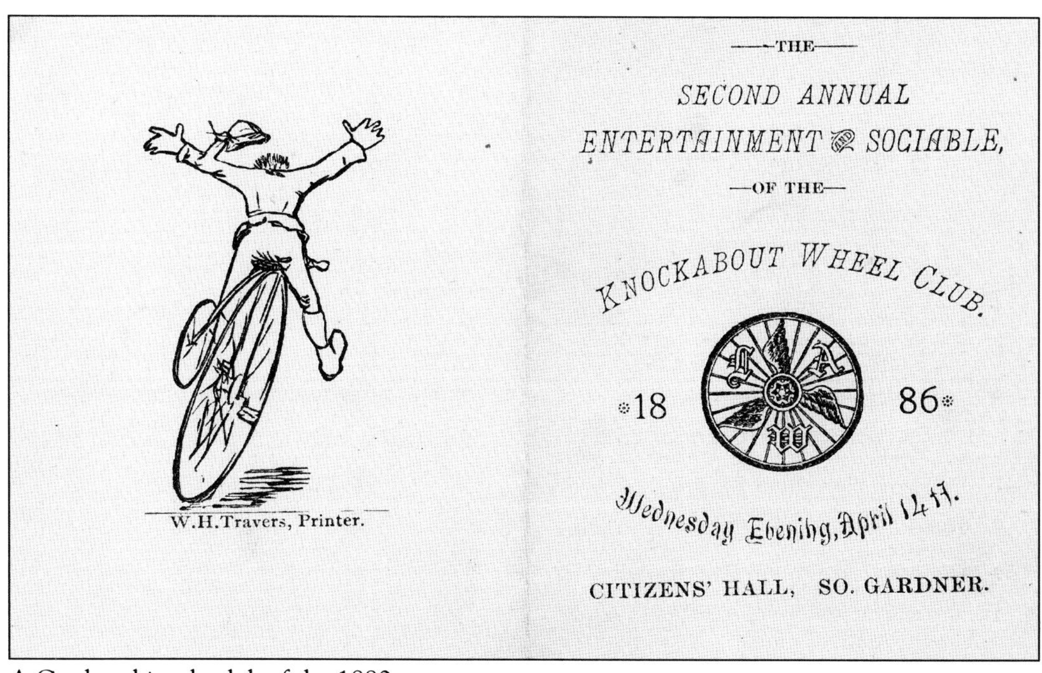

W.H.Travers, Printer.

—THE—

SECOND ANNUAL

ENTERTAINMENT & SOCIABLE,

—OF THE—

KNOCKABOUT WHEEL CLUB.

1886

Wednesday Evening, April 14th.

CITIZENS' HALL, SO. GARDNER.

A Gardner bicycle club of the 1880s.

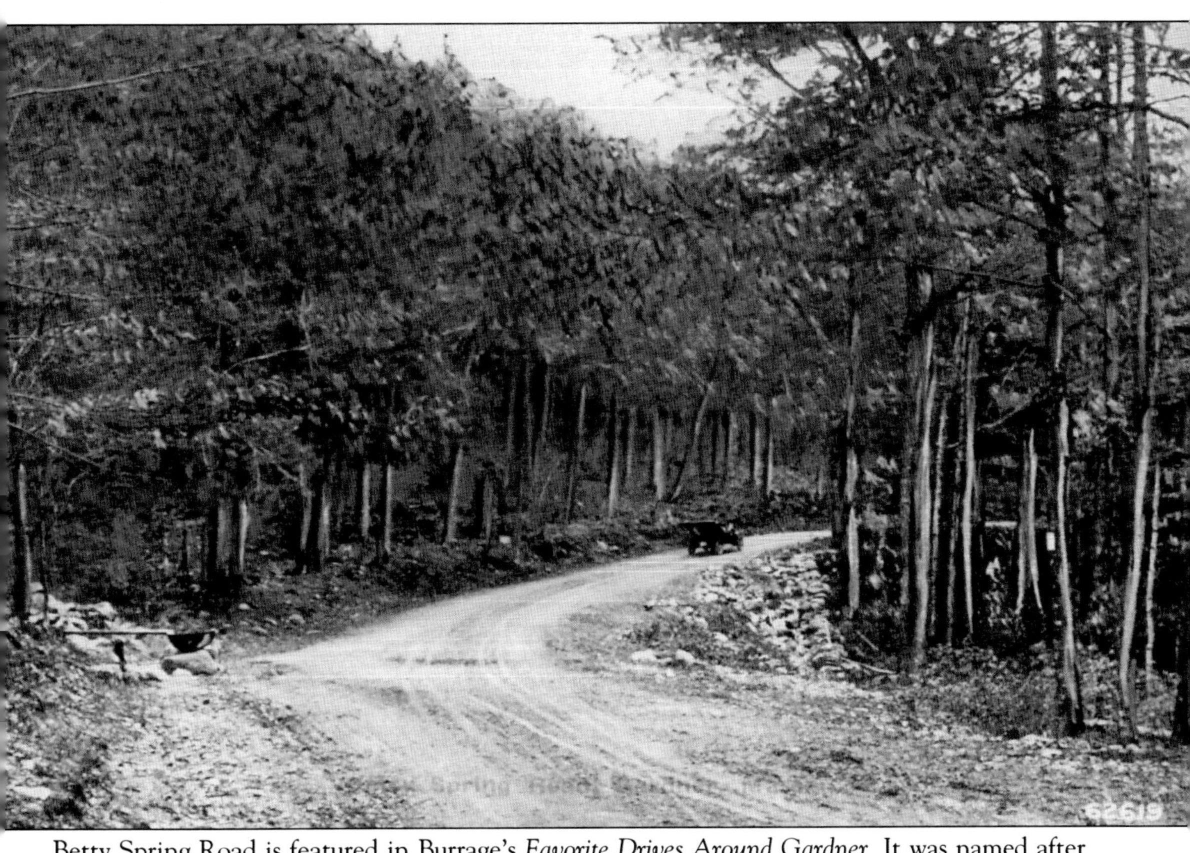

Betty Spring Road is featured in Burrage's *Favorite Drives Around Gardner*. It was named after two Native American inhabitants, Jonas and Betty Obscue, who used the spring.

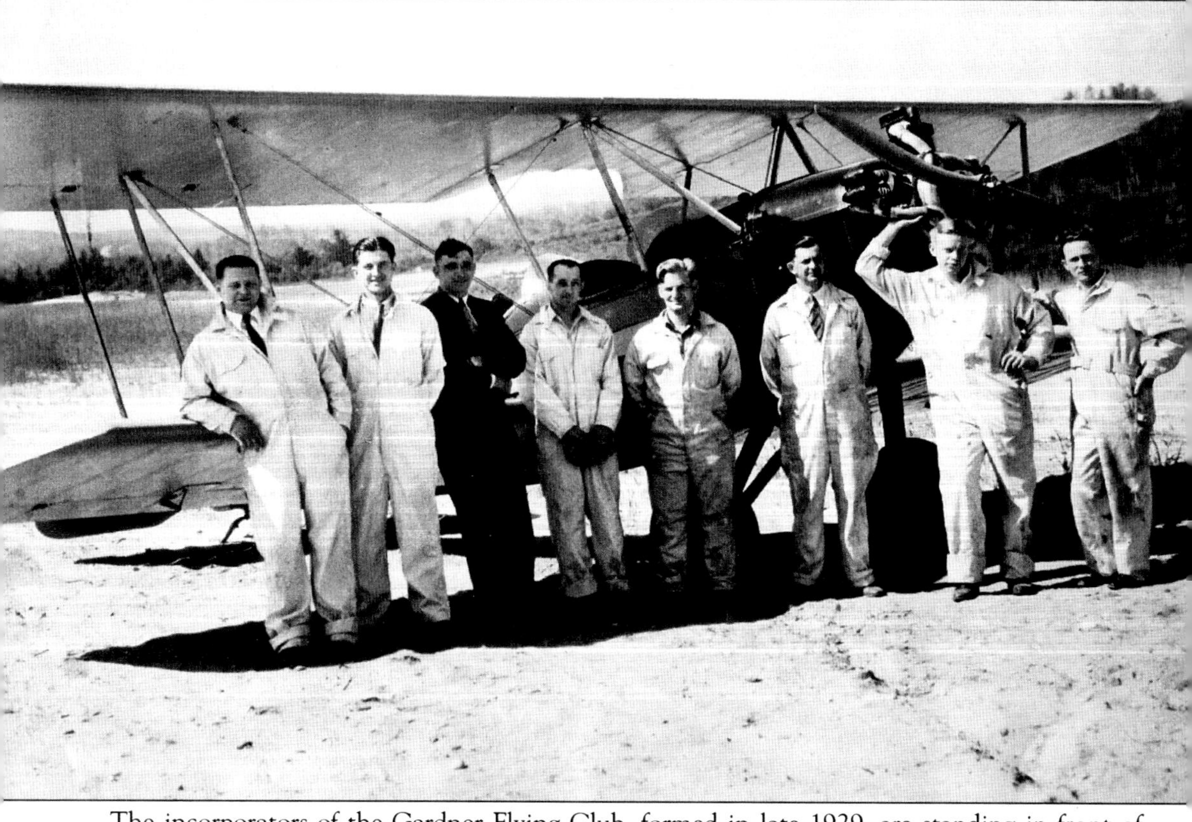

The incorporators of the Gardner Flying Club, formed in late 1929, are standing in front of their red and white American Eagle biplane. From left to right are: Edward "Cliff" LaFortune (president), Joseph Renes, Walter Gerber (pilot and instructor), Joseph Vincent (secretary), Bernard O. Page (treasurer), William N. Crabtree, Ernest C. Pearson, and John A. Halkola. Missing from the photograph was Joseph Berlo. Rides were given in this plane at the airport for $3 and $5.

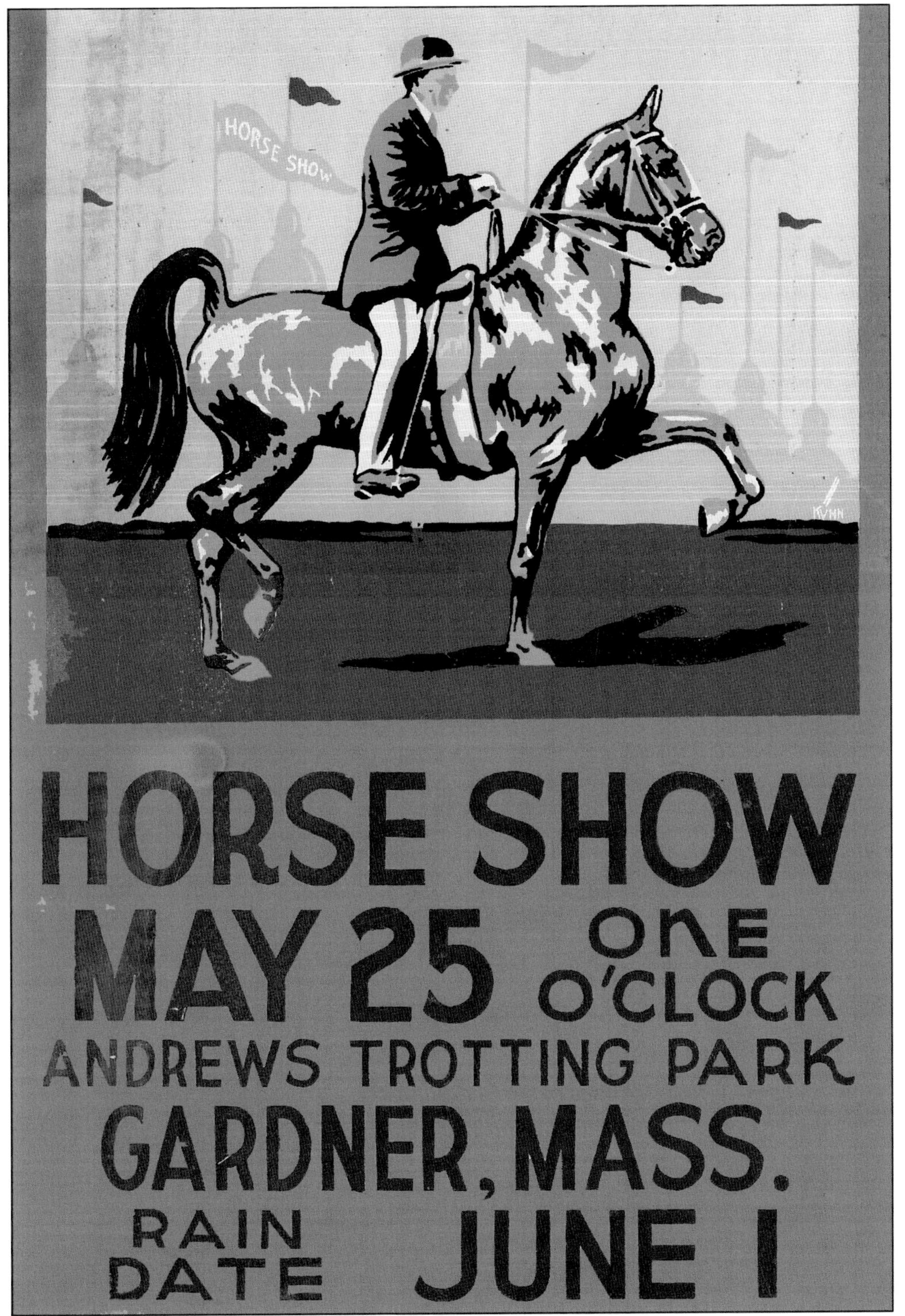

The Andrews Trotting Park was named after Dr. Robert Foster Andrews, president of the Gardner Driving Park Association, which was formed in 1874. The first meet at the park was not held until 1875.

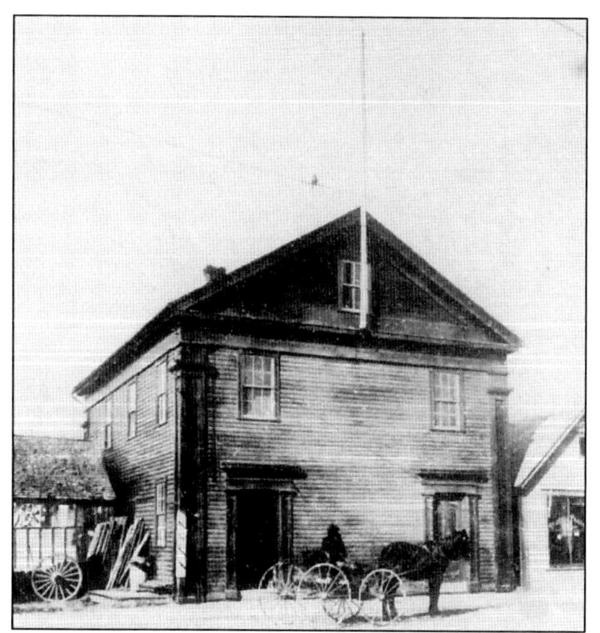

The Centre School was built about 1845. The building was located near 55-57 Green Street. This continued as a grammar school until 1857 when the new Centre, or School Street, School was built. From 1866 to 1874 the building was used as the first high school in Gardner. In 1875 the building was moved to Union Depot and used by Howe Brothers as a grain store. In 1914 it was moved to 362 Elm Street.

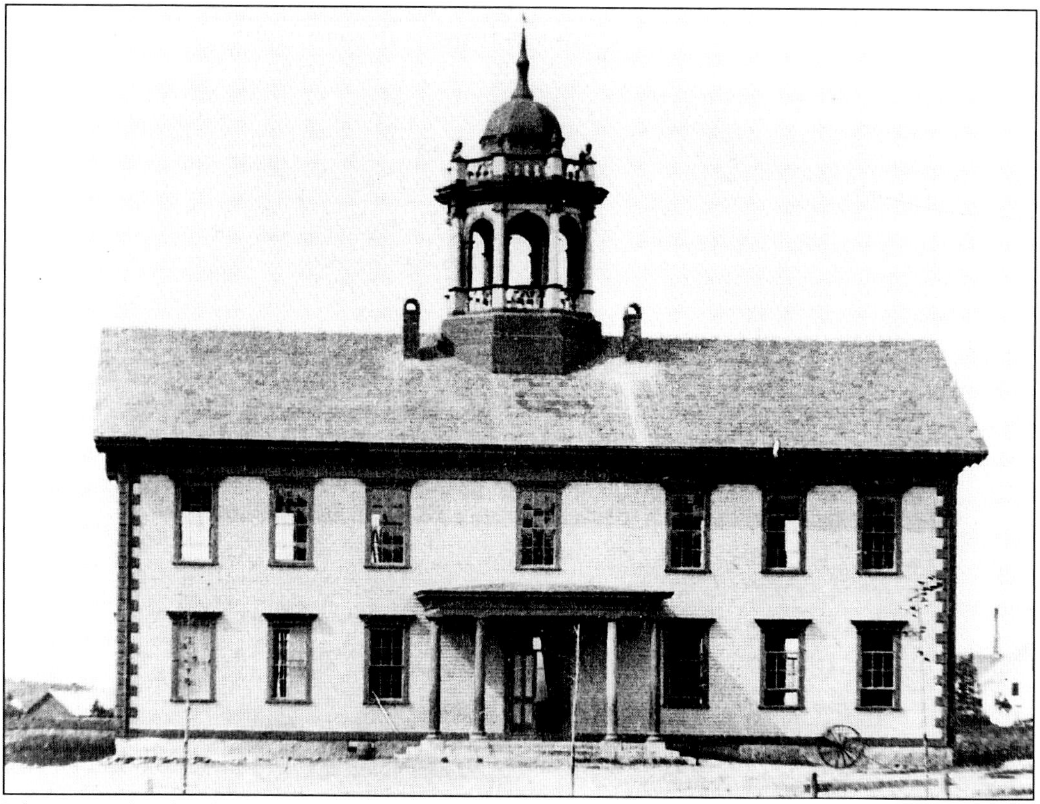

The original School Street School, or Centre School, was built in 1857. This wooden structure was used until 1903 when it was determined a new structure, the current brick School Street School, was needed. To allow rapid building of the new school the old building was raised upon stilts and moved forward; the children continued to meet in the upraised school.

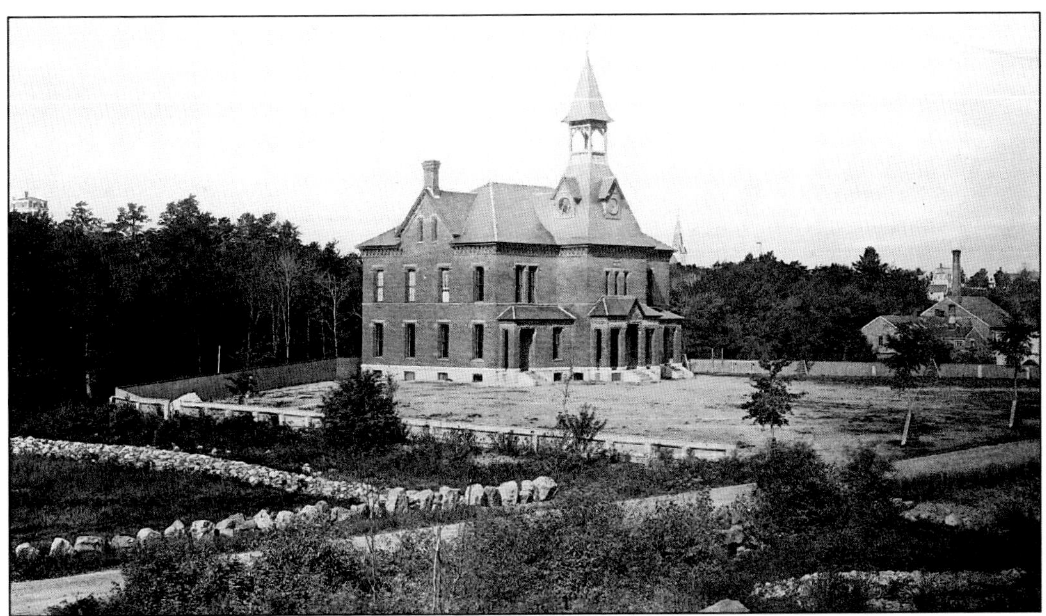

The brick high school was built in 1874 and was located on Chestnut Street near the corner of Logan and Chestnut Streets. It served as the high school until 1898, when it was converted into a grammar school. It served in this capacity until 1927 when it was abandoned. The building was subsequently torn down.

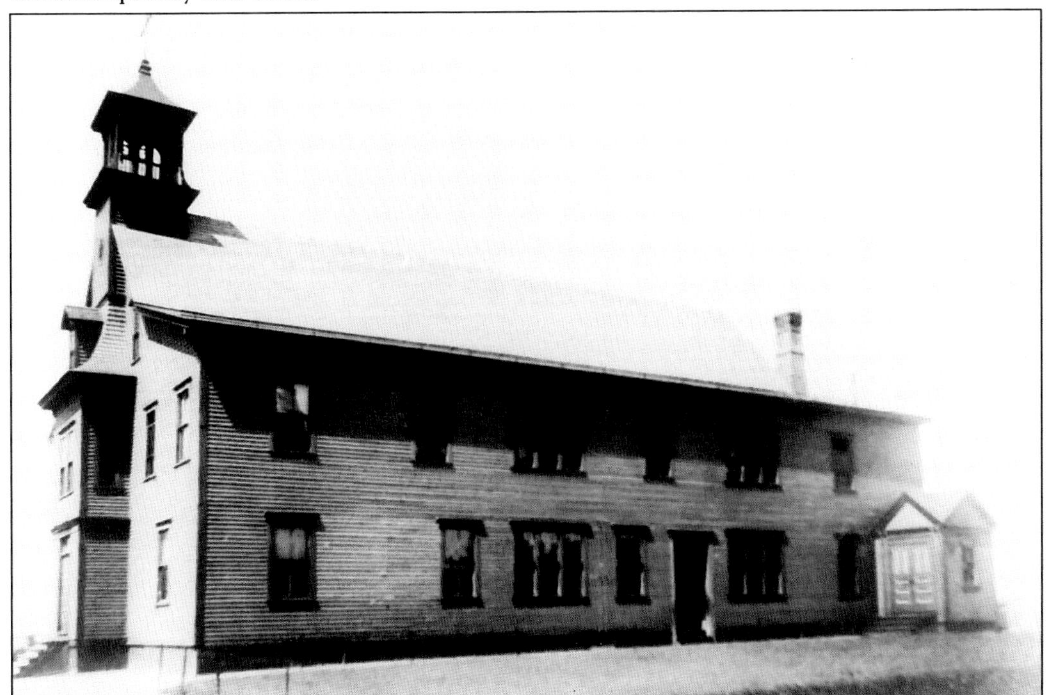

The Holy Rosary School began in 1886 and used the wooden church building as a meeting place. The school continued until 1896 when it was suspended until 1903. The wooden church, which had been moved to make way for the new brick church, again served as the school. This building continued as the school until the brick school building was completed in 1925.

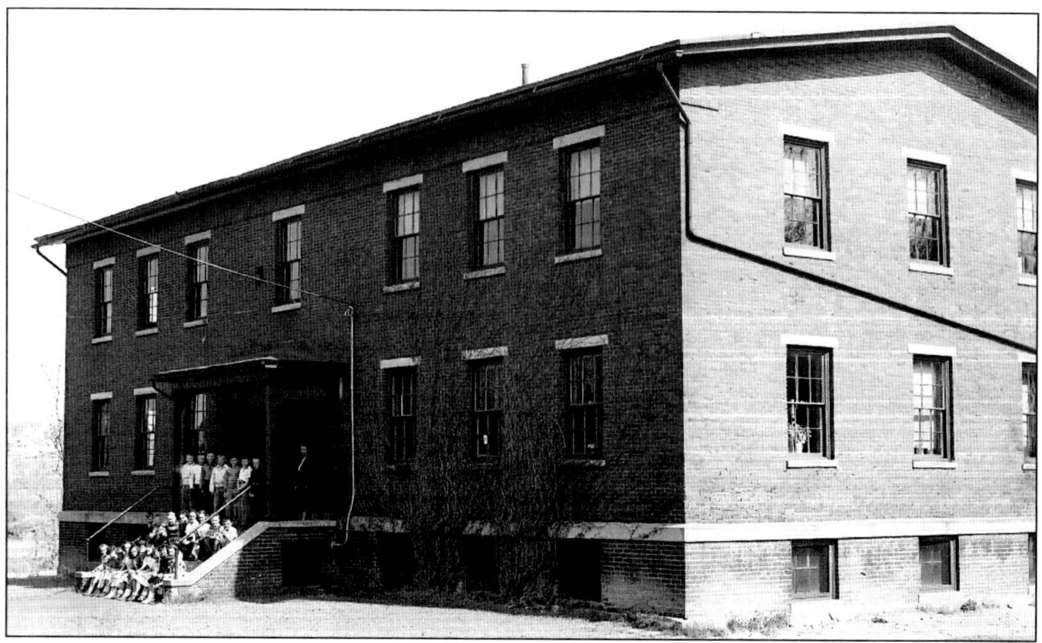

The Broadway School was built in 1858 on what is today West Broadway. Originally it served eight grades but in latter years the number of grades dropped to six by 1913, and later to four, with the higher classes going to the Prospect Street School. In 1912 the building was raised and a basement added. It served until 1953 when it was abandoned and torn down to make way for the National Guard armory.

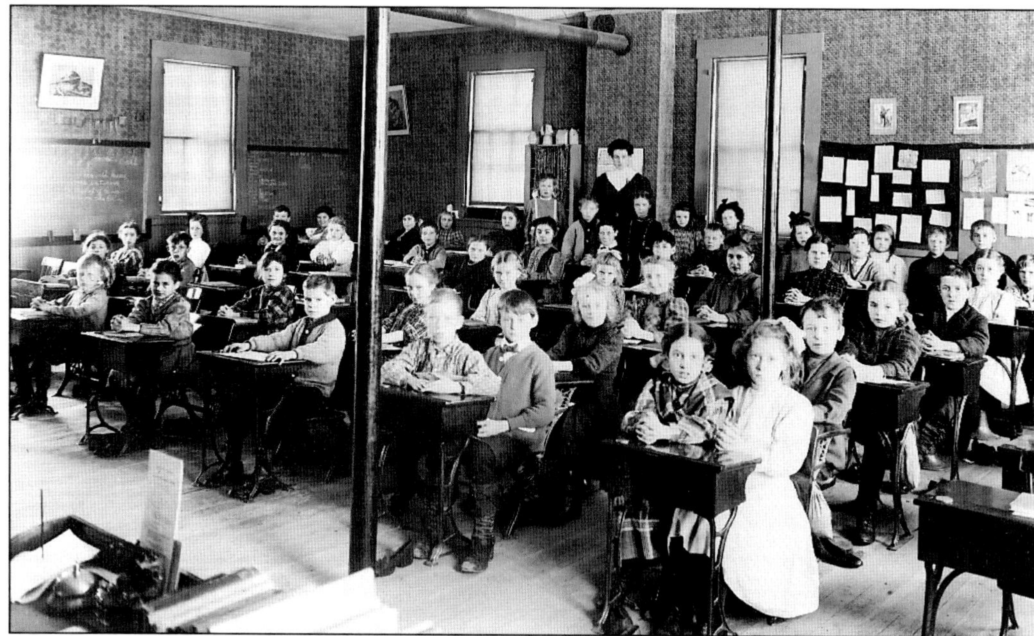

The third and fourth grades of the Broadway School, with their teacher Miss Cole, 1910–1911. Note the stove pipe across the ceiling which came from the wood stove. Bags tied to some of the desks held children's individual drinking cups. Students formerly drank from a common dipper in the hall. Outdoor privies were then in use.

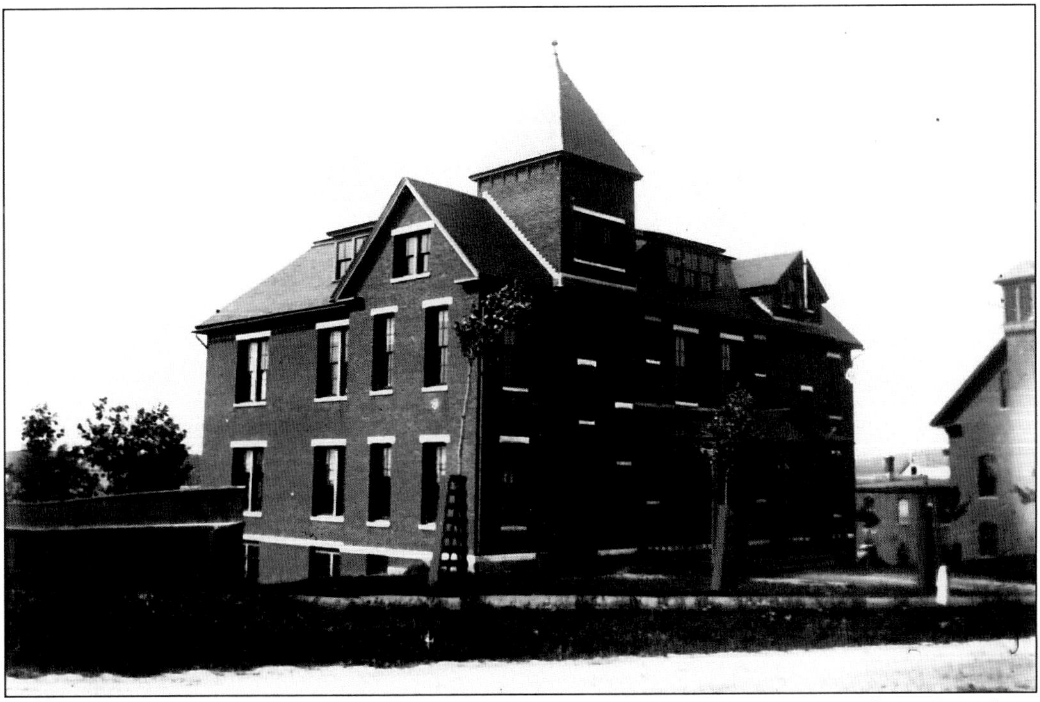

The Prospect Street School was located behind the Fire Station on the corner of East Broadway and Prospect Street. The building was built in 1887 and was remodeled and enlarged in 1904. When the Prospect School was built across the street the building housed the first grade for a number of years, with Ida Bradshaw as the teacher. The building was demolished in 1946.

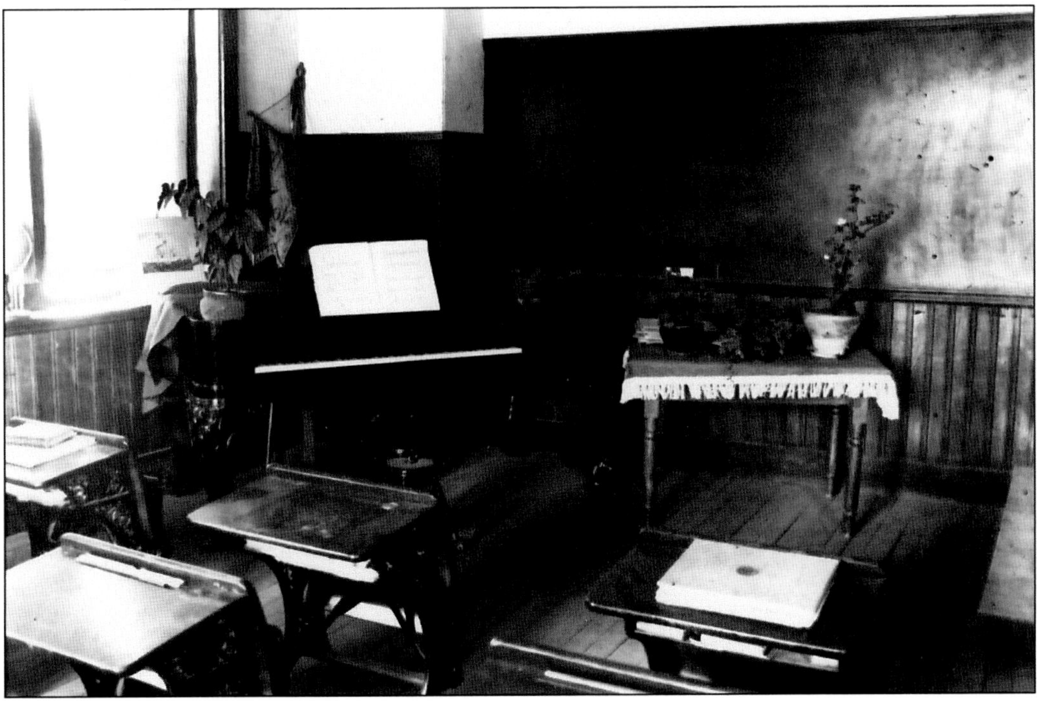

The interior of the Prospect Street School.

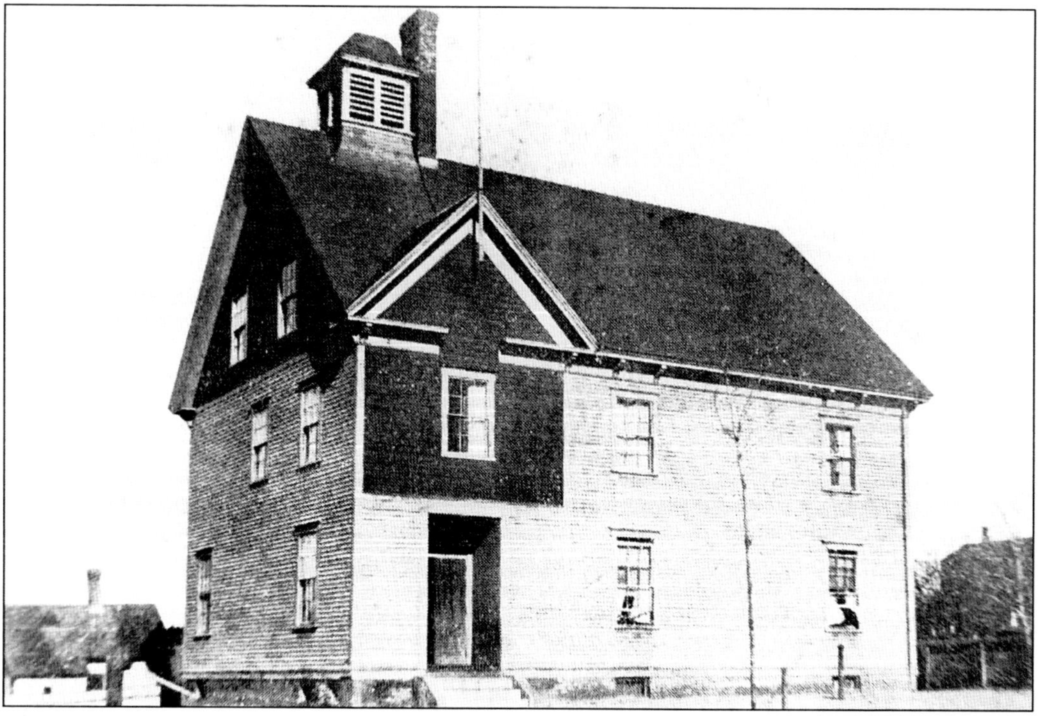

The Stuart Street School was erected in 1888 and served as a neighborhood school until it was closed in 1926. This building still exists on the corner of Stuart and Nadeau Streets.

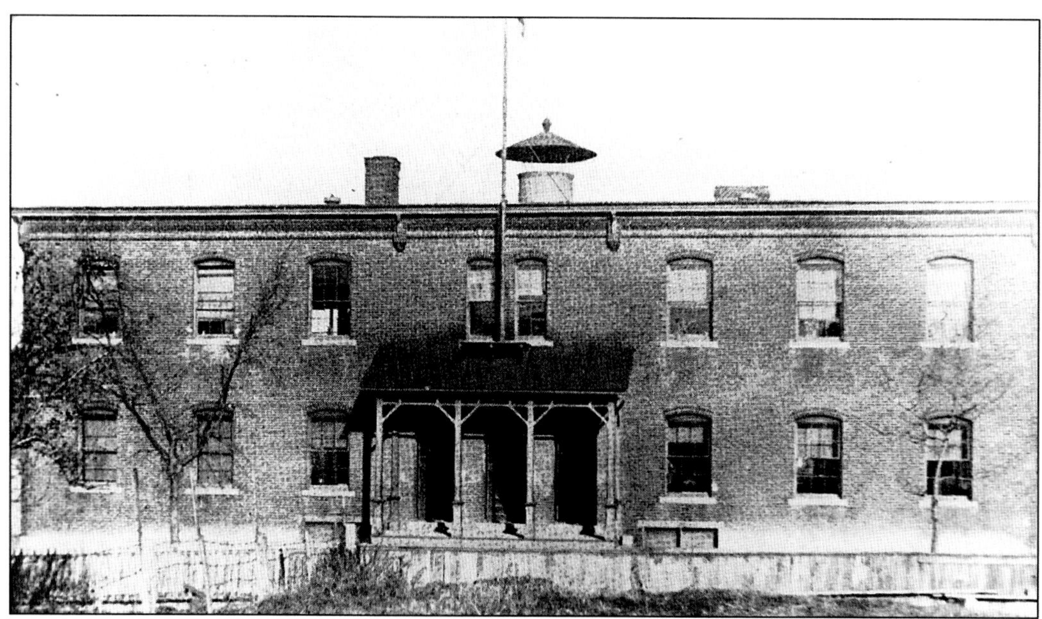

The Pleasant Street School was located next to the PACC Building on Pleasant Street. The school was opened in 1881, and remodeled in 1914. The building was finally abandoned in 1953.

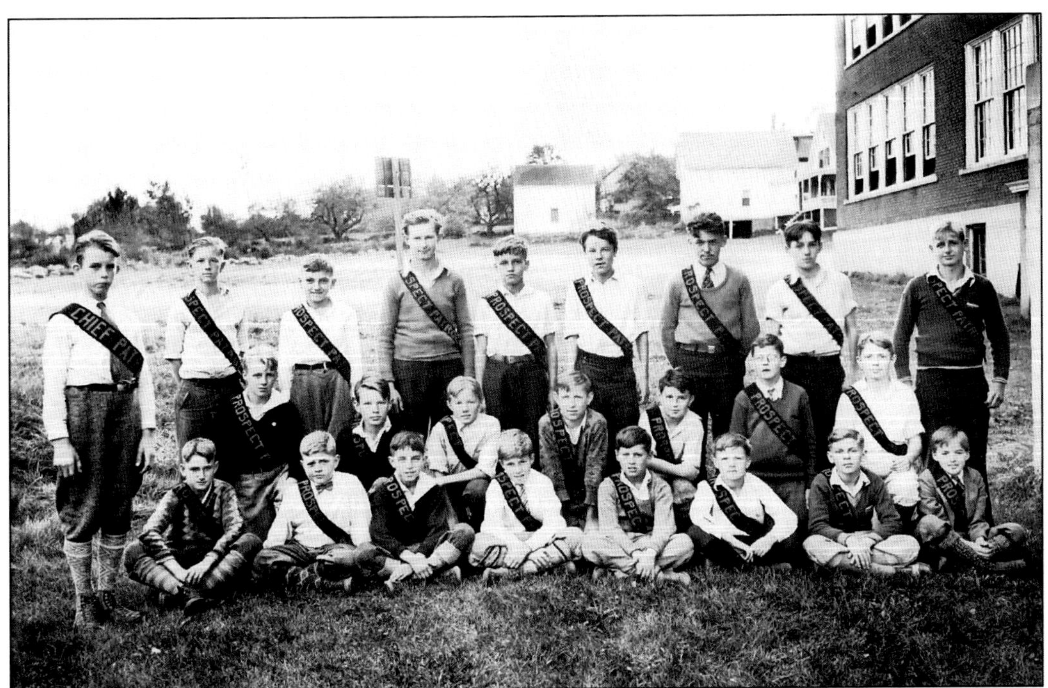

Chief Cyrille Leblanc and Fremont Antelle of the Wachusett Auto Club organized the patrol leader system in 1932. Patrolman Clayton McKean supervised the system in the schools. This shows the patrol leaders at Prospect School in 1932.

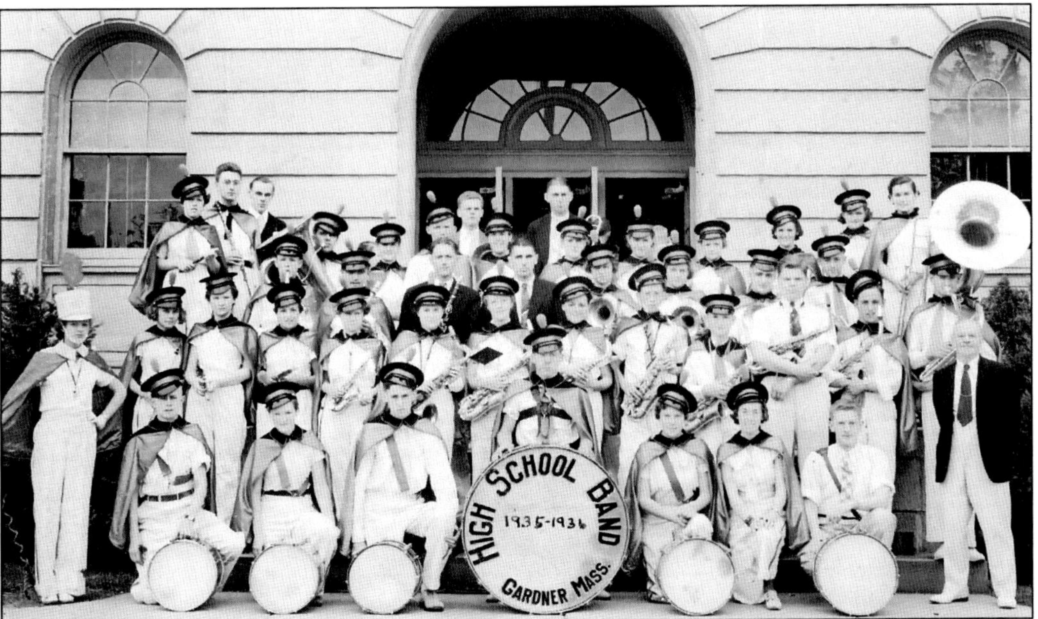

The Gardner High School Band for 1934–35, under the direction of John Redmond, appeared in the Sesquicentennial Parade, with the presence of alumni who came back to give Mr. Redmond, and the band, a hand. The Rotary Club had brought Mr. Redmond to Gardner in 1928 to help build the band. For the next twenty years, before retiring in 1947, John P. Redmond did just that.

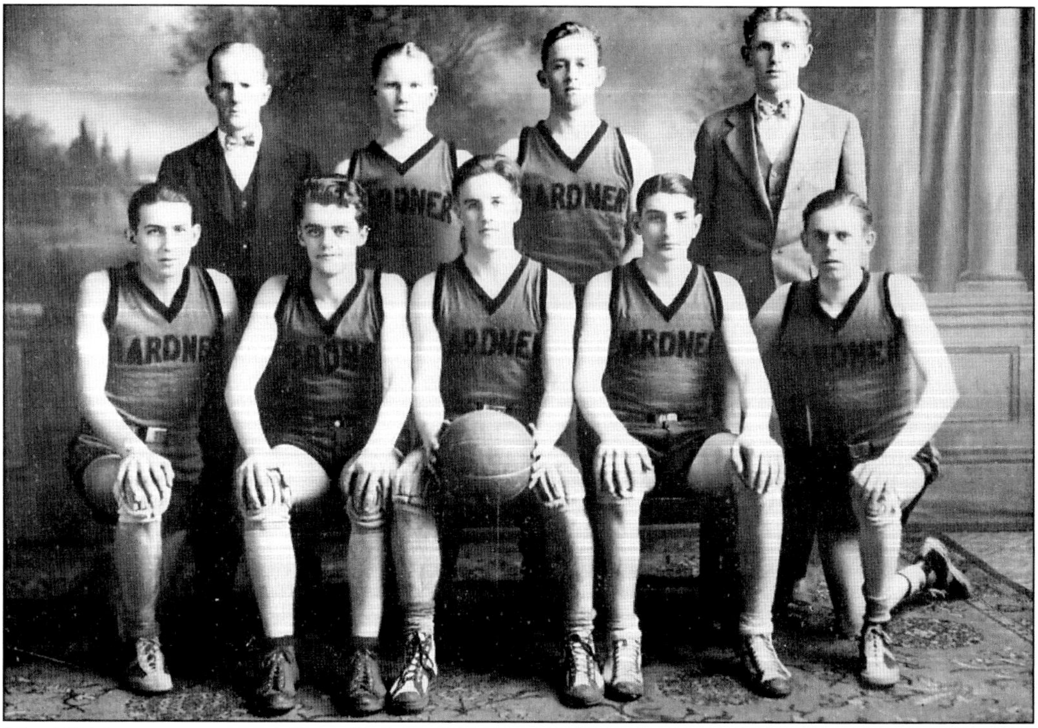

The Wildcats were originally called the "Orange and Black." Donald "Bennie" Bennett shot a wildcat in late October 1923 in Templeton. A news story followed shortly thereafter mentioning the Gardner High Wildcats.

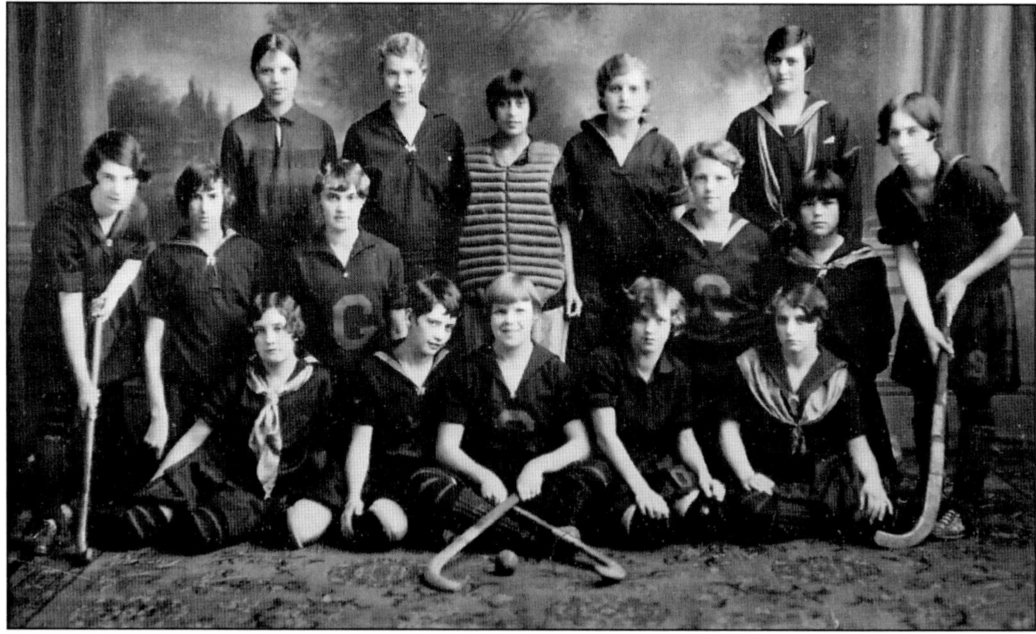

Women's sports, such as basketball, track, and field hockey, were introduced in 1925. Minerva Cutler and Thelma B. Greenwood were coaches in the women's athletic program. Thelma Greenwood was the coach of the 1929 field hockey team.

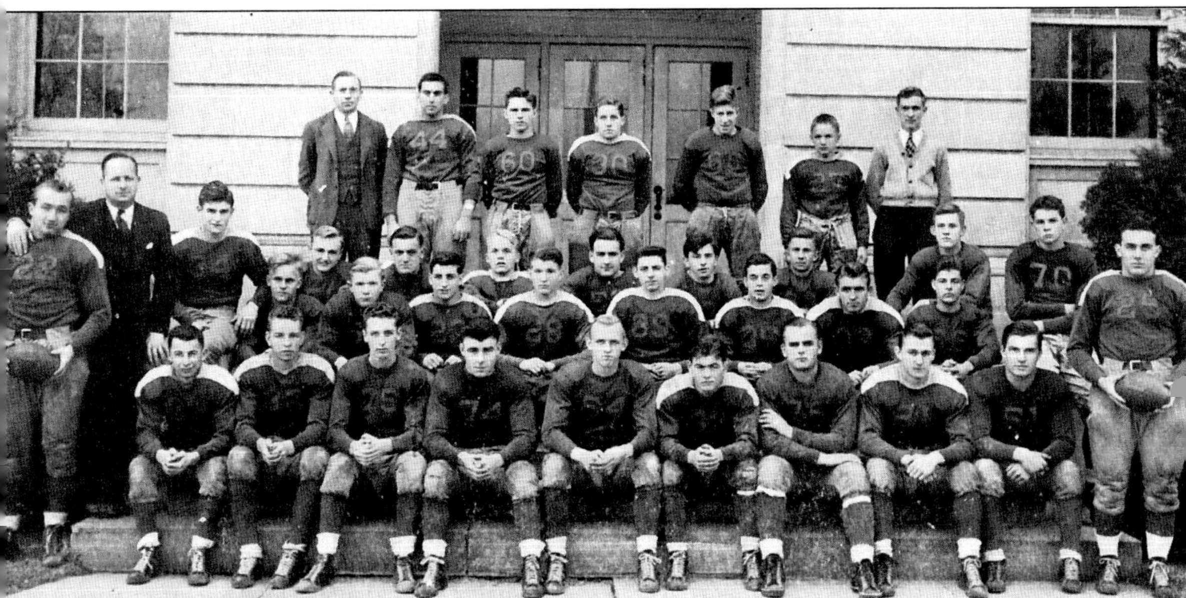

The football team of 1937. From left to right are: (front row) W. Dubzinski (captain), D. Kaplan, C. Butenas, R. Nelson, D. Leamy, C. Yablonski, G. Lison, C. Norbutus, E. Kodys, J. Wesnoski, and E. Zoldak (captain); (second row) Coach Tarpey, D. Delay, E. Nivell, J. Dowal, R. St. Jean, Z. Ladroga, R. Corsiglia, R. Dorval, J. Matukas, E. Leclair, and F. Donovan; (third row) J. Dubzinski, F. Miciewicz, R. Mattila, F. Bourgeois, N. Bliss, A. Turczynski, and J. Nazarow; (back row) Mr. Baker (faculty manager), L. Suglia, I. Chapman, R. Fredette, R. Antaya, E. Taavitsainen, and A. Janski (manager).

Phil Tarpey came to Gardner in 1928. His football team of 1929 won the Worcester County Championship. On March 9, 1963, at Harvard University, he was named to the Massachusetts High School Football Coaches Hall of Fame.

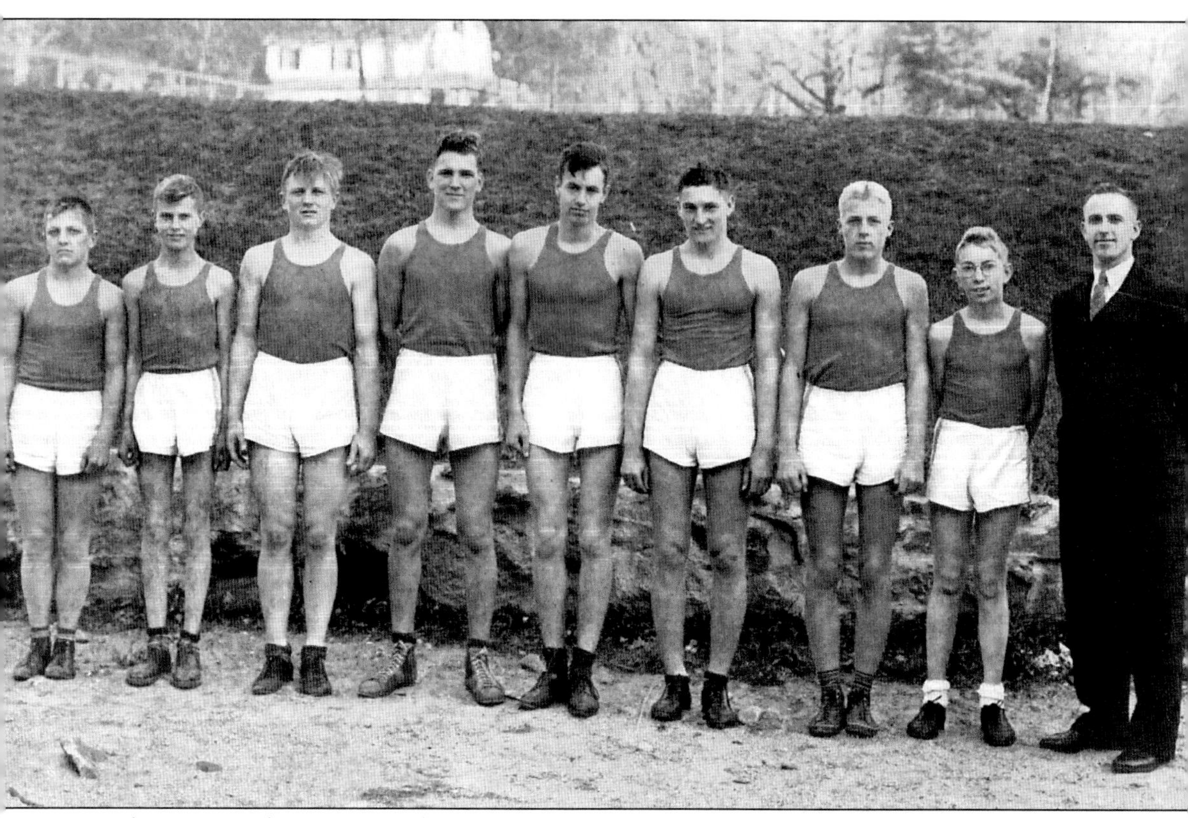

The 1939 track team. From left to right are C. Gronlund, E. Larkin, H. Gronlund, E. Gonyer, A. Shephard, E. Kowlzan, J. Kauppinen, S. Berg, and Coach W. Footrick.

In 1940–41 William Footrick's cross country team won the Massachusetts State Championship and the same team took third place in the Eastern United States High School Championships at Seton Hall College in Orange, New Jersey.

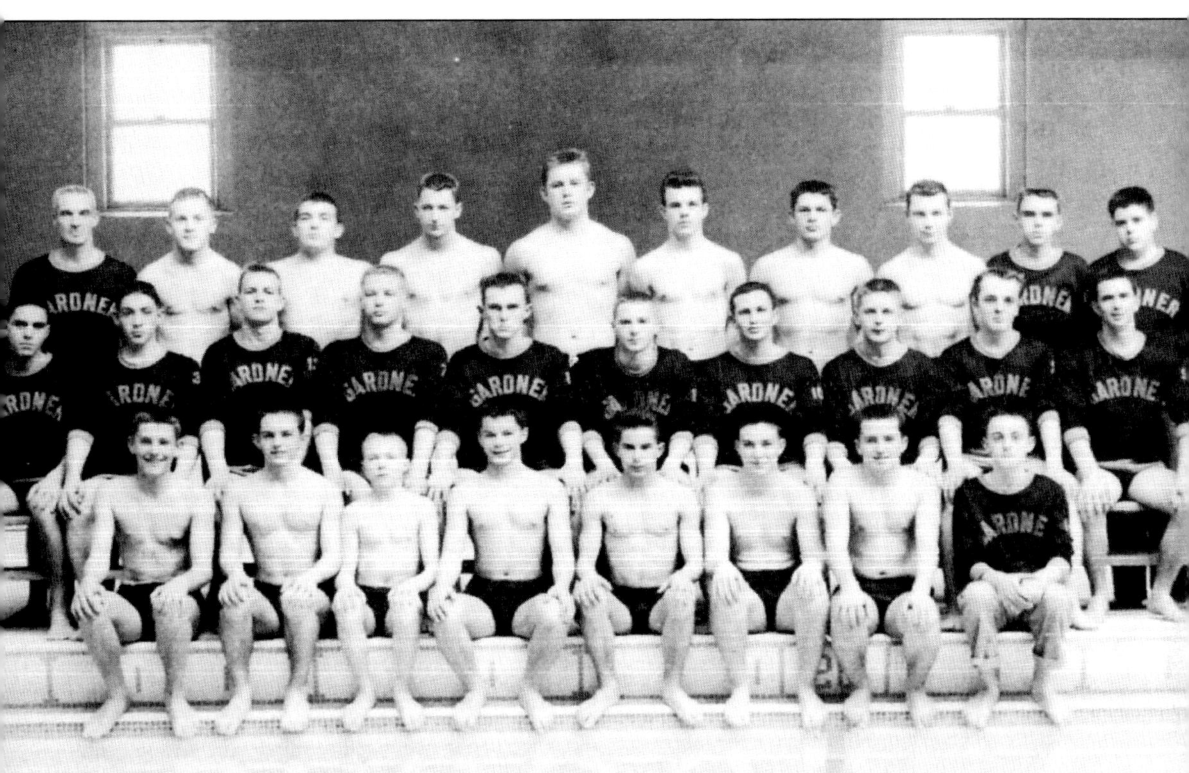

The swimming team of 1957. In this photograph are: Coach John R. Tinker; Managers Dexter Hedstrom, Larry Popple, and James Powers; Captains Thomas Crowley and Larry Chapman; and members Thomas Crowley, Larry Chapman, David MacDonanld, Daniel O' Connell, William Fontaine, Jeffrey Glinski, Peter Evans, Stephen Erickson, Francis Richard, Roger Sharron, Jonathan Rice, Michael Gajdukow, John Olechnicki, Leon Jazinski, Michael Clavien, Moran Beauregard, Donald Sweet, Ronald Rogers, Paul Hagen, Jerome Pierce, Creighton Morris, Dennis Erickson, Donald Diemdowicz, Glenn Theodore, Brian Bjurling, Martin Anderholm, Gerald Richardson, Albert Vallee, and Robert Dill.

John Tinker came to Gardner High School in 1937. He took over the boy's high school swimming team in 1939, and started the Massachusetts High School Swimming Championships in Gardner in 1947. The Gardner boy's swim team won the championship for the next thirteen years. He retired in 1975, after teaching for thirty-eight years.

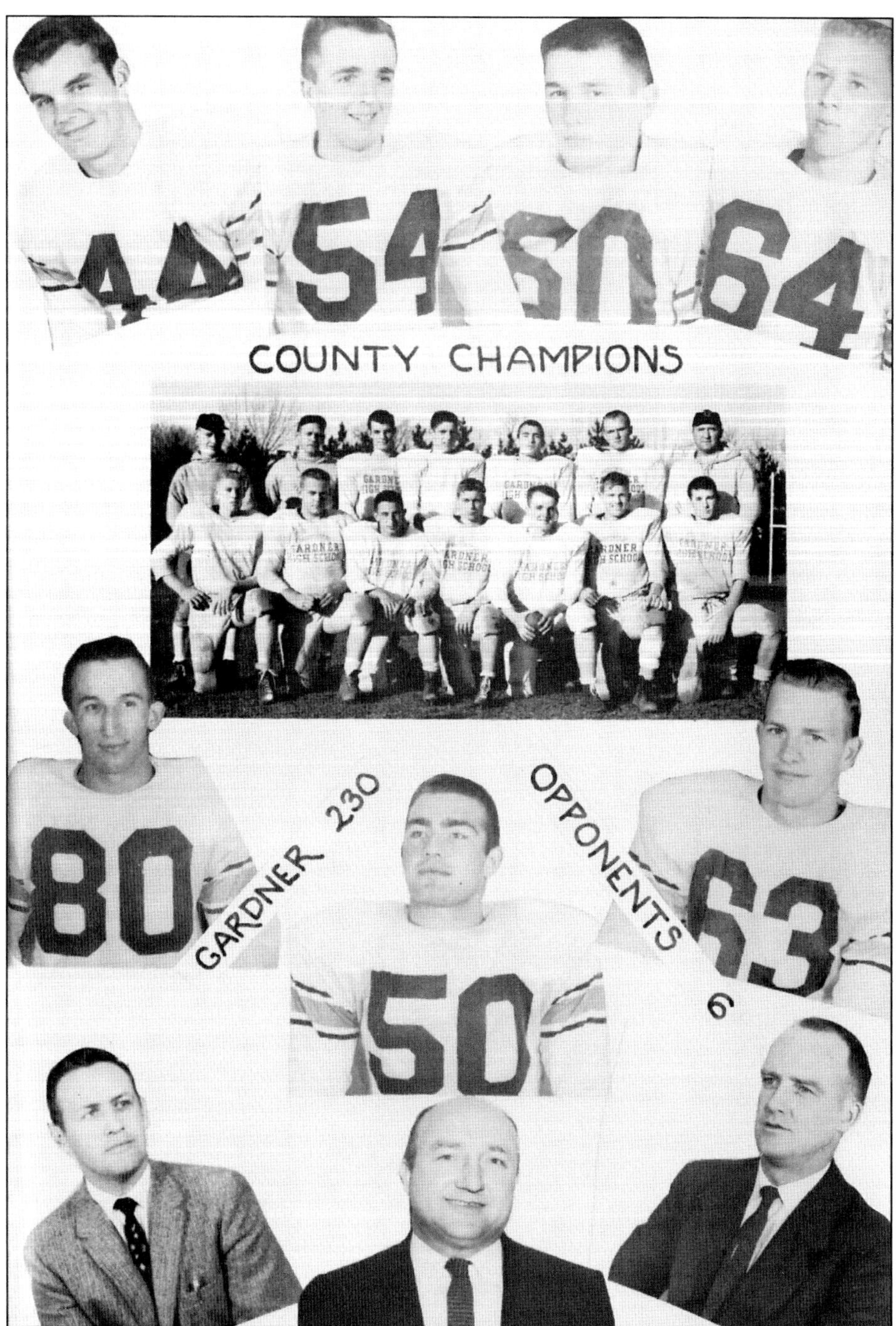

Walter Dubzinski played with the professional football teams the New York Giants in 1943, and the Boston Yanks in 1944. He came to Gardner in 1946. In the 1950s he coached winning football teams. In 1958 the football team won the Worcester County Championship with a record of 9–0. Martin Anderson was a football coach for twenty-eight years and the head coach at Gardner High School for ten years starting in 1966. Robert Duncan was the assistant football coach and the head track coach beginning in 1955. Between 1961 and 1965 the track team was Worcester and Northern Worcester County champions.

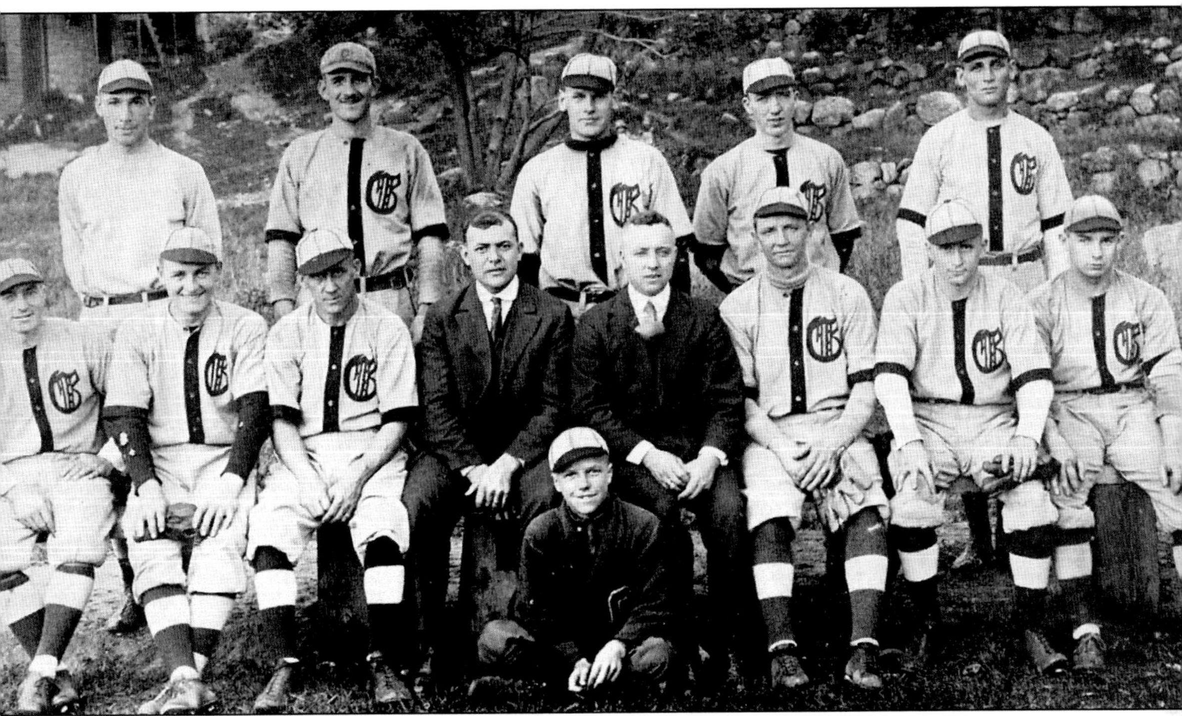

The Gardner Athletic Association baseball teams were part of a larger organization which comprised, among other cities and towns, Worcester, Clinton, Gilbertville, Shirley, Winchendon, and Malden.

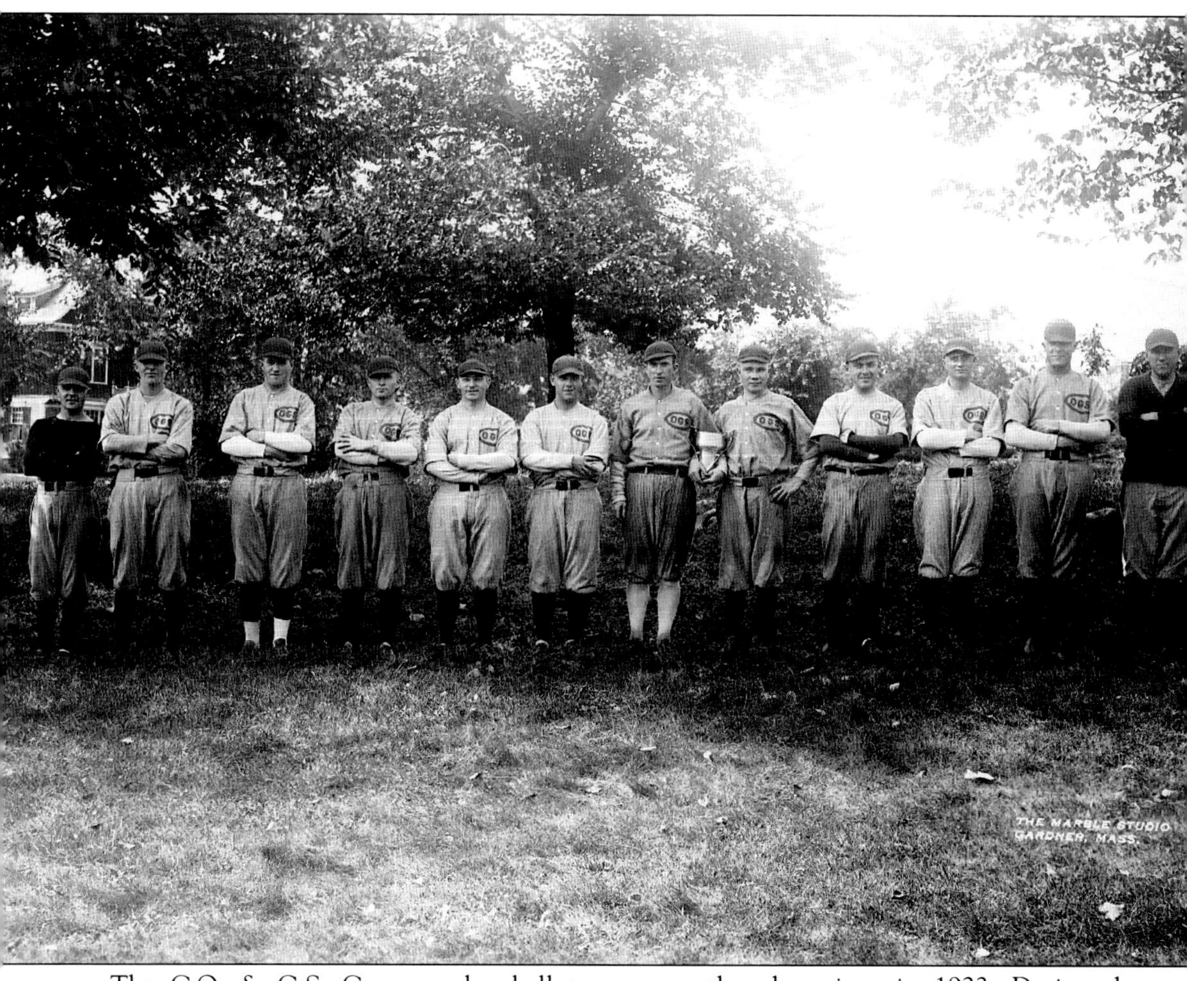

The C.O. & G.S. Company baseball team were the champions in 1922. During the 1920s there was an active industrial baseball league not only in Gardner but in all of central Massachusetts.

Six

Entertainment, Celebrations, and Parks

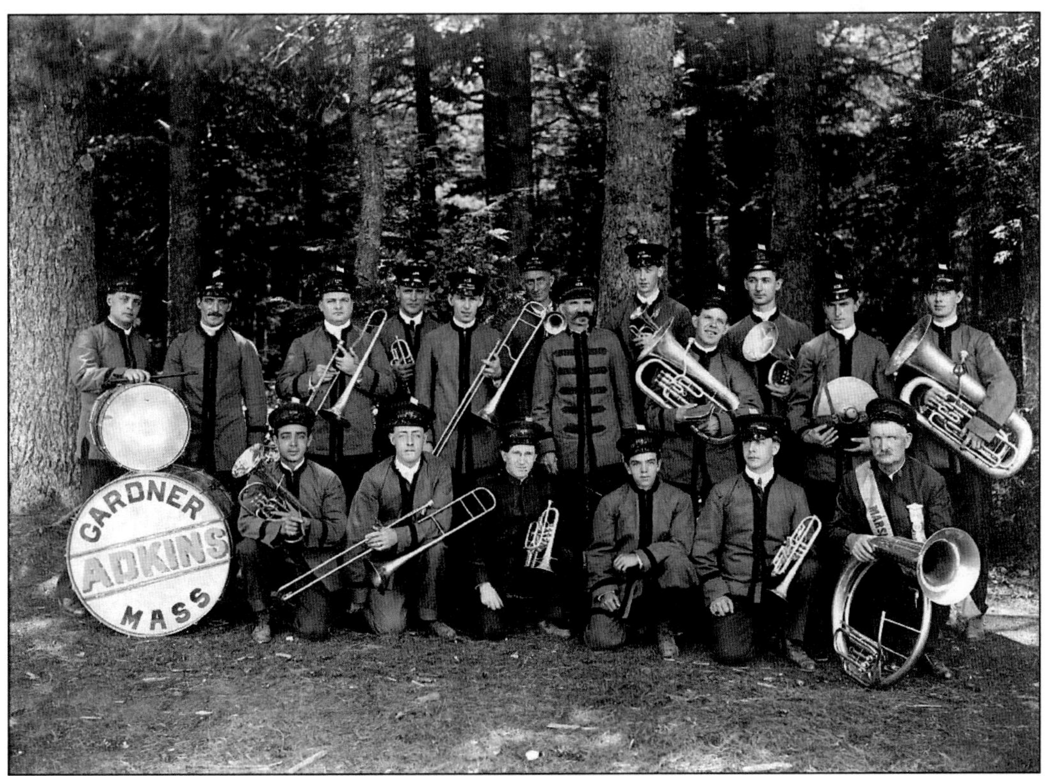

The Adkins Brass Band was a well-known marching and concert band in Gardner during the early 1900s. The leader, Charles Adkins (at center in band masters uniform), came from England at the turn of the century and recruited many South Gardner musicians into his organization. To the right of Charles is his son George and behind him to the left is M. Riley. Charles died in 1927 at the age of sixty-eight.

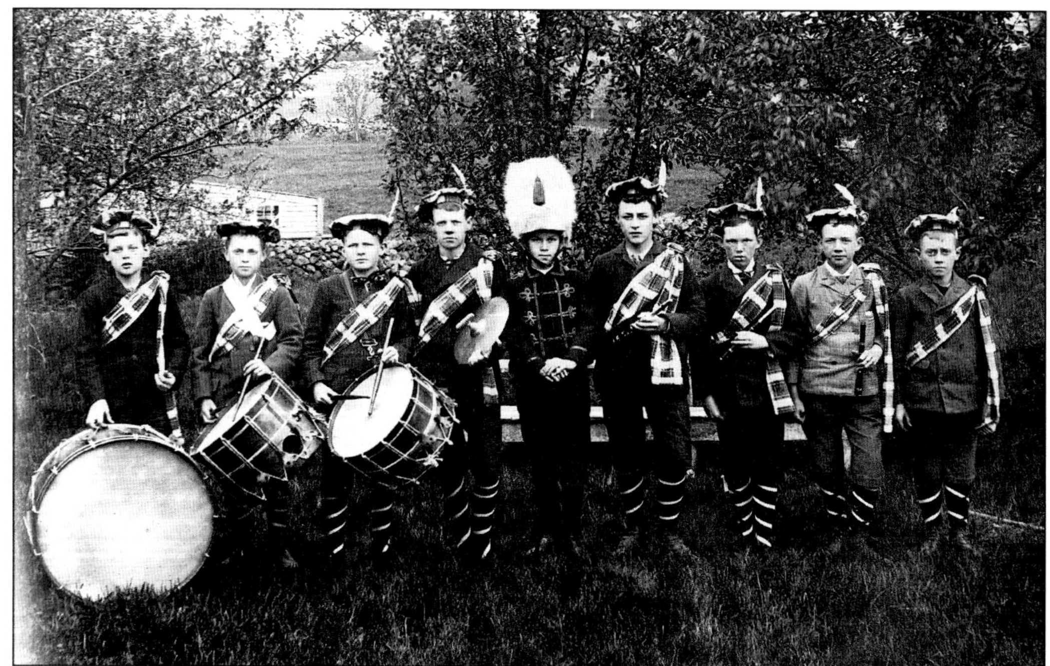

The October 26, 1892 *Gardner Journal*, regarding the Columbus Day Parade of October 21, 1892, states: "The South Gardner's Boys' Drum Corps made a fine appearance in their natty scotch plaid caps and sashes."

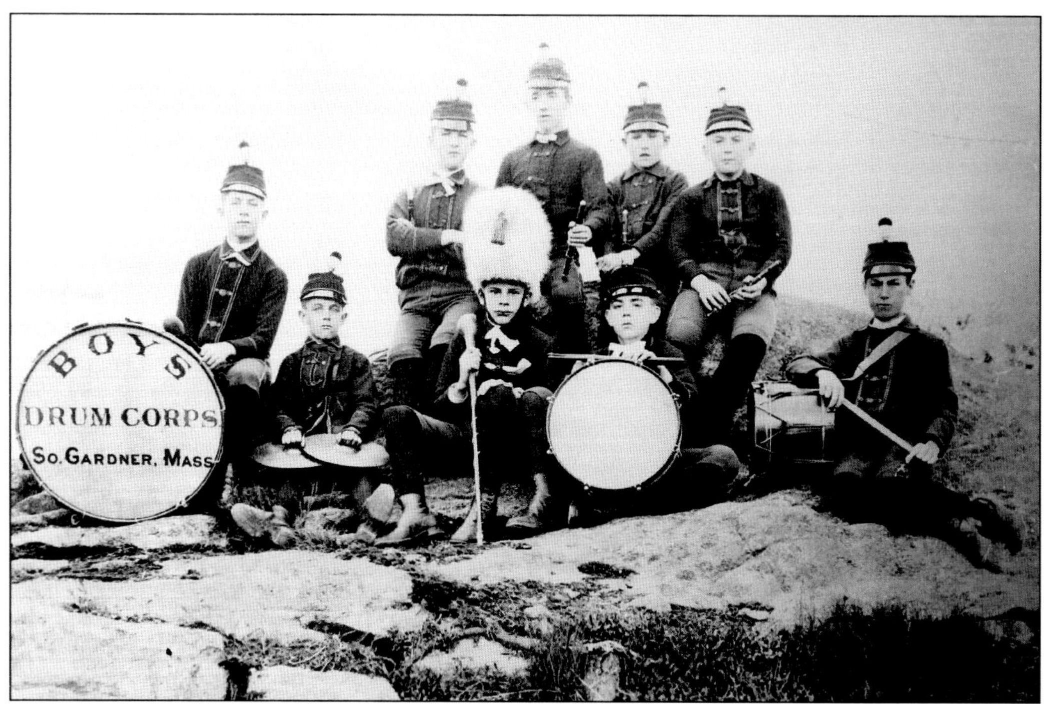

The South Gardner Boys' Drum Corp consisted of Harry Jillson, Thomas Burke, John Burke, Louis Hartwell, Bert Moore, Pete Cornish, Roland Bent, James Beckman, and Frank E. Lavallee.

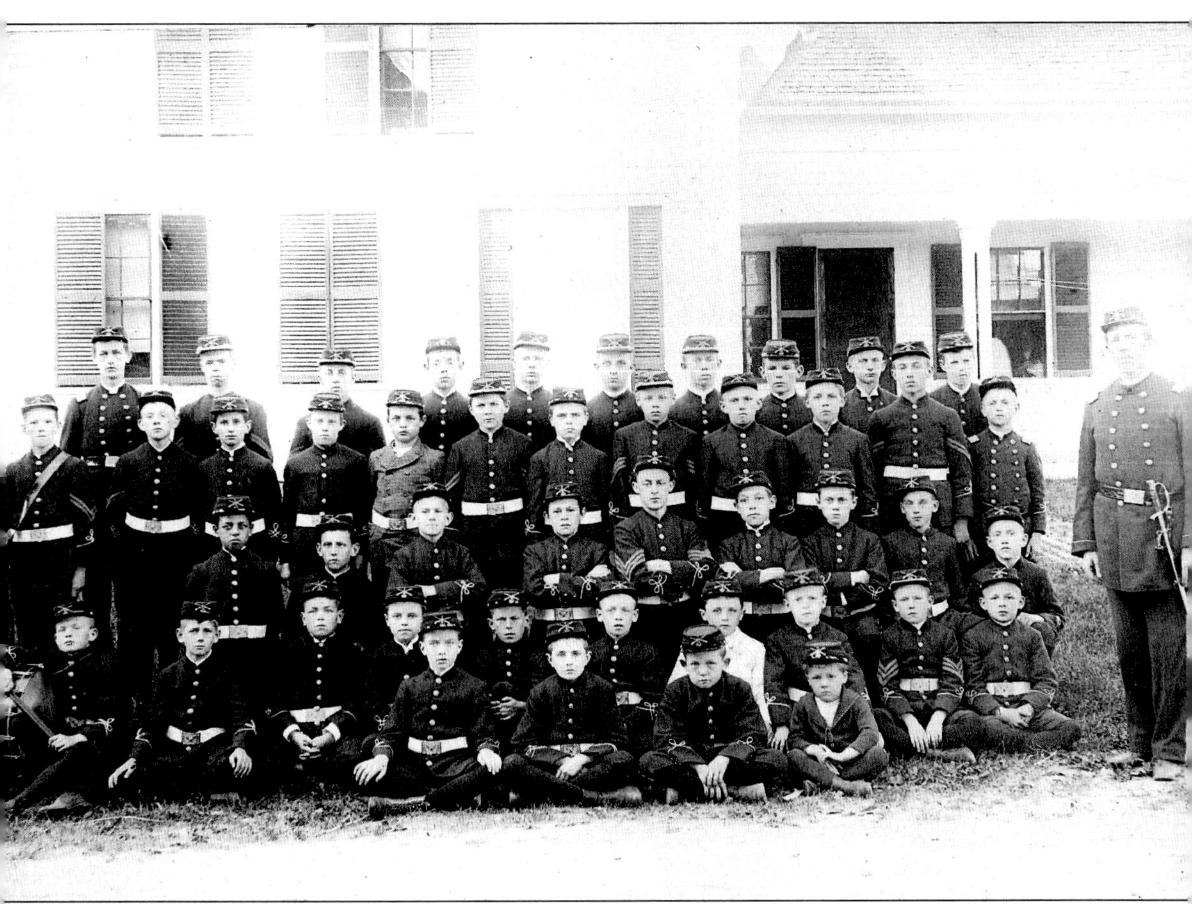

The First Gardner Company Boys' Brigade was under the leadership of Captain Reverend E.M. Fuller. He was at the Baptist church from September 1892 to September 1897. Rules governing the brigade stated the members must abstain from intoxicating liquor, refrain from profane language, and not use tobacco in any form.

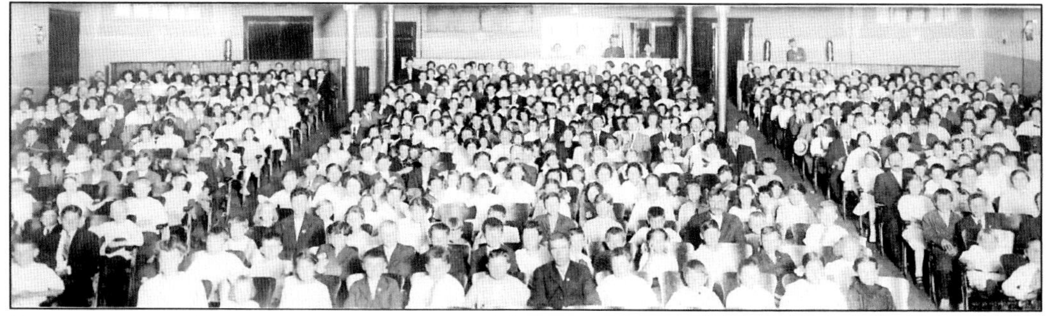
The opening of the Orpheum Theatre in 1913 was a major event in Gardner as the number of people in attendance shows. The theatre was remodeled once and then was broken down into several smaller theatres called the Gardner Cinemas. It was located at 34 Parker Street.

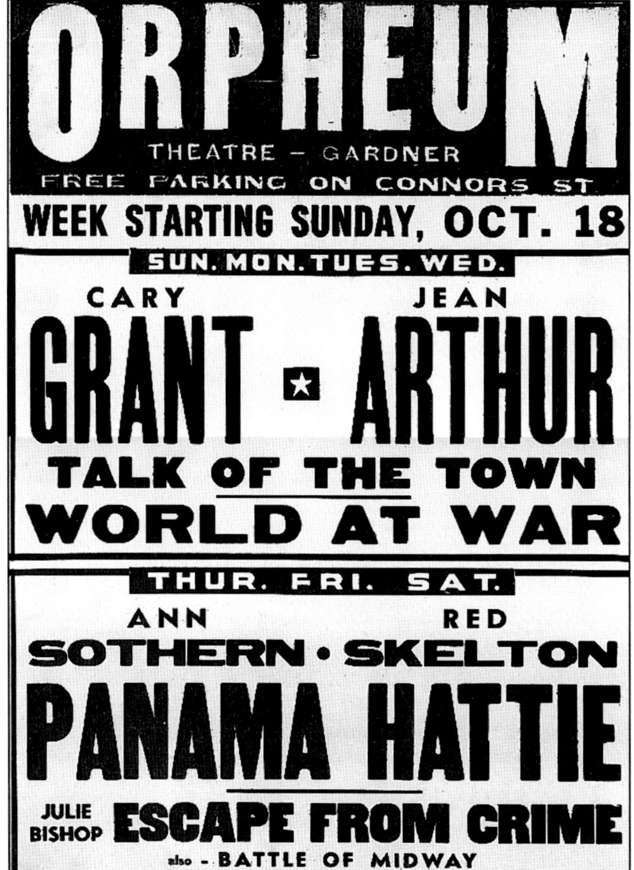

One of the many posters distributed to stores to be posted in their windows promoting the Orpheum Theatre.

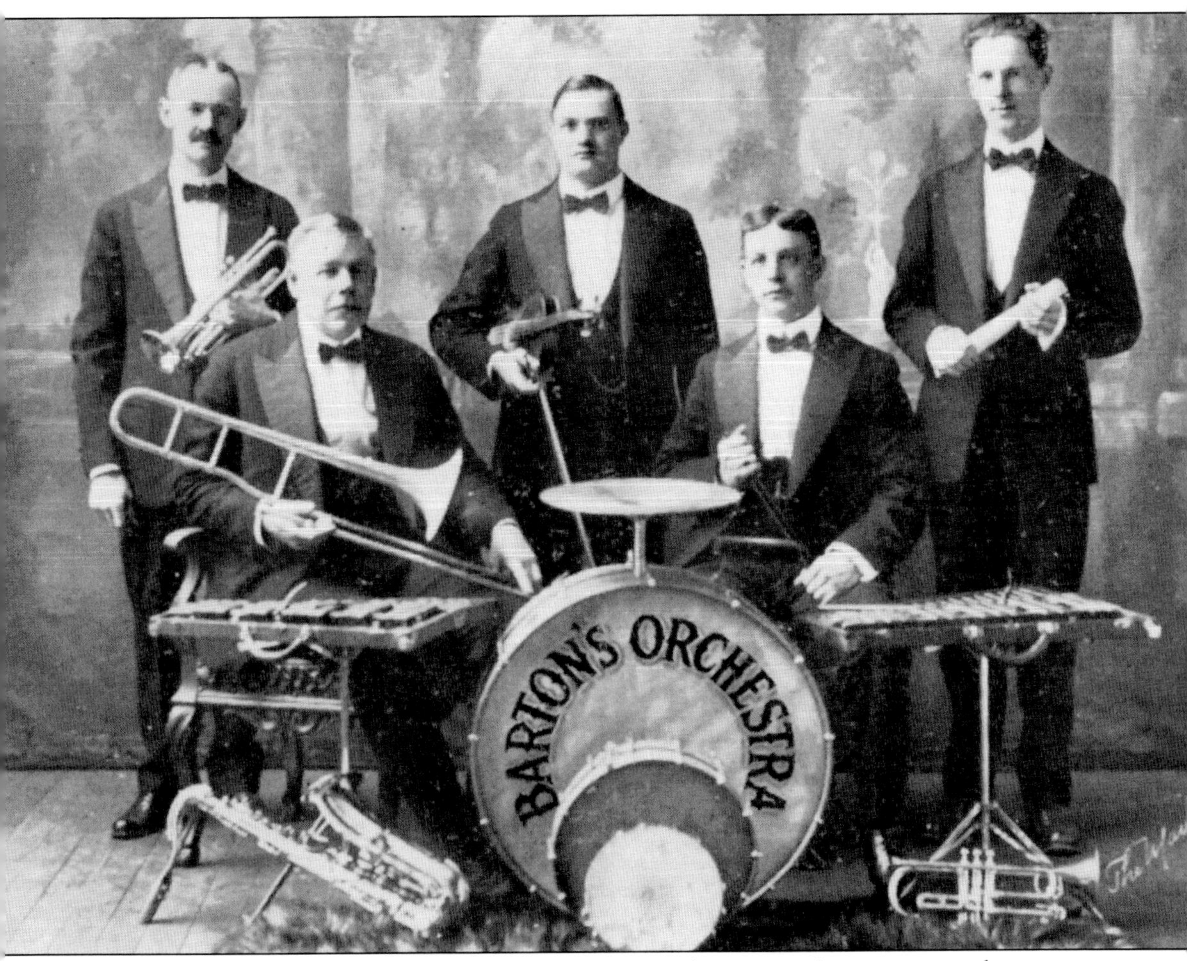

Barton's Orchestra existed in the early part of the twentieth century. Among its members were Daniel N. Burbank (trumpet), Elof Zetterberg (violin), Oscar Bergstrom (piano), George A. Barton (trombone), and Erik Sandstrand (drummer).

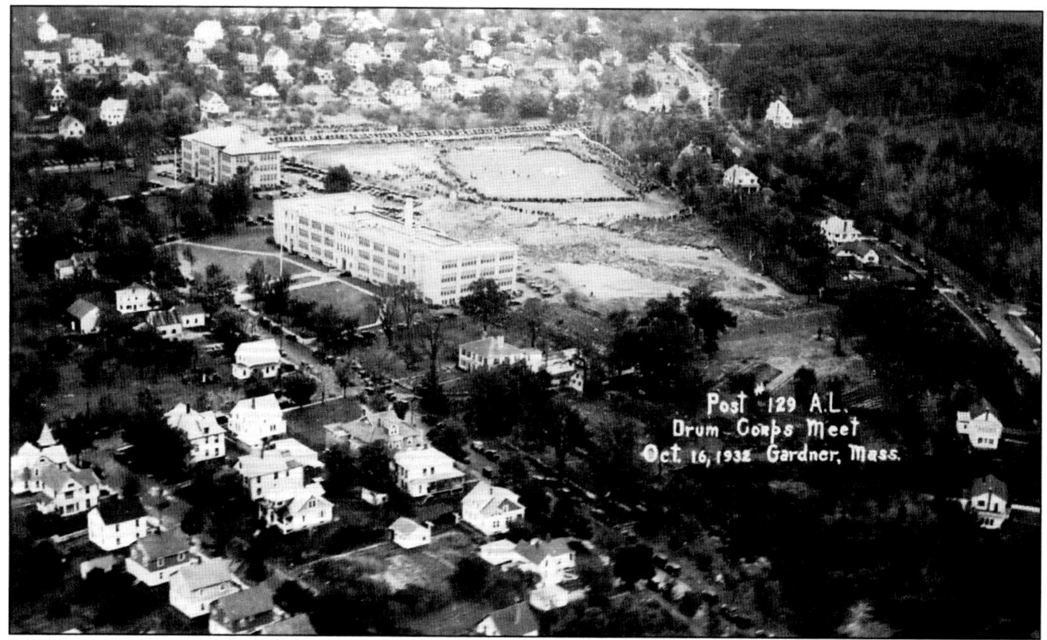

The American Legion hosted a Drum Corps meeting at Stone Field in 1932.

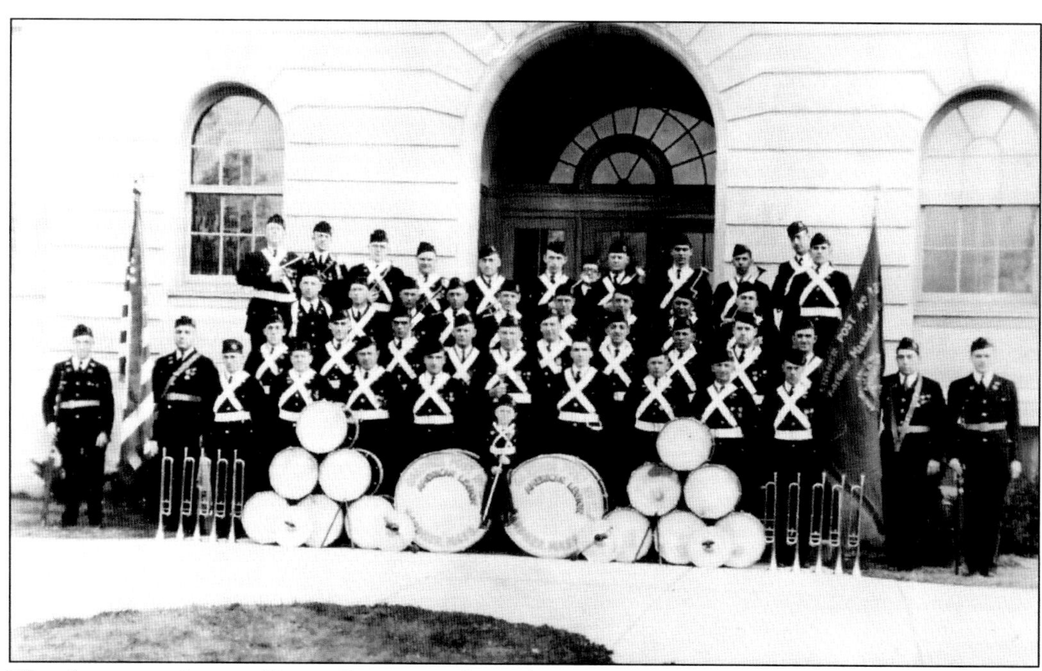
The American Legion Drum Corps was formed in 1928. It assisted the high school band by performing at football games during the 1920s and early 1930s.

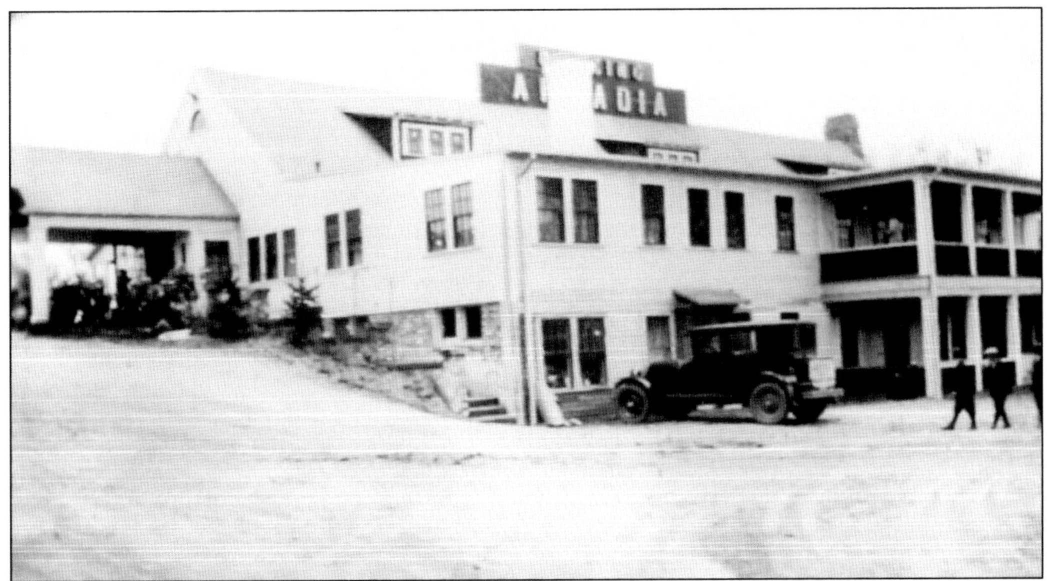

Arcadia by the Lake, or the Arc, was built in 1925 as a dance hall and exhibition center. It was located on the old Marcus Wright Mill site on High Street. Many well-known bands and leaders played the Arc, one of them being Paul Whitman and his Steamboat Orchestra. An outdoor ballroom was added that attracted people and bands from near and far. The dance hall closed in the mid-1940s, and after use as a manufacturing facility, was razed in 1973.

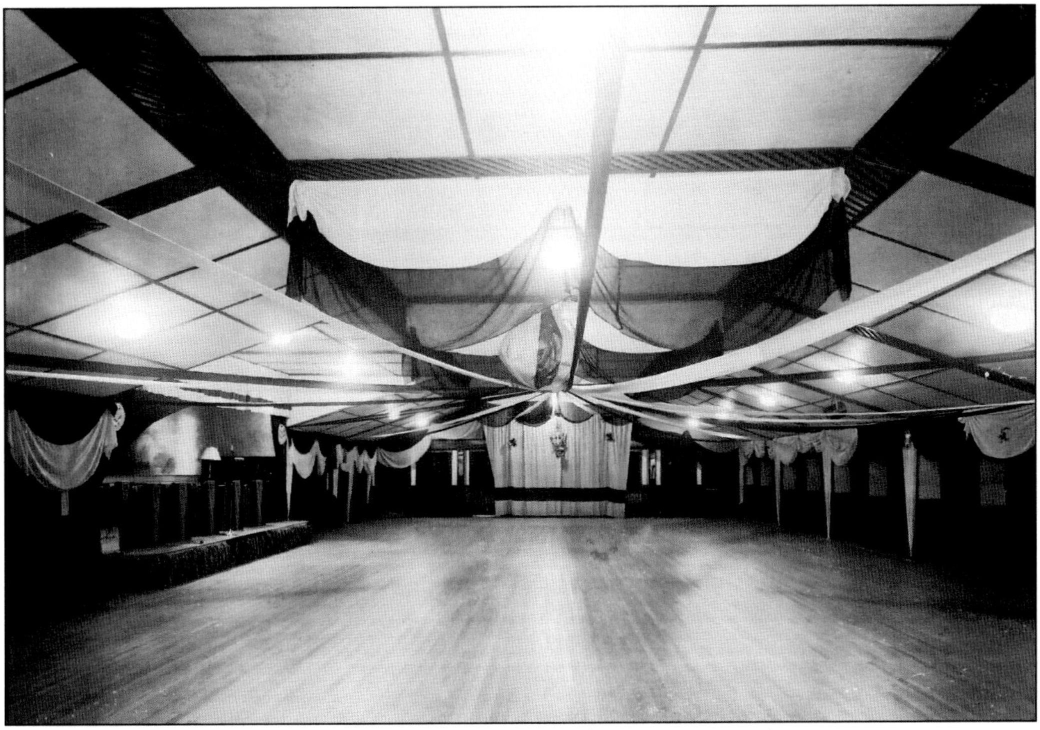

The interior of the Arc decorated for a dance. Bands were among the many entertainments and exhibitions that performed in this room. It was recognized as having one of the finest springboard dance floors in New England.

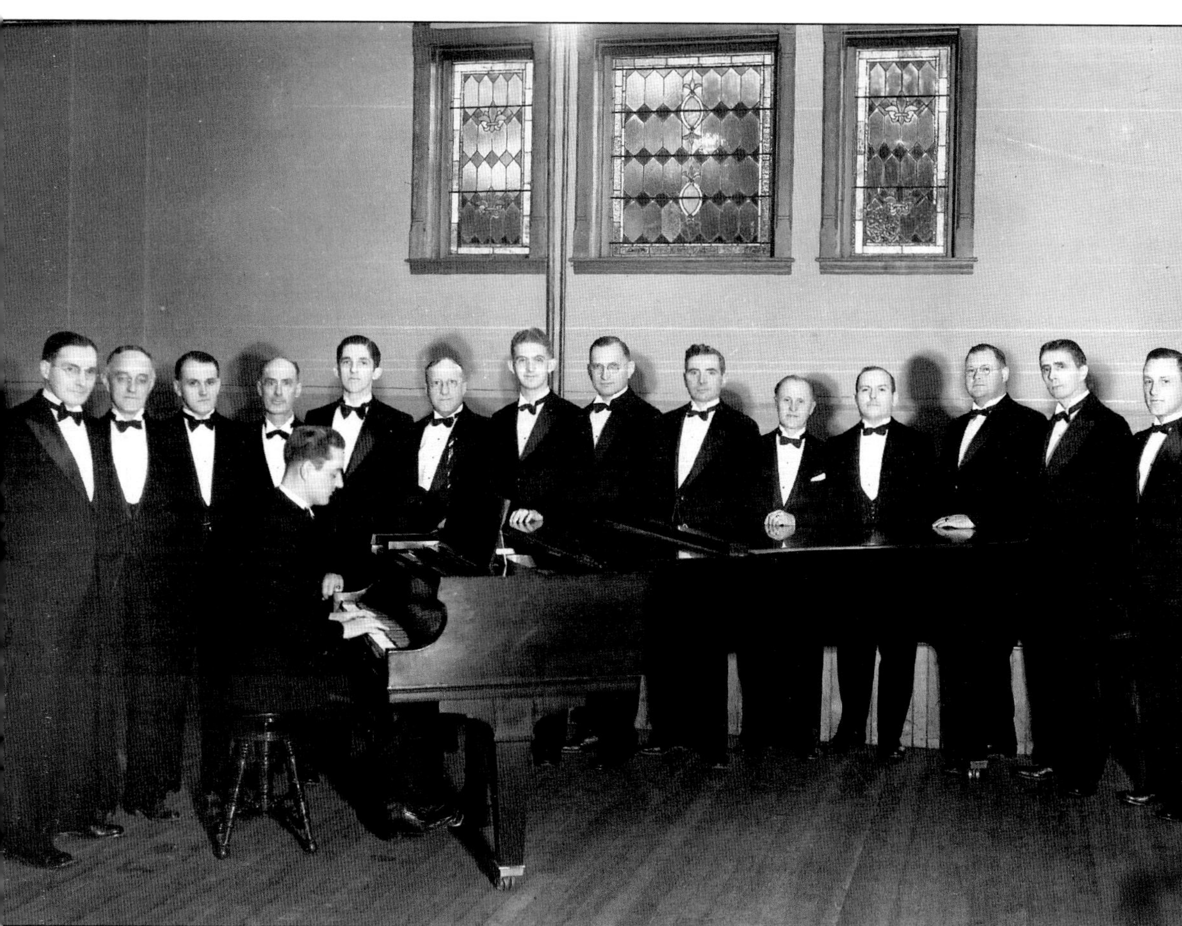

The Nevin Glee Club in the First Congregational Church, 1931. From left to right are: Clifford Webber (at the piano), Robert Little, L. Warner Howe, Robert Boone, Frank Lavallee, Arthur E. Crouch, William Aker (director), Robert M. Crouch, Dr. Earle M. Munson, David Black, Anton Scholz, Llewelyn E. Jones, Edwin J. Bjurling, Gustaf H. Nordstrom, and George Carrick.

Gardner Chapter,
Daughters of the American Revolution
Mrs. Enos R. Bishop, Regent

Presents

The Nevin Glee Club of Gardner

Sixteen Male Voices. Mr. William Aker, Director
and

CLIFFORD WHITE WEBBER, Pianist

in Concert at Pearson Auditorium in
Gardner High School, May 11, 1932

PROGRAM

Glee Club—TO THEE, O COUNTRY,	Eichberg
Tenor Solos—a. AH, MOON OF MY DELIGHT,	Lehmann
b. TREES,	Rasbach
Mr. Howard B. Roche	
Glee Club—BENDEMEER'S STREAM,	Old Irish Air
Baritone Solos—a. OUT OF THE DEEP,	Lohr
b. WHERE MY HEART FINDS REST,	Brown
Mr. Robert Crouch	
Piano Solo—PRELUDE in C SHARP MINOR,	Rachmanioff
Mr. Clifford Webber	
Glee Club—SOLDIER'S CHORUS from "Faust"	Gounod
Duet—IN THE GARDEN OF MY HEART,	Ball
Mr. Little and Mr. Roche	
Glee Club—KINGS OF THE ROAD,	Bevan
Baritone Solos—a. INVICTUS,	Huhn
b. SHIPMATES O' MINE,	Sanderson
Dr. Earle Munson	
Glee Club—THE GARDEN OF DREAMS,	Aker
Piano Specialty—SONG HITS from recent "MINSTREL-REVUE"	
Mr. Clifford Webber	(Webber
(requested)	
Glee Club—DARLING NELLIE GRAY,	arr. by Aker
Favorite Scotch Songs—ROAMIN' IN THE GLOAMIN'	Lauder
I THINK I'LL WED IN THE SUMMER	Lauder
Mr. Robert Little	
Glee Club—NATURE'S PRAISE,	Beethoven

A Daughter of the American Revolution broadside shows a typical presentation of the Nevin Glee Club.

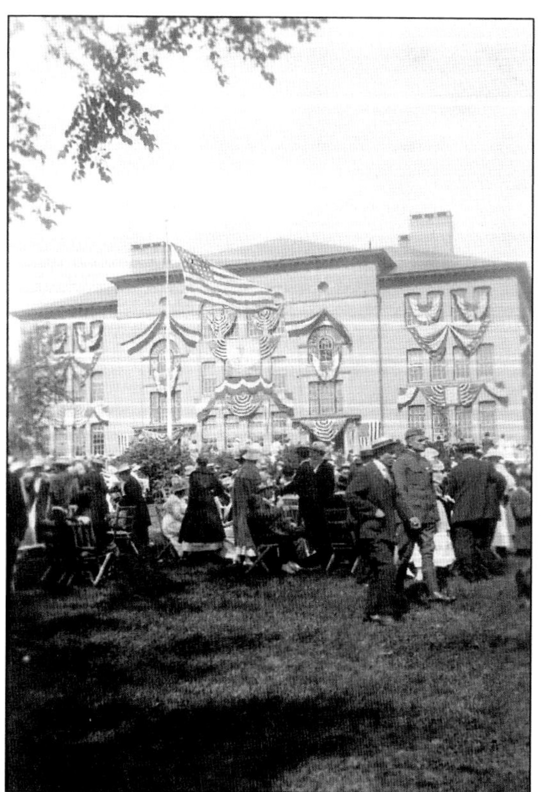

A Welcome Home celebration honoring service men and women who had served in World War I was held on August 2, 1919. The speakers at the high school, now the Helen Mae Sauter School, were Major-General Clarence R. Edwards and Joe Mitchell Chapple.

The Victory Quartet, part of the Welcome Home celebrations after World War I, sit in their conveyance in front of the Kirby Newton home at 75 Union Street. Leroy Morris is shown directly behind the boy in the sailors uniform, and Delphis Fleurant, Joseph LaFountain, and Nathan Lampert were the other members of the quartet.

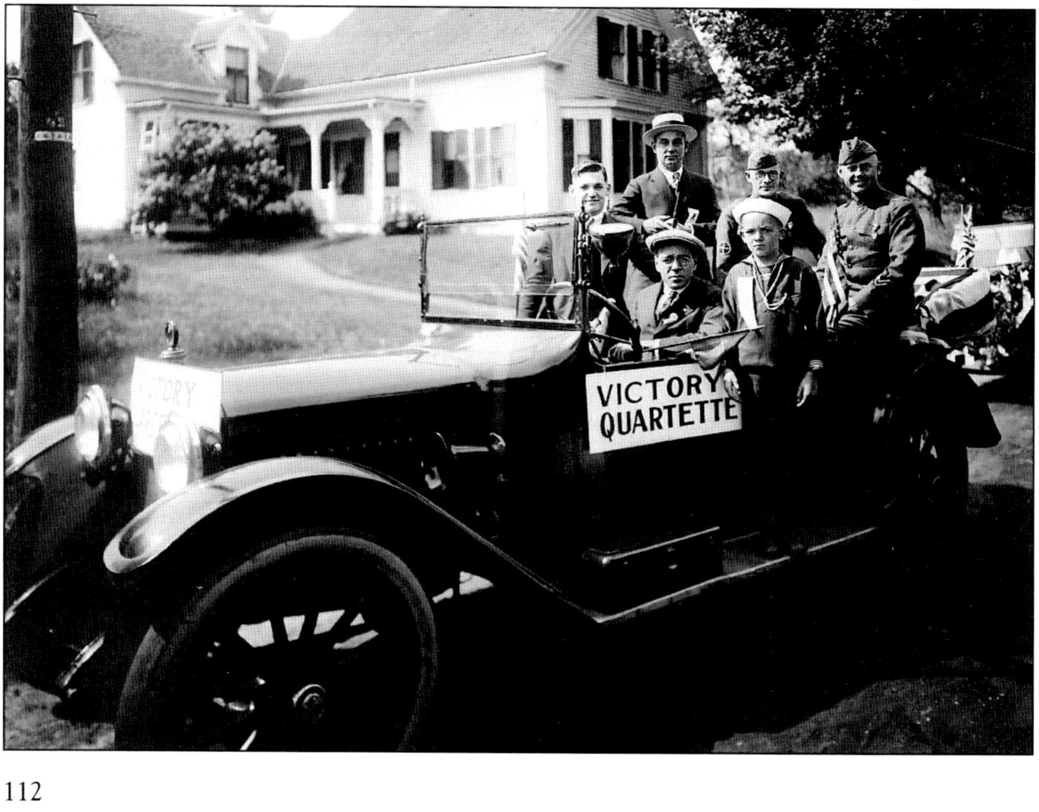

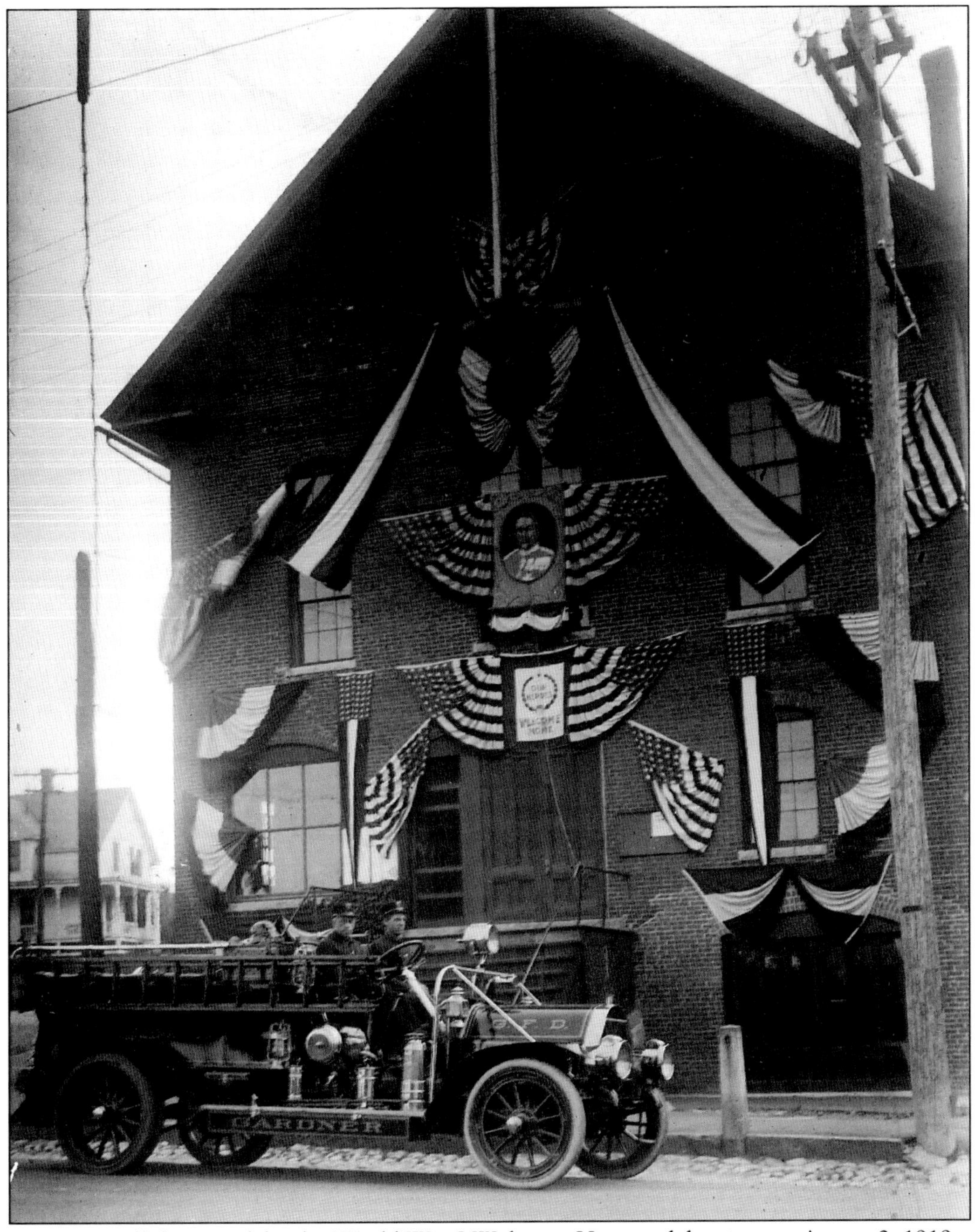

Citizen's Hall decorated for the World War I Welcome Home celebration on August 2, 1919.

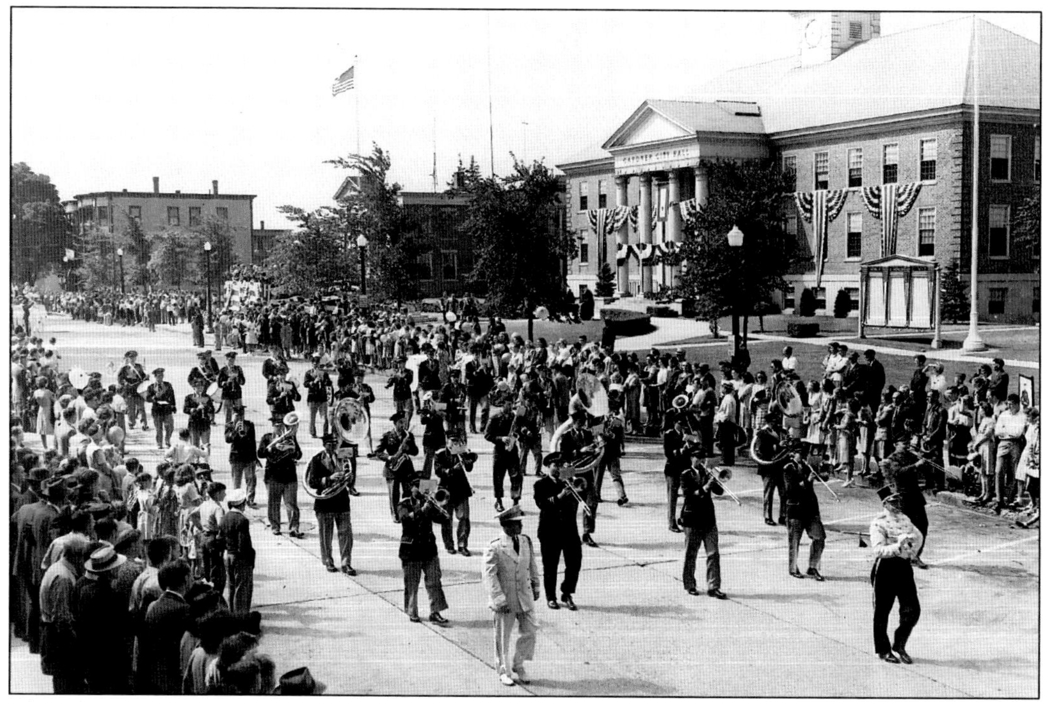

The Florence Rangers Band, one of several bands sponsored by local manufacturers such as Heywood Wakefield and Simplex Time Recorder Company, is shown marching in front of the City Hall on August 17, 1946, during the Welcome Home parade for World War II veterans.

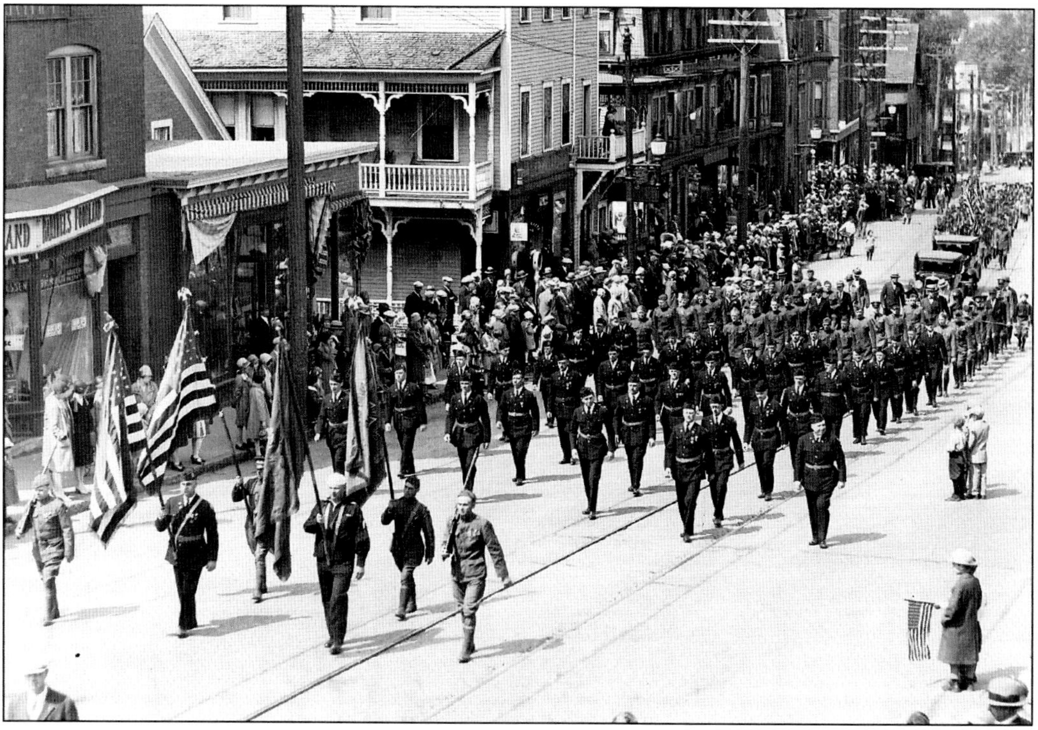

A veteran's group is shown marching up Parker Street during a Memorial Day parade.

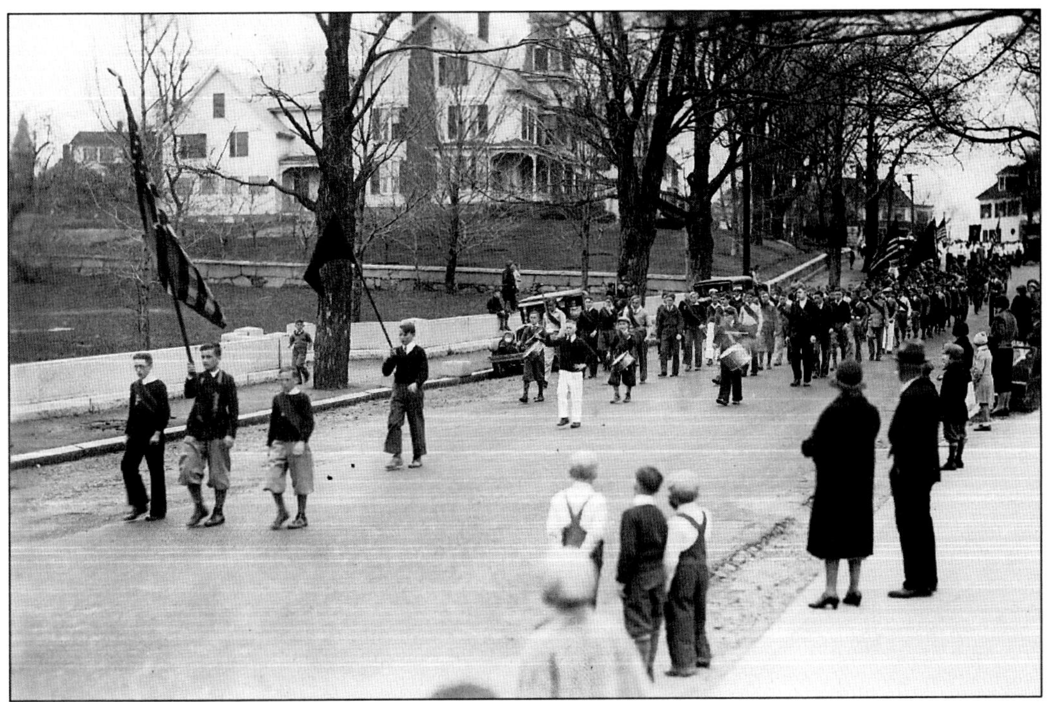

A parade marking the end of Boys' Week in 1932. During the week the boys from the city schools participated in many events, including "running" Gardner for a day as mayor and city councilors.

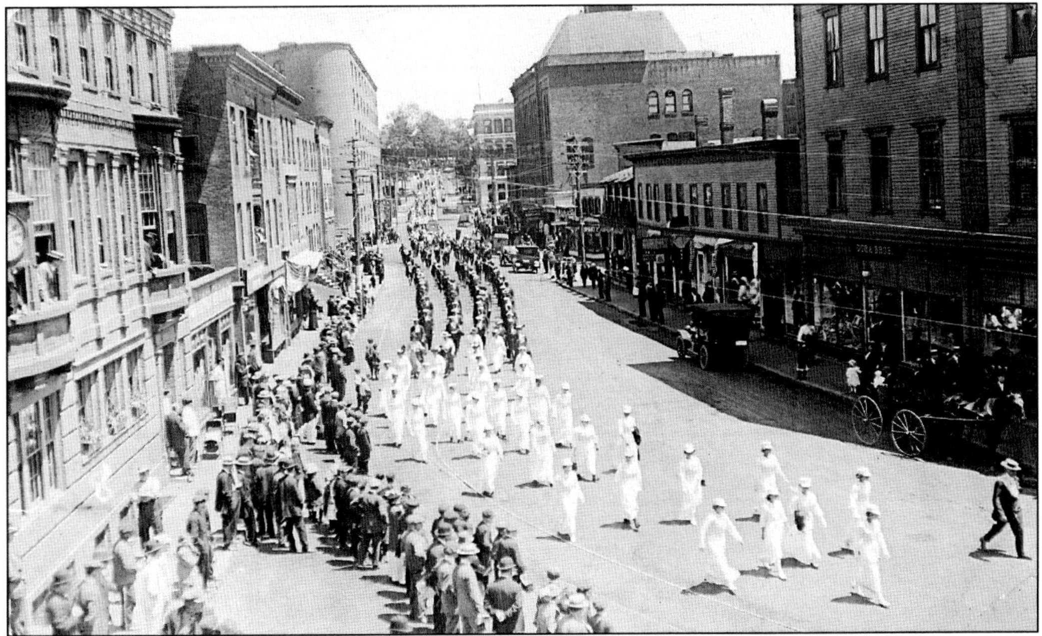

The Ladies of Kaleva, a prominent Finnish women's society, march on Central Street after the turn of the century. They are still active today.

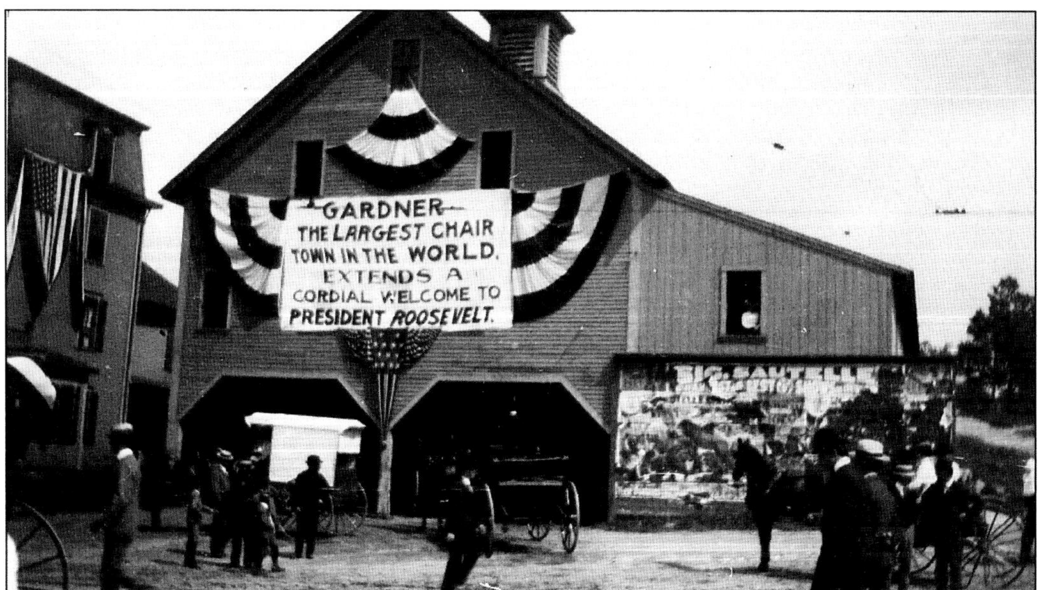

On September 2, 1902, the town of Gardner awaited the arrival of President Theodore Roosevelt. This sign of welcome was on the barn next to the Gardner House across from Union Station.

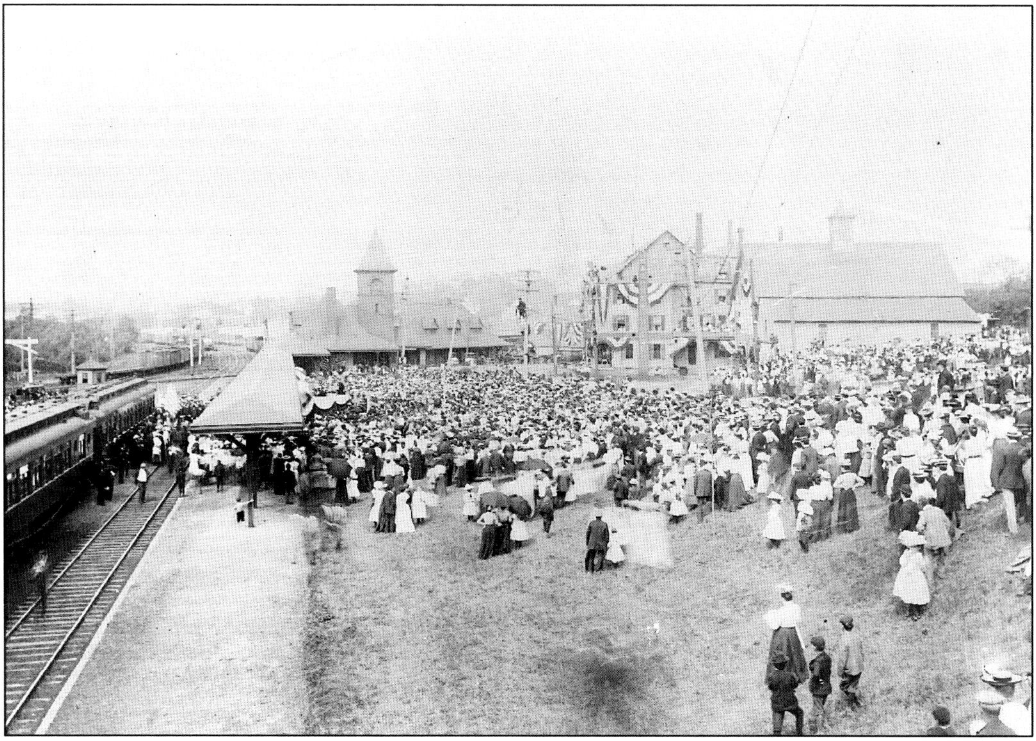

The massive crowd of people gathered at Union Station of September 2, 1902, to hear President Roosevelt speak.

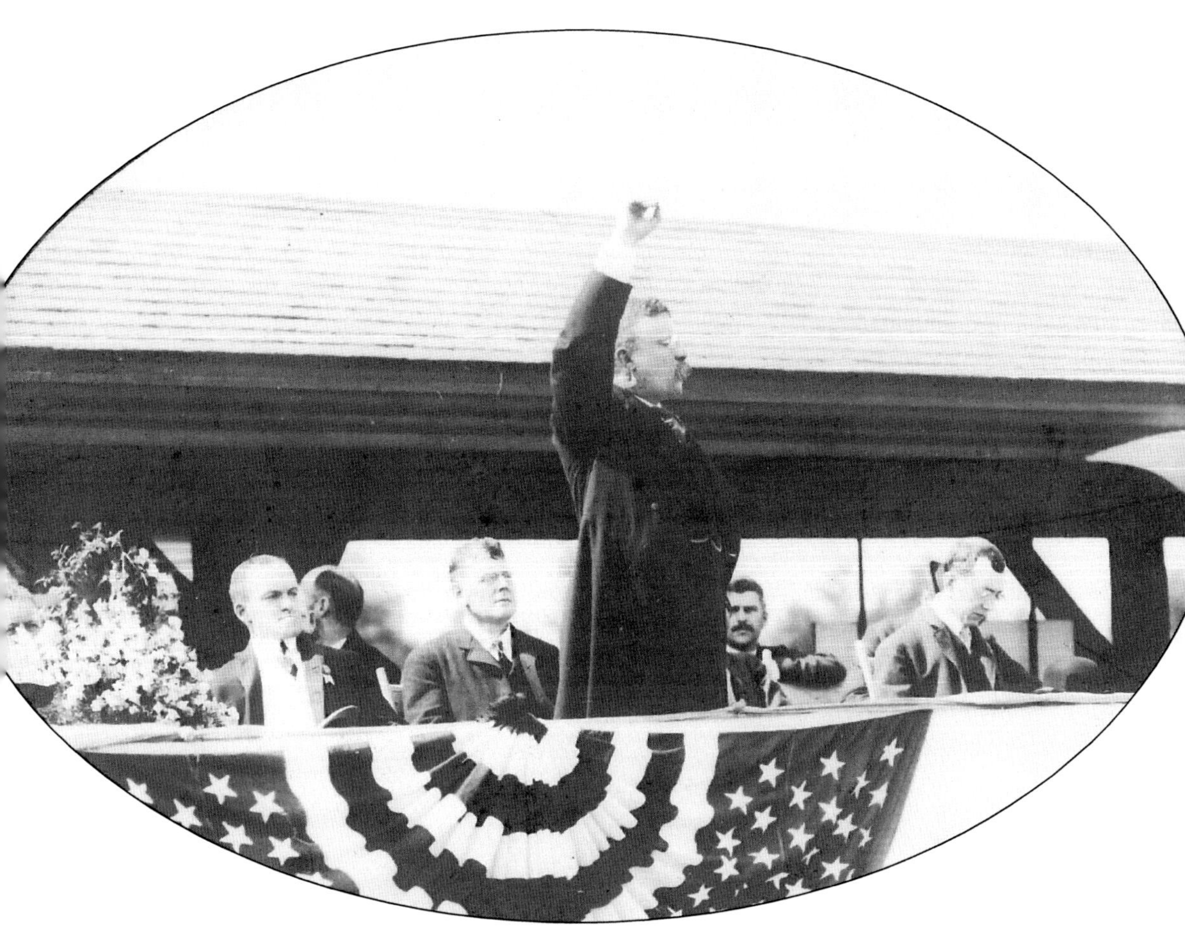

President Theodore Roosevelt addresses the gathering at Union Station on September 2, 1902. He arrived at 10:08 and left at 10:27 a.m. Mr. Craig, one of his secret service guards, who may be visible on the platform, was killed the next day when the President's chaise was struck by an electric trolley car in Pittsfield, Massachusetts. The President was hurt and his health was never the same.

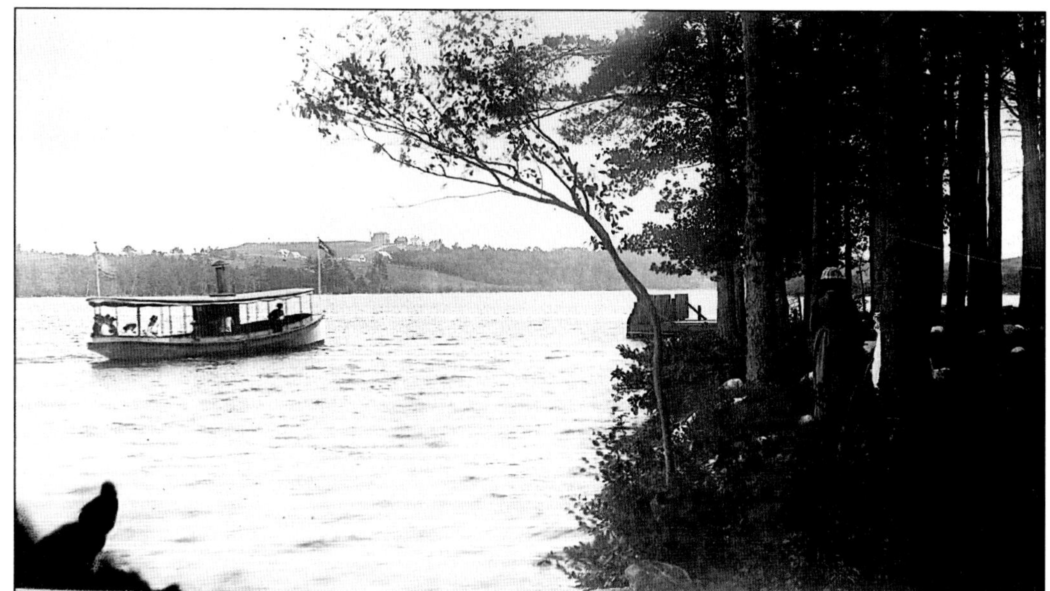

For a period of time from 1875 until about 1900 the waters of Crystal Lake were open to boating. The steamer shown here was one of a series that plied the waters taking tourists to Crystal Lake Park. The first was the *Little Favorite* in 1875, then there were the *Waukegan* and the *Zephyr*.

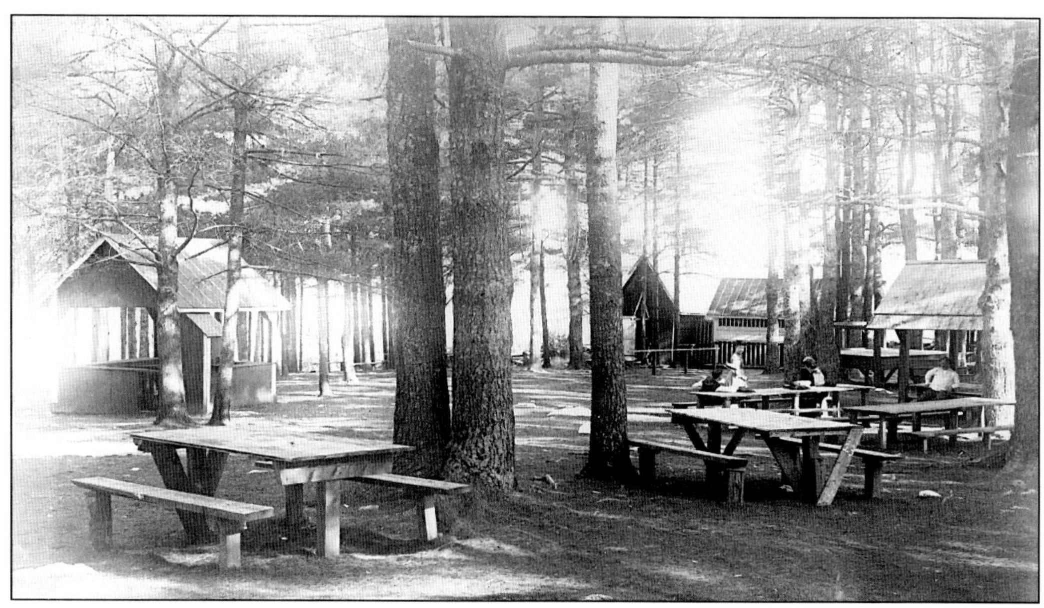

There was a picnic grove at the park.

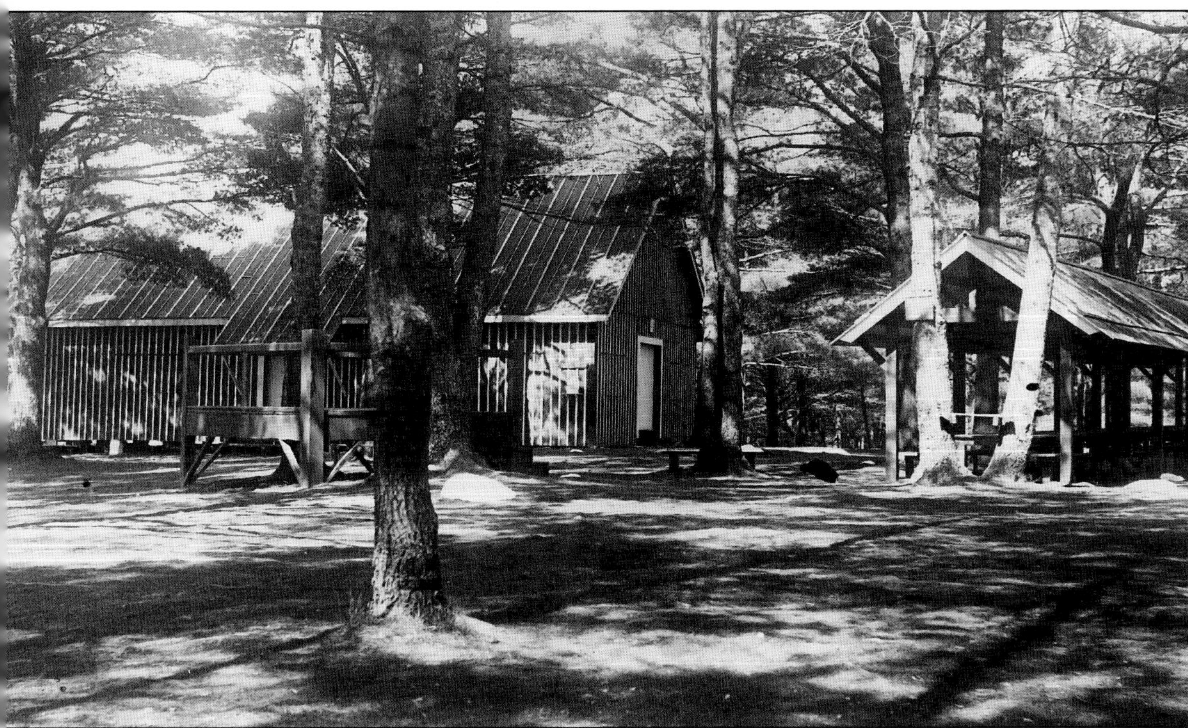

Crystal Lake Park was located on the northwest shore of Crystal Lake. The site is now partially covered by the golf course. It was originally called Heywood Grove until the Heywood's gave the park to the Boston, Barre, and Gardner Railroad in 1875. The railroad improved the area, adding ball fields, bowling, a bicycle track, dance pavilions, and a wharf. The park closed soon after 1900 when the state took control of all lakes used as water supplies.

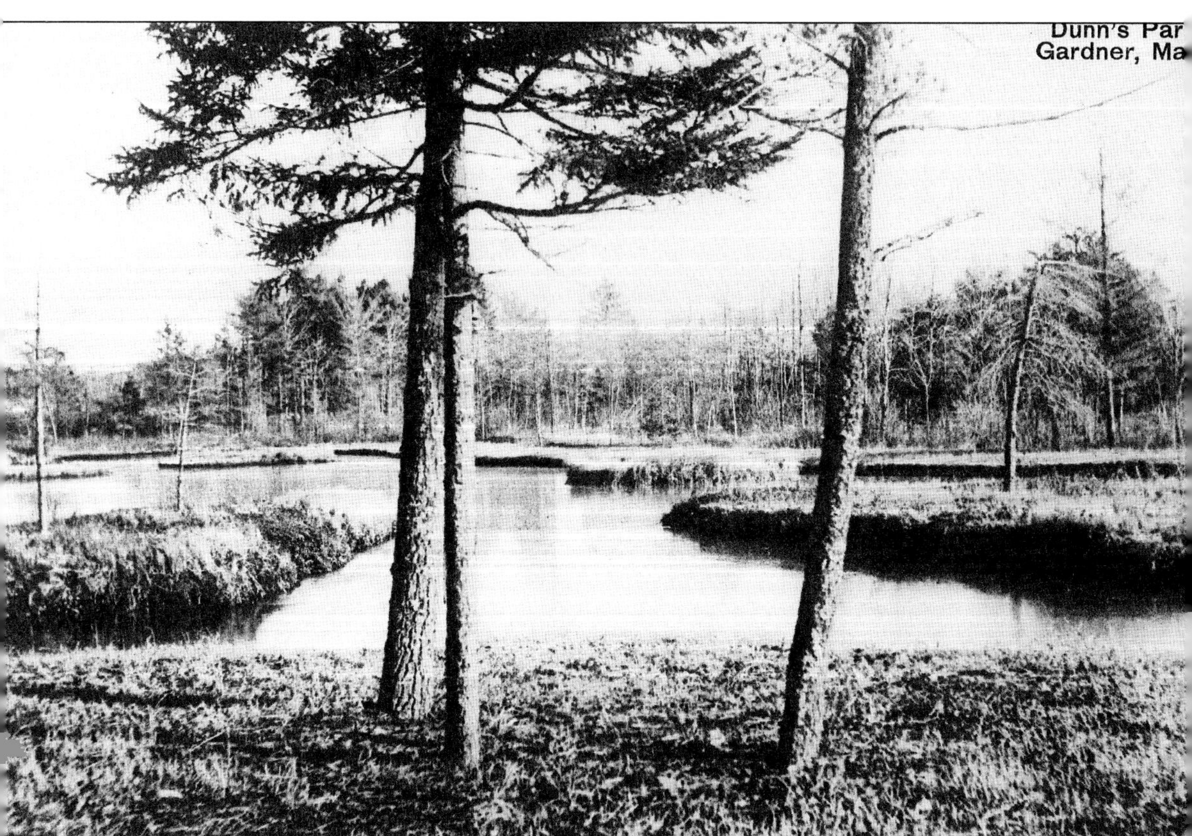

At the end of the nineteenth century John A. Dunn bought up land surrounding what is today Dunn's Pond. He made it known that upon his death the land would revert to the town of Gardner for a park. At his death in 1919 Gardner acquired the tract and was custodian of the land and lake until it was turned over to the state to become part of the Heritage State Park.

Seven

Industry and Commerce

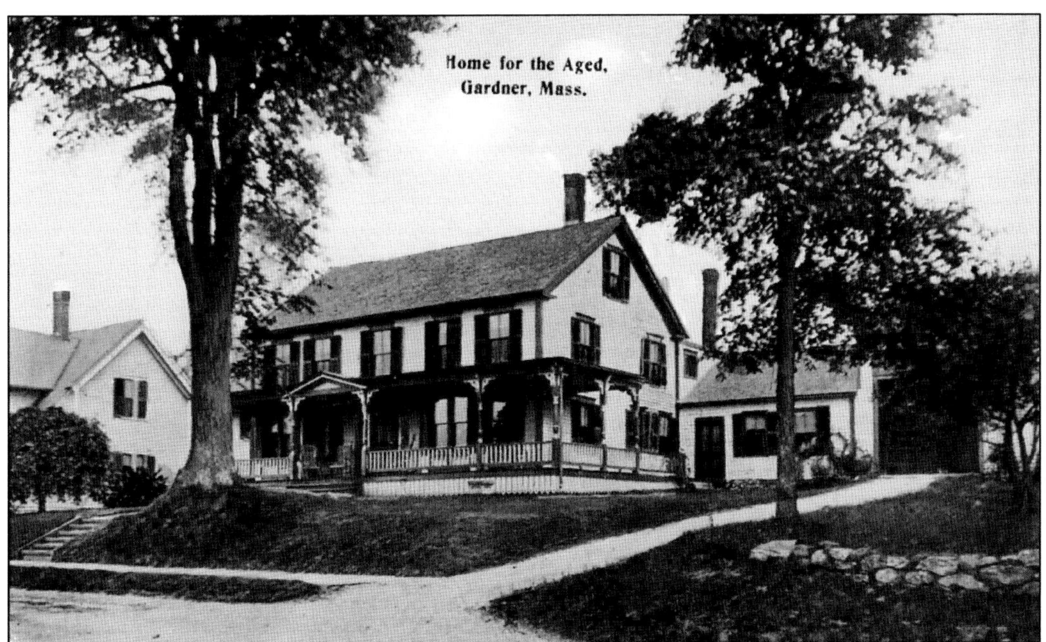

James Comee began the manufacture of chairs in a barn attached to this house in 1805. This small shop is where many of the later chair shop owners began as apprentices to Mr. Comee.

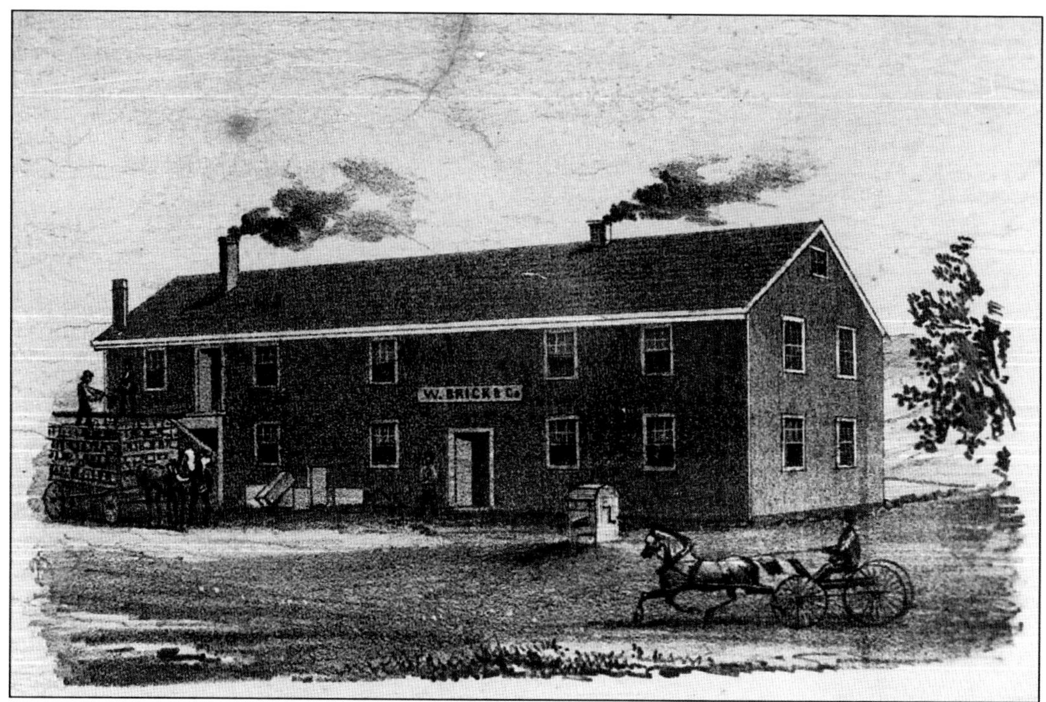

W. Brick and Company operated a chair business on Green Street in the area of the small pond near Mount Wachusett Community College on Green Street. The Brick's were noted for the use and beauty of the stencils they made to decorate their chairs and other company's chairs. Mr. Brick was one of many apprentices of James M. Comee.

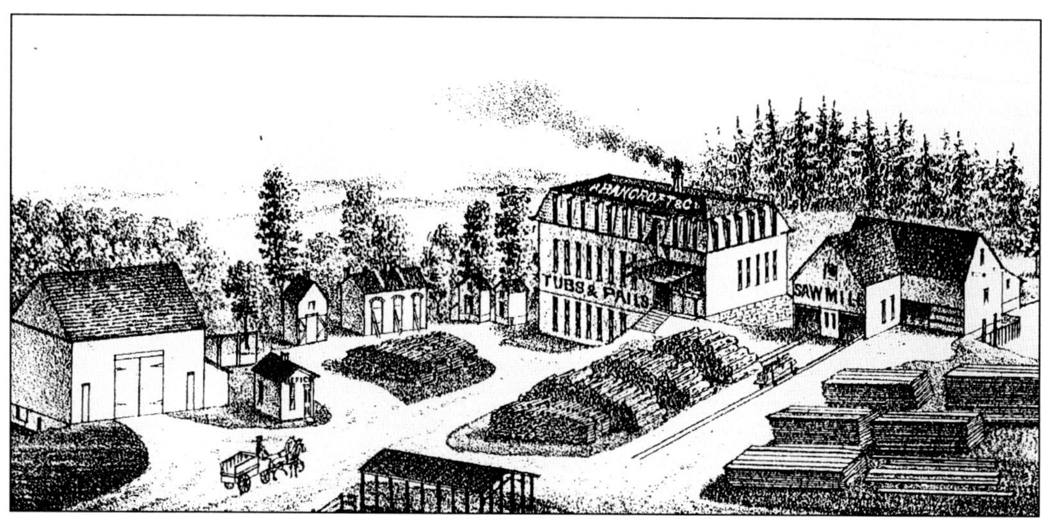

The Amasa Bancroft and Company pail and tub manufacturing operation used the early Joshua Whitney sawmill site on the present lower Mill Street. Proprietors from 1822 on produced wooden ware until Bancroft expanded the pail-making business in 1840. In later years former mayor Fred Perry milled various wood products and fine turnings. His plant burned in the early 1930s.

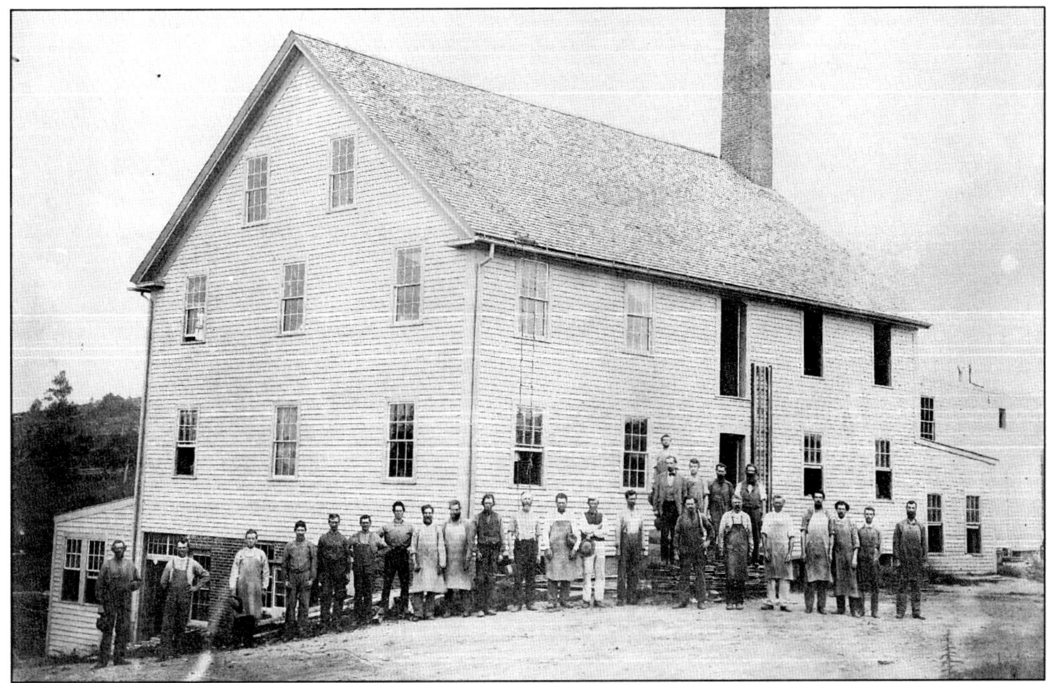

The help standing in front of Conant Brothers and Company chair factory and plant, on West Broadway on Pond Brook near the present Doctors Professional Building, about 1866. Originally the site was occupied by Aaron Jackson and Aaron L. Greenwood beginning in 1852. In 1875 the name was Conant, Ball, and Company, and in 1888 the business was moved to the present site of its vacated buildings on West Lynde Street, originally owned by L.H. Sawin and Company.

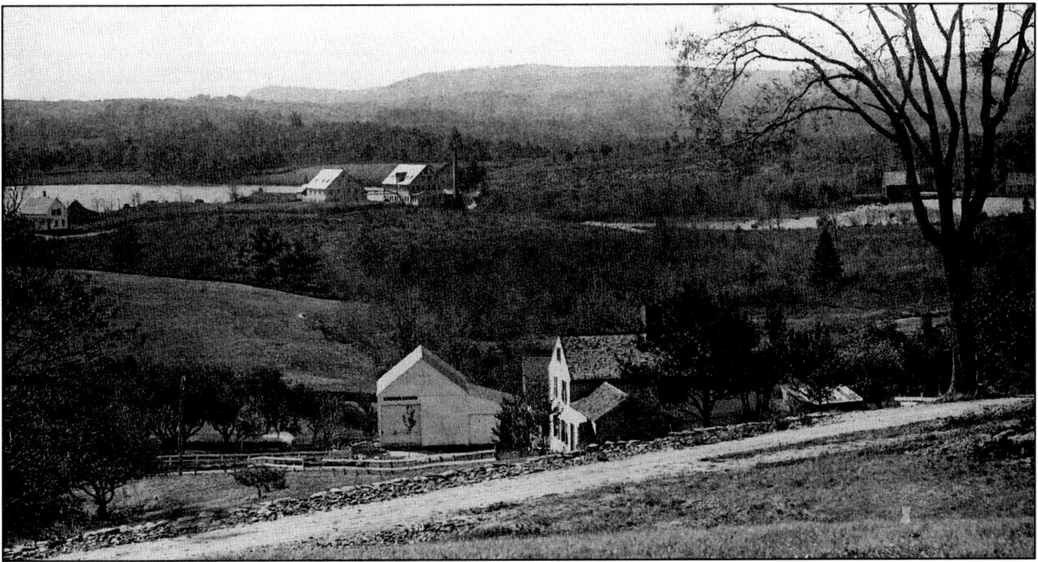

Kendall Street is in the foreground. Just beyond is the rear of Sullivan Jackson's home on West Broadway. In the background is the L.B. Ramsdell Shop, originally built by Levi Warren, which was to become the largest manufacturer of doll carriages in the country in 1897 . At the right is the Howe Brothers' Gristmill where Timpany Boulevard now passes.

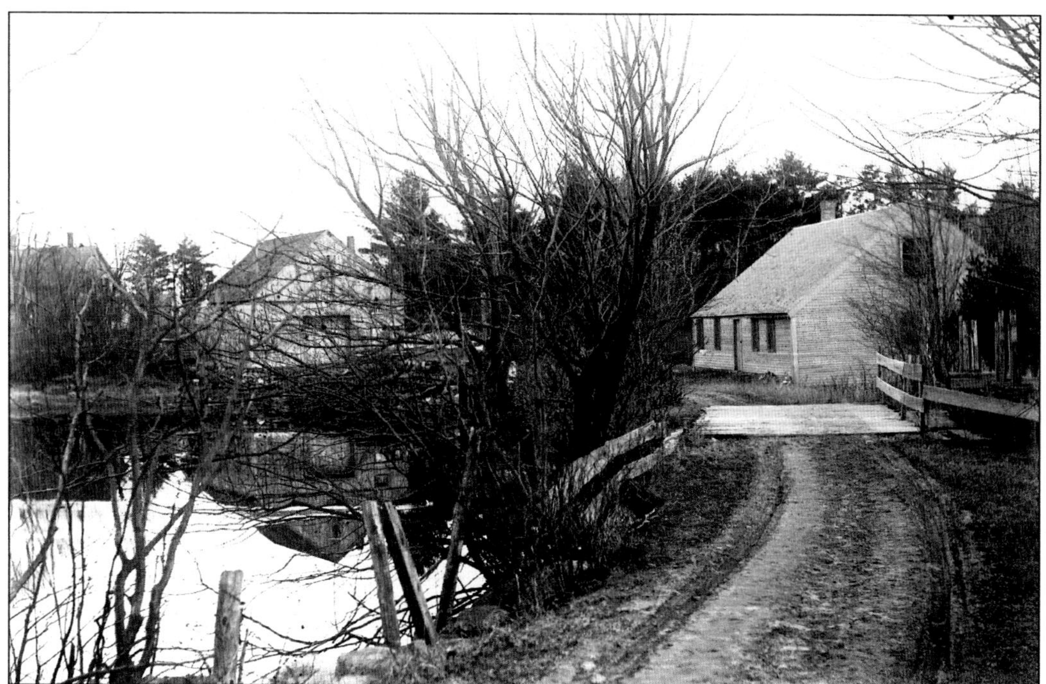

The Howe Brothers began operating at this site in 1871, succeeding the same business of C. Webster Bush. Luke Sawin and Dr. David Parker built the dam and a small plant here in the 1820s for getting out chair stock, and were followed by several other operators before the mill stones were introduced. This scene was between Mill and Dyer Streets, below the present bridge on Route 68, near the Garbose Metal Scrap Yard.

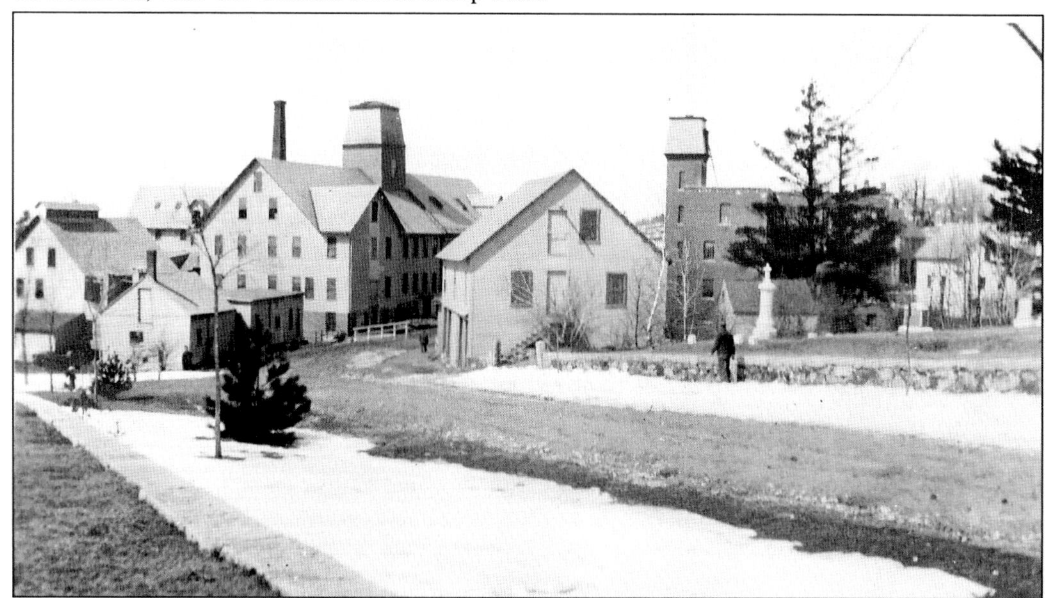

The S. Bent and Brothers site was first occupied by John Merriam in 1822. About 1860 A. Allen Bent became involved in the business. He sold his interest to his brother Charles who involved his brothers Roderic L. and Samuel in the business under the name Samuel Bent and Brothers. When Samuel Bent died in 1883 the name was changed to S. Bent and Brothers.

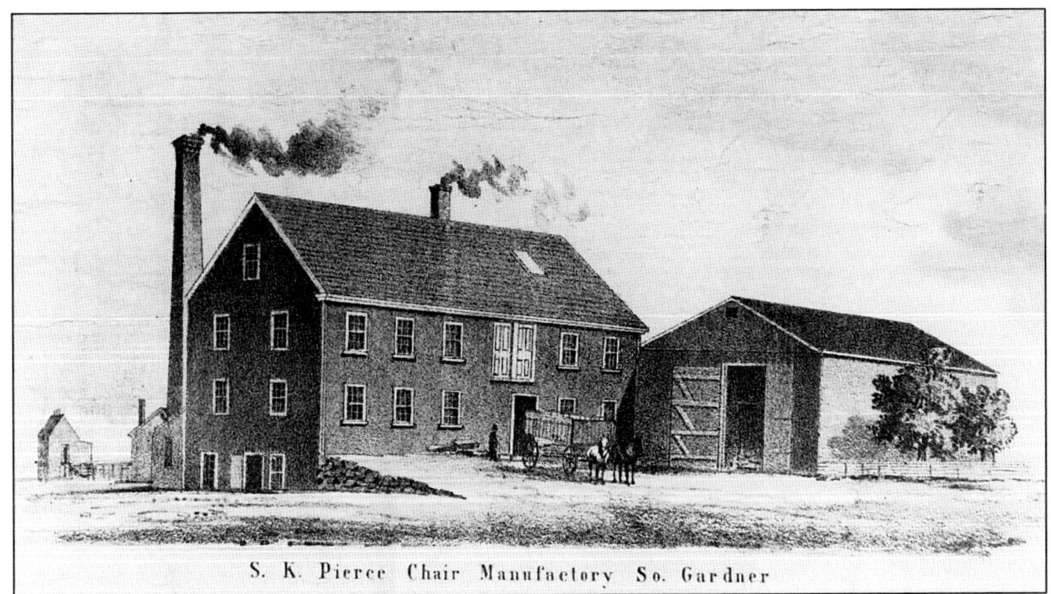

The early S.K. Pierce Shop. Very early on William Bickford used this site as a potash works. In 1830 Stephen Taylor bought the privilege. He sold out to Sylvester K. Pierce and Jonas Pierce, who employed Philander Derby for a time. This is the early plant of Mr. Pierce.

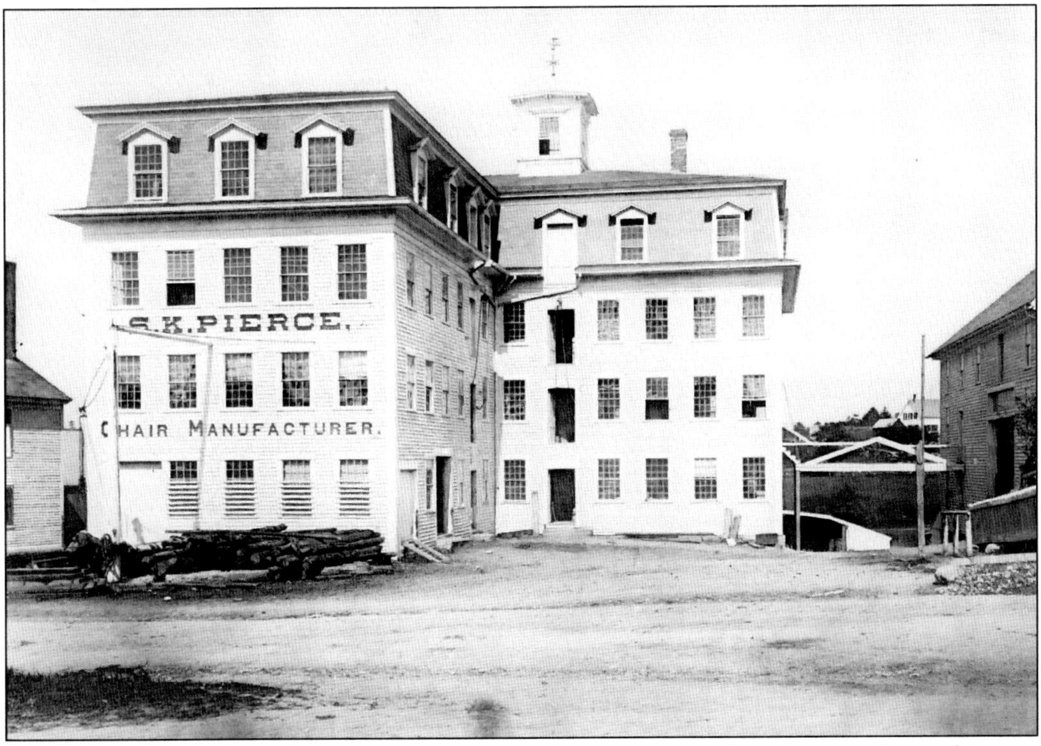

The rebuilt S.K. Pierce plant. Upon the death of Sylvester in 1888, Frank J. Pierce, his son, assumed control of the S.K. Pierce and Company. The company closed in 1937 and the building and was subsequently destroyed by fire on February 25, 1938. Standard Chair now occupies the site.

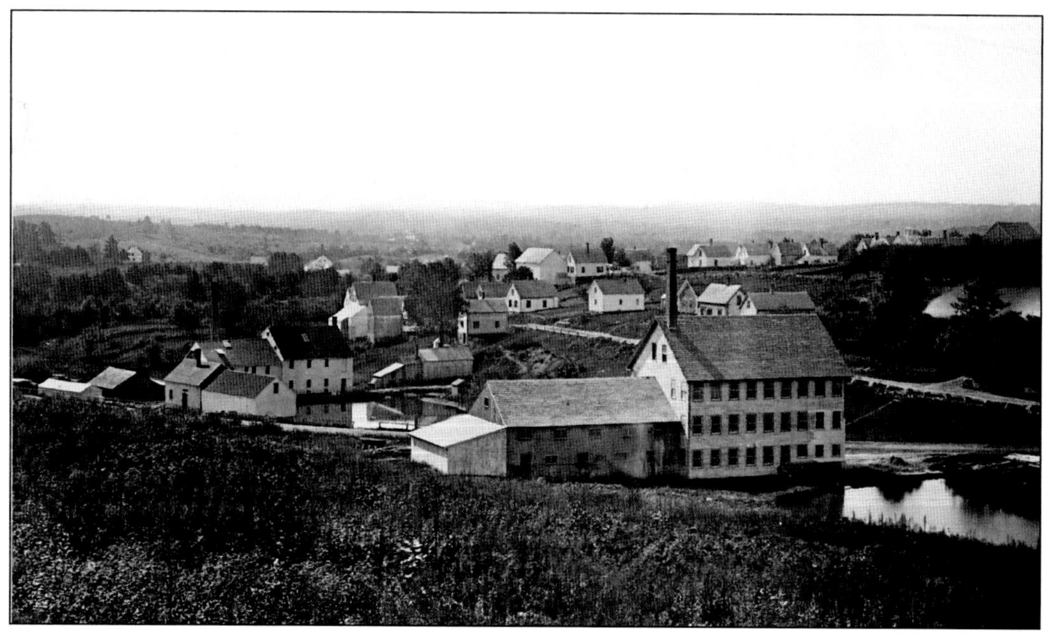

Two privileges are visible here. One, on the left, was first developed by Abner White in 1848. Later Alex and H.C. Knowlton used the site. The buildings were destroyed by fire. The other privilege was also improved by Abner White about 1845. E. Wright eventually bought the site and used it for many years. GEM Industries bought the plant in 1916. The building was partially burned and then demolished in 1994.

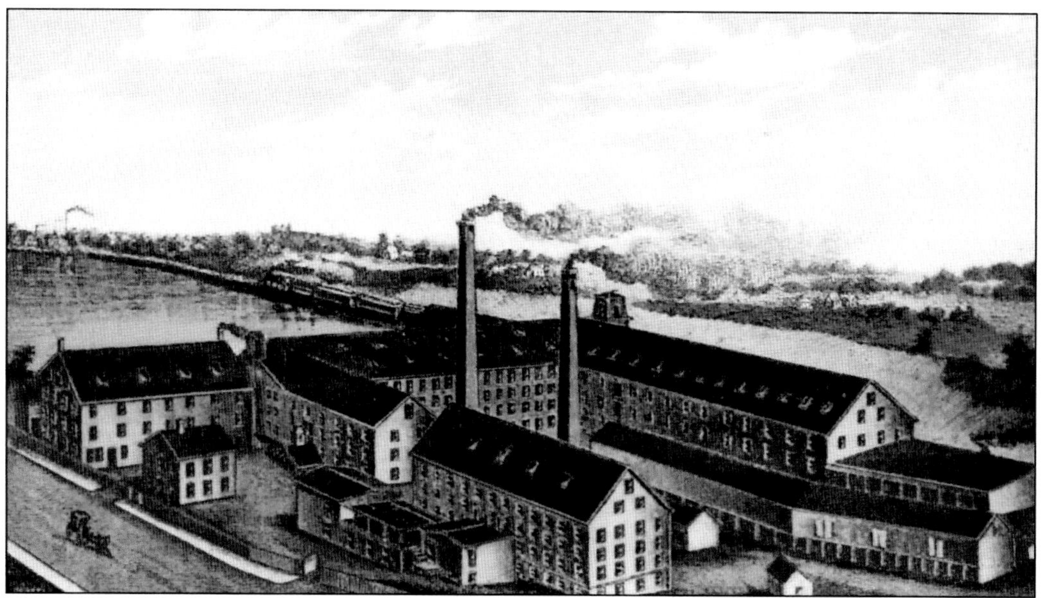

The P. Derby Company. The site was originally owned by William Lynde who sold it to Benjamin Heywood in 1834. Through many owners it came to be owned by Philander Derby and Augustus Knowlton in 1863. By 1868 Philander Derby had gained control of the shop. This company produced the first "large" Gardner chair which stood at the depot for many years. The company which was listed in 1897 as being the second largest chair manufacturer in the world, closed in 1935. The complex was torn down in 1997.

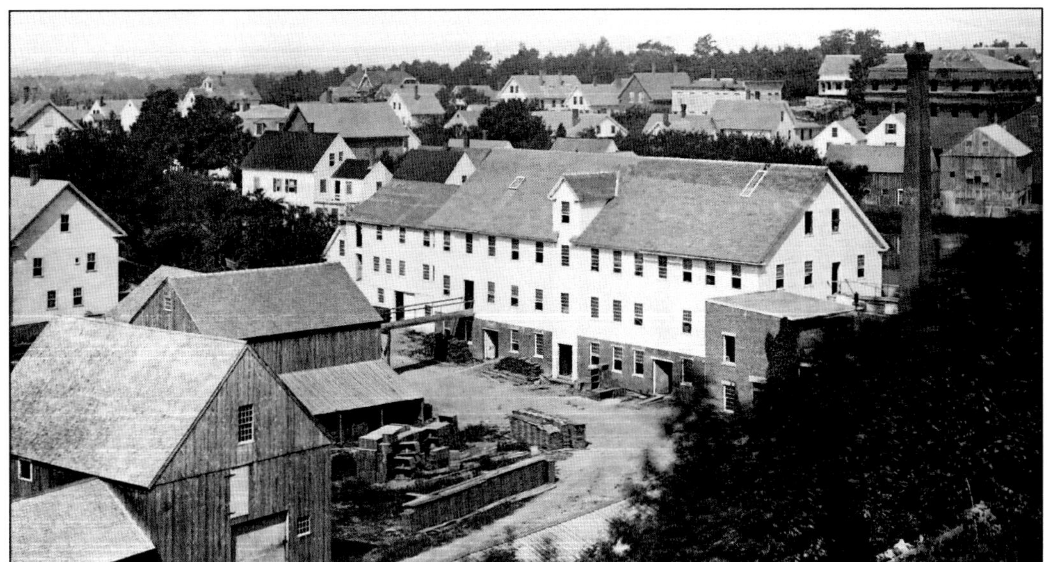

The J.A. Dunn Company. This site was also purchased from William Lynde. Elijah Putnam built a dam here in 1838. Various companies occupied the site until John A. Dunn became associated with Eaton and Holmes. The Dunn family gained control in 1886 under the name J.A. and I.J. Dunn. John A. bought out his brother and the John A. Dunn Company came into existence. The company closed in 1930.

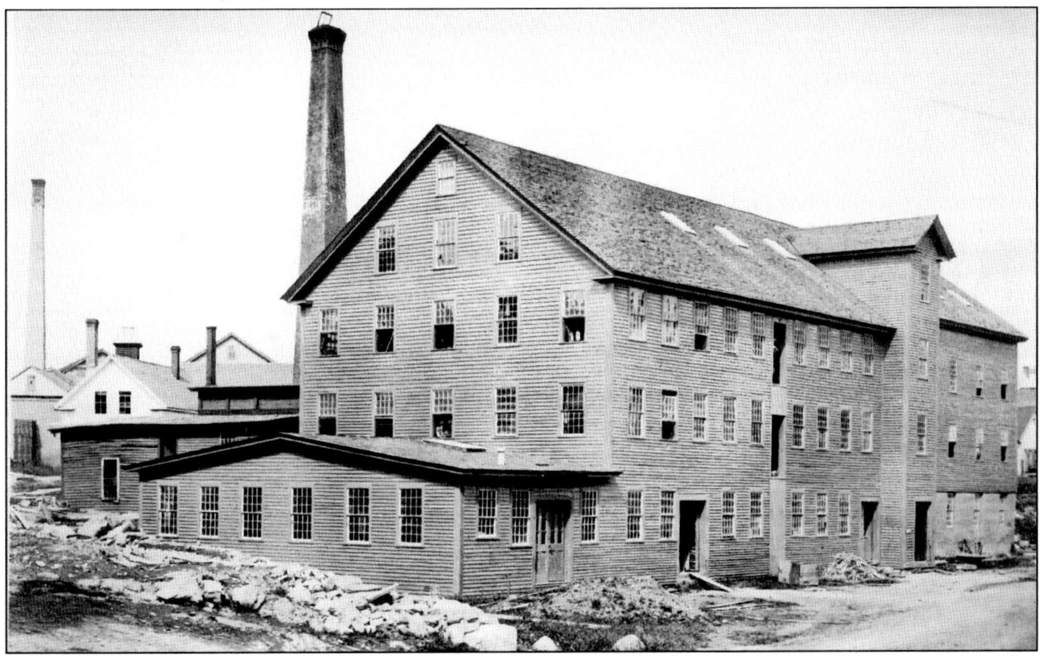

The L.H. Sawin/Conant Ball Company site was first used by Noah Fairbanks as a gristmill about 1800. This was the first privilege on Pond Brook which drains Crystal Lake. He later sold it to Elijah Putnam, who introduced cane seating to Gardner. In 1851 Levi Sawin became involved in the plant which eventually became known as L.H. Sawin and Company. In 1888 they moved the operation to New York State and Conant Ball bought the privilege. This National Register property was torn down in 1997.

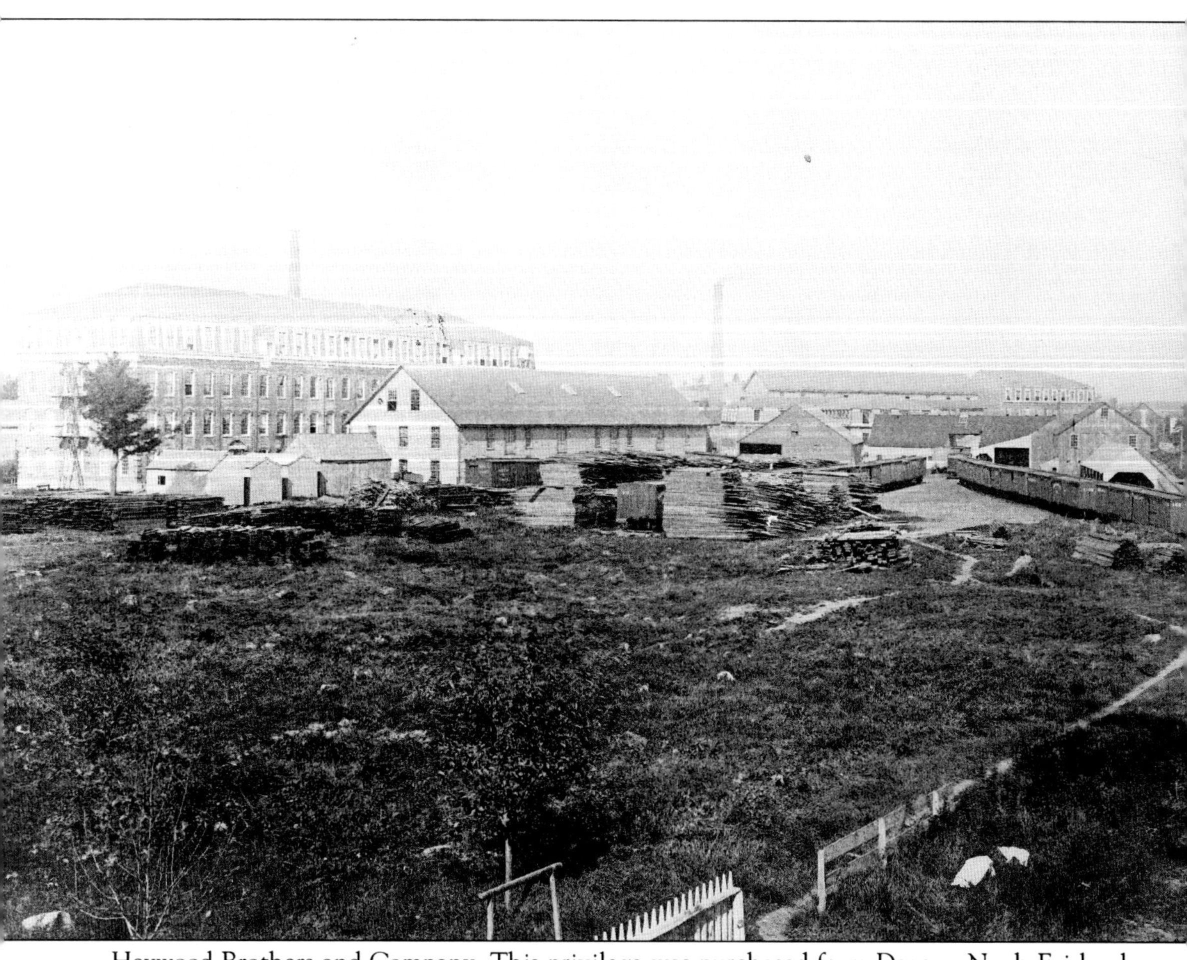

Heywood Brothers and Company. This privilege was purchased from Deacon Noah Fairbanks by Merrick Wallace in the early part of the nineteenth century. The company, begun by the Heywood brothers—Levi, Seth, Benjamin, Walter, and William—at their father's house in 1826, bought this privilege. Heywood Brothers and Company, later the Heywood Wakefield Company, became the largest manufacturer of chairs in Gardner and the world. The massive complex still exists on Central, Pine, Cross, Park, and Lake Streets.

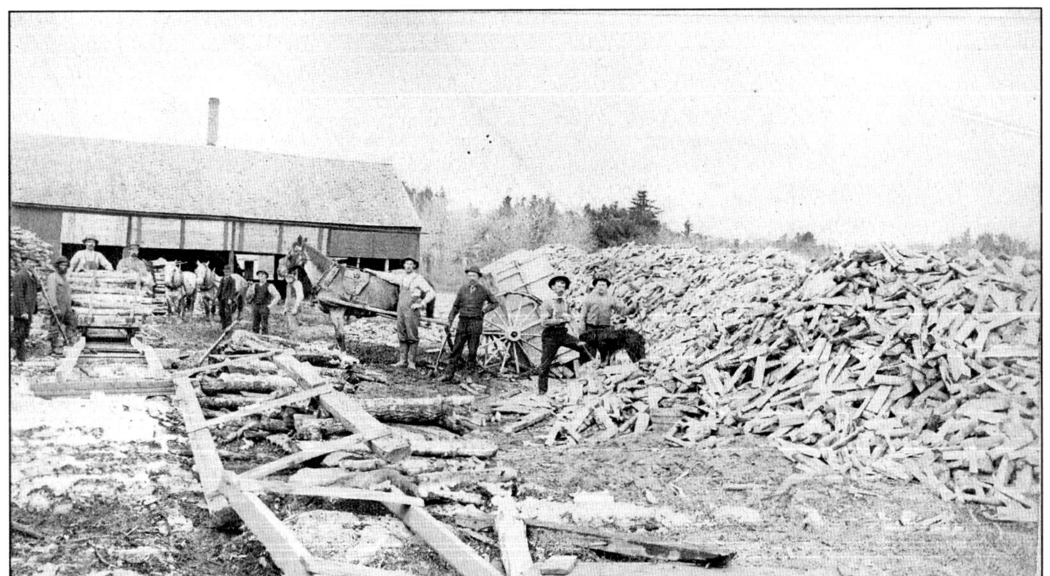

C.B. Kendall first ran a coach line between Gardner and Hubbardston. But this ended about 1874 and by 1875 he was in the business of supplying first wood and later coal, both retail and wholesale. His establishment was off South Main Street behind Grossman's.

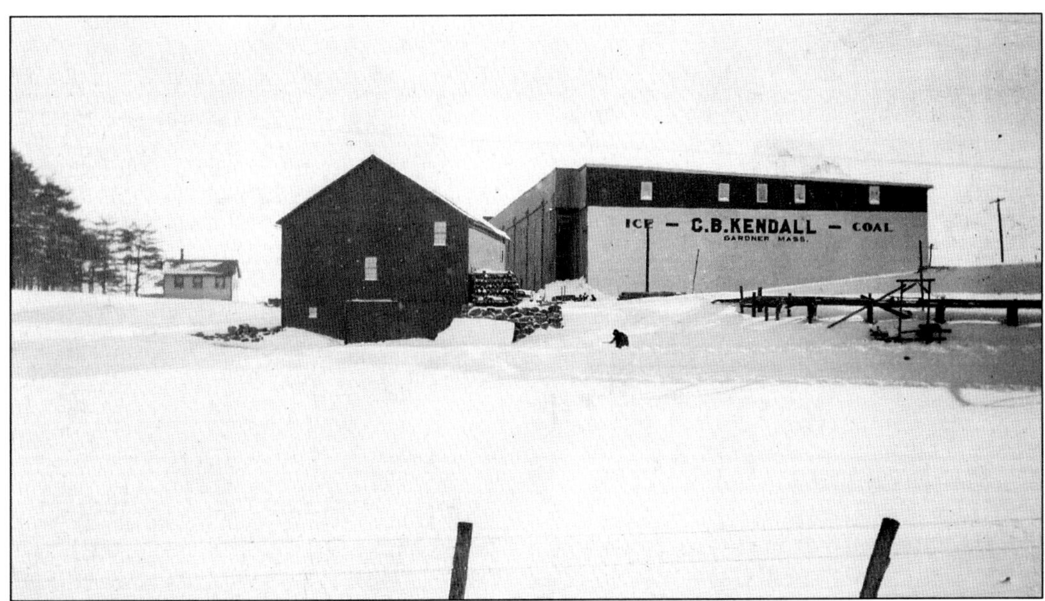

Mr. Kendall next began the harvesting of ice in 1876. He began on Mahoney's and later bought C.W. Morse's ice house on Crystal Lake in 1877. It being too small, he then moved to the park at the entrance to Crystal Lake Cemetery. He finally built a large ice house at the northwest corner of Crystal Lake. The business lasted into the late 1930s.

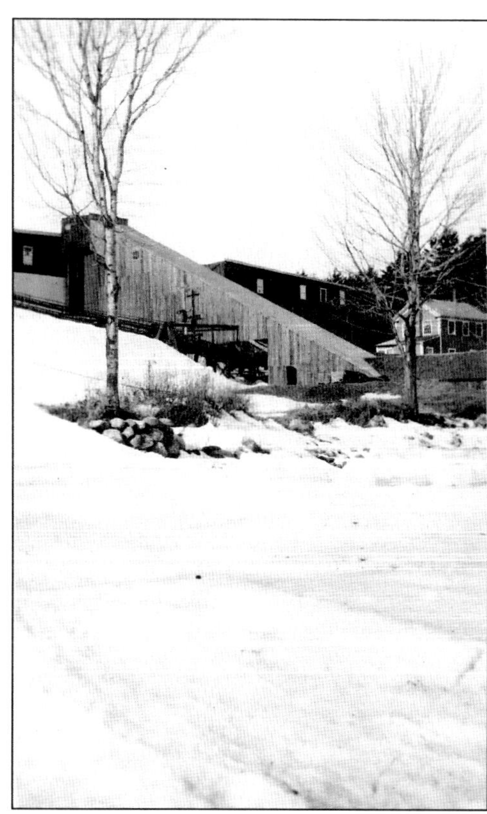

This powered run moved ice from the lake into the ice room. After being shaved, it was then packed in sawdust insulation and awaited shipment.

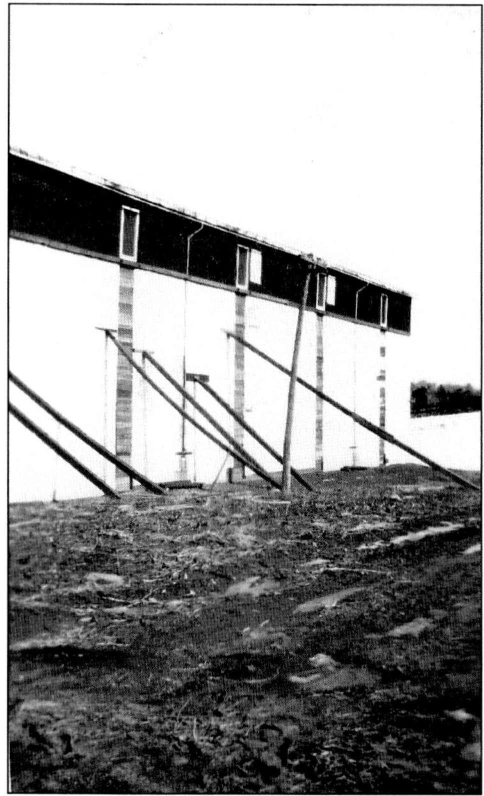

This ice house could hold more than 10,000 tons of ice. As the *Gardner News* put it, the ice was "as clear as a Christian's eye." Mr. Kendall shipped his ice all around the country and the world.

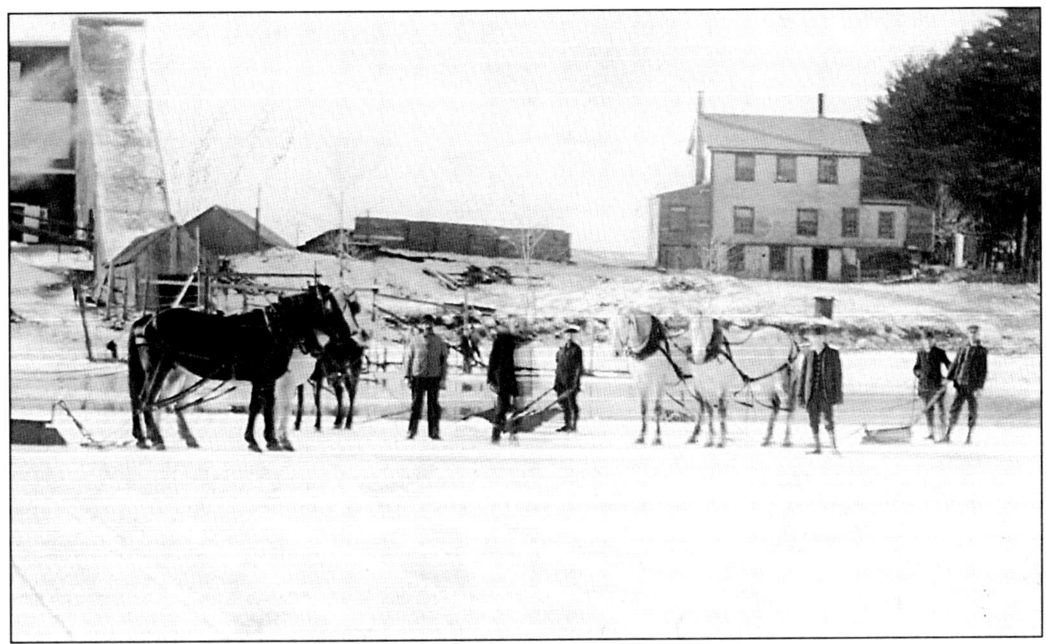

The men are using horses to draw saws over the ice to mark the lines where the ice will be sawed into uniform cakes. The cakes, or a raft of them, was then drifted to the bottom of the run where they were loaded for the trip to the ice house.

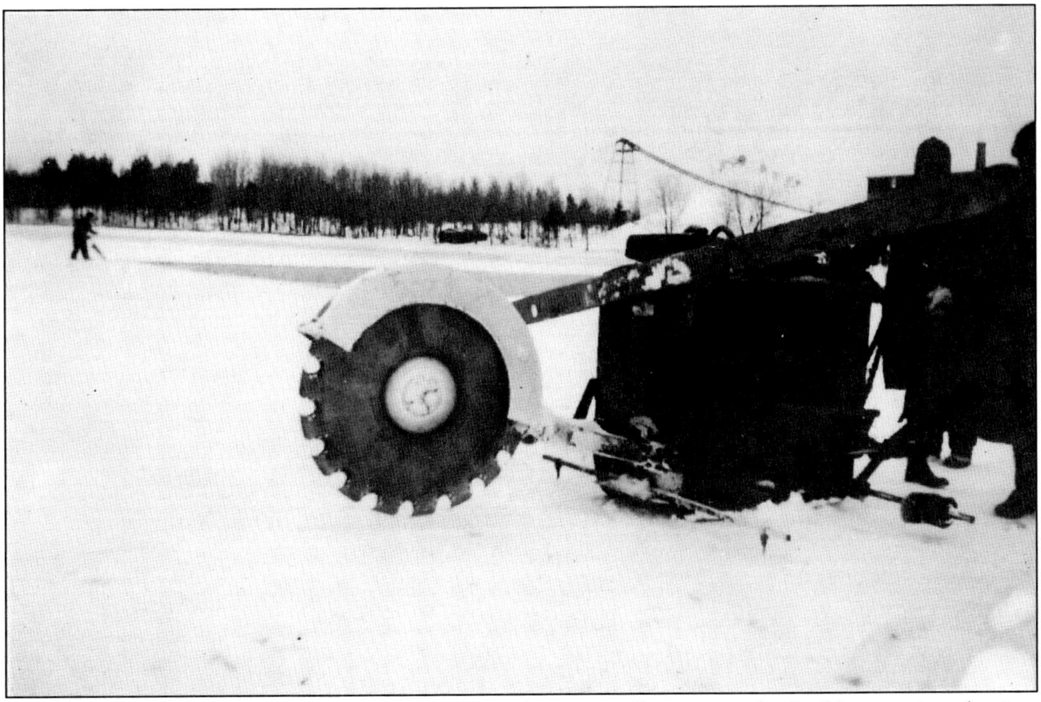

In later years the motor replaced the horse as the most efficient method of harvesting the ice. Once the ice was harvested it was loaded onto special freight cars and sent to its destination.

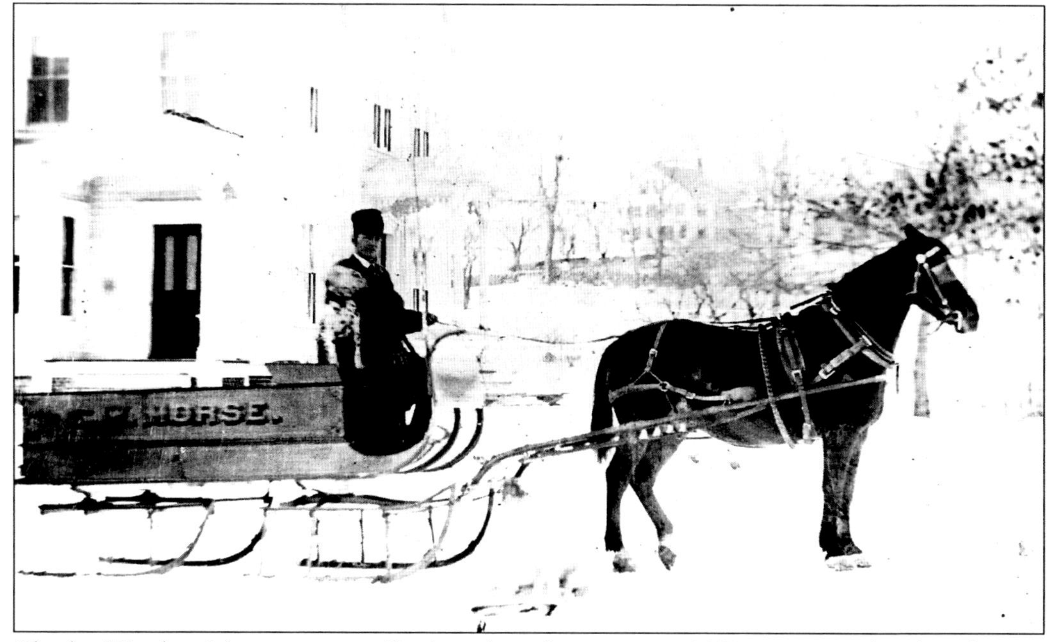

Charles Windsor Morse came to Gardner from Lancaster in 1851 to open a butcher shop in South Gardner. After several years at this stand he bought land on School Street and erected a barn and slaughter house. About 1859 he erected his home on the same site, 65 School Street. He is shown here in his sleigh about 1860, which was used for meat delivery in the winter.

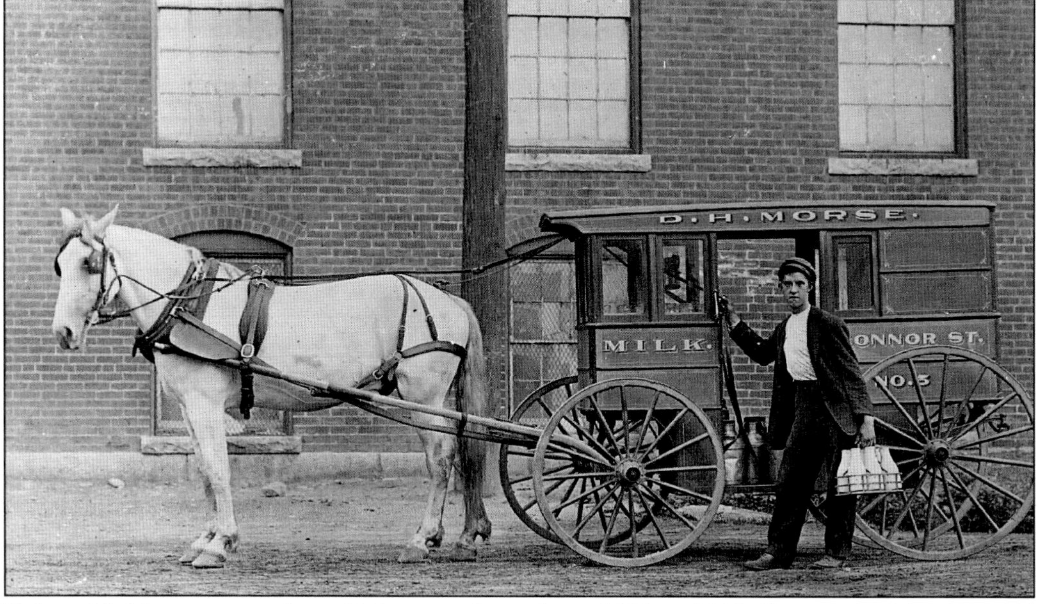

Delmar H. Morse operated a milk business from about 1900 to 1912. He operated from several locations including Green, Parker, and Connors Streets. The driver is Chester W. Baker. He was part of a large group that delivered milk to customers' homes, including such businesses as the Heywood Farm, Taavitsainen, Racette, the Rockland Farm, the United Co-Operative Society, Gardner Creamery, the Guertin Brothers, Chicoine , Korhonen, Dubzinski, Anderson, Johnson, Binnall, and Tappin, to name just a few.

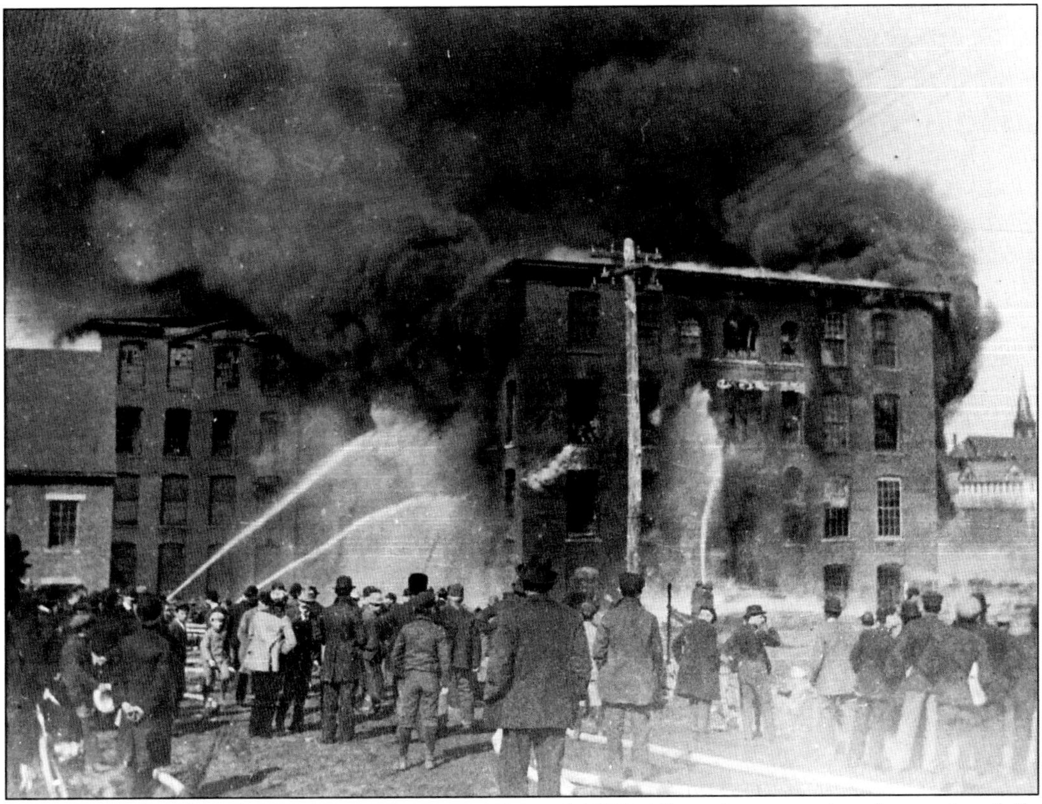

The Central Oil and Gas Stove Company fire of 1899. The plant was just becoming fully engulfed at this time.

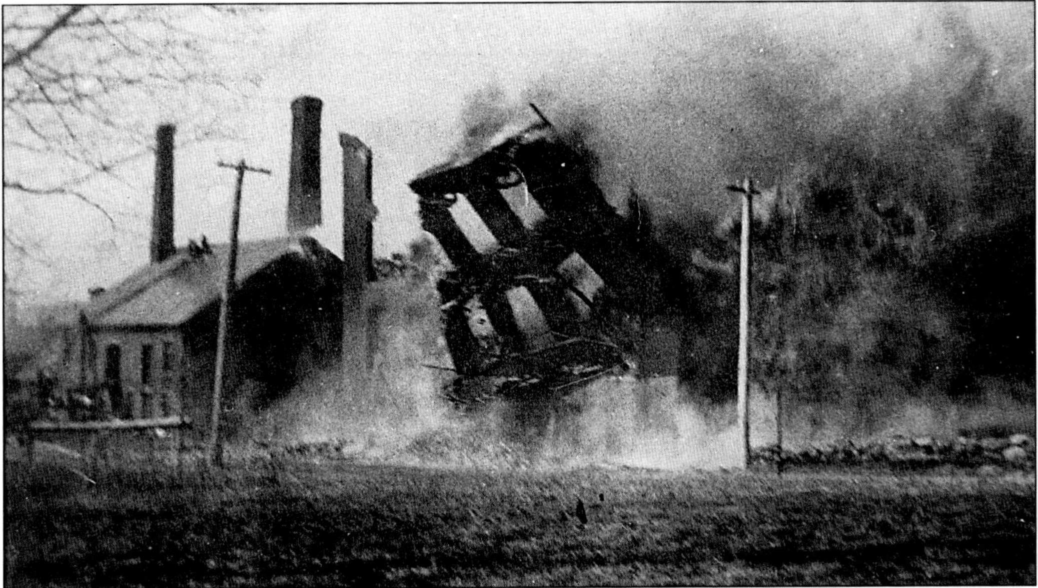

By now the fire had run its course and the brick building was collapsing in upon itself. The company rebuilt and became the Florence Stove Company. Today the buildings are the headquarters of the Simplex Time Recorder Company.

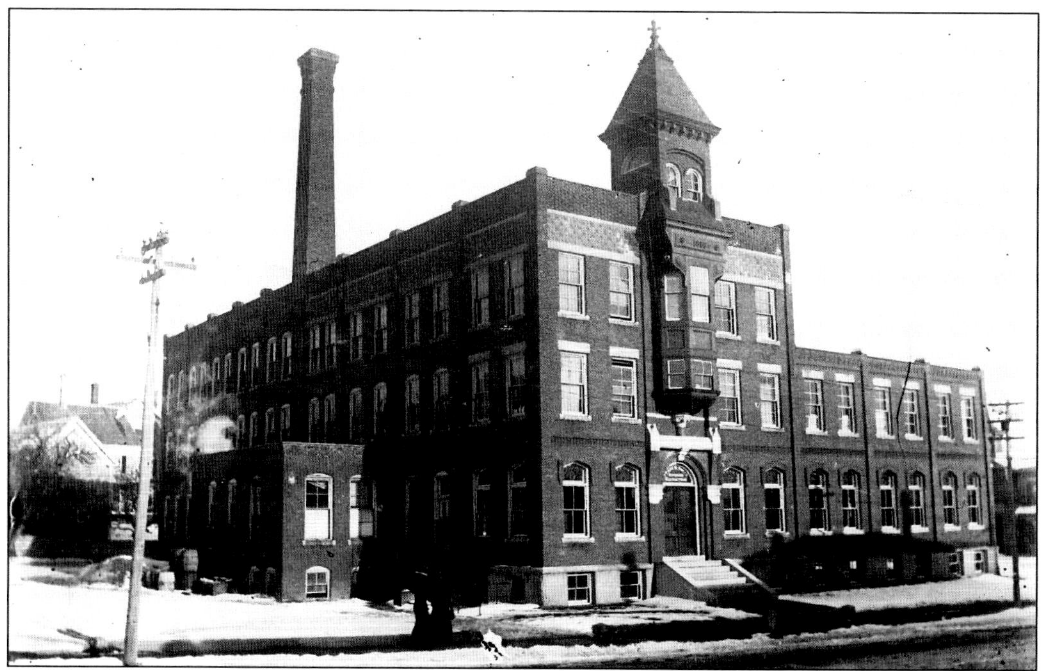

Frank Wyman Smith came to Gardner in 1886 from the Durgin Silver Company in Concord, New Hampshire. He began the Frank W. Smith Silver Company which produced fine sterling silver until 1958. The Smith Company created a punch service for the Battleship *Louisiana* designed by Pierre Cheron. Queen Elizabeth of England and Princess Grace of Monaco received pieces of Smith sterling. Marie Louise, one of their flat ware patterns, was used in United States embassies all over the world.

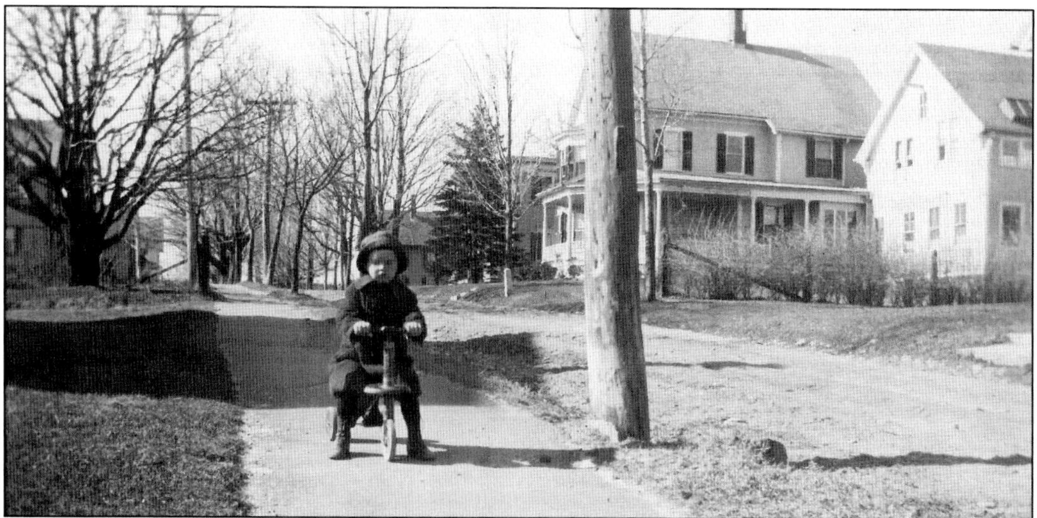

Arthur J. Stone first came to the United States in 1884 to work for Durgin Silver Company in Concord, New Hampshire. In 1887 Mr. Stone came to Gardner to work for the Frank W. Smith Silver Company. He established the holloware department and served as superintendent and designer for eight years. In 1901 he set up his own silver shop at 17 Winter Street, shown here at the far right. He was honored by the Boston Society of Art and Crafts, with the rating of Master Craftsman and Medalist. He died in 1937.

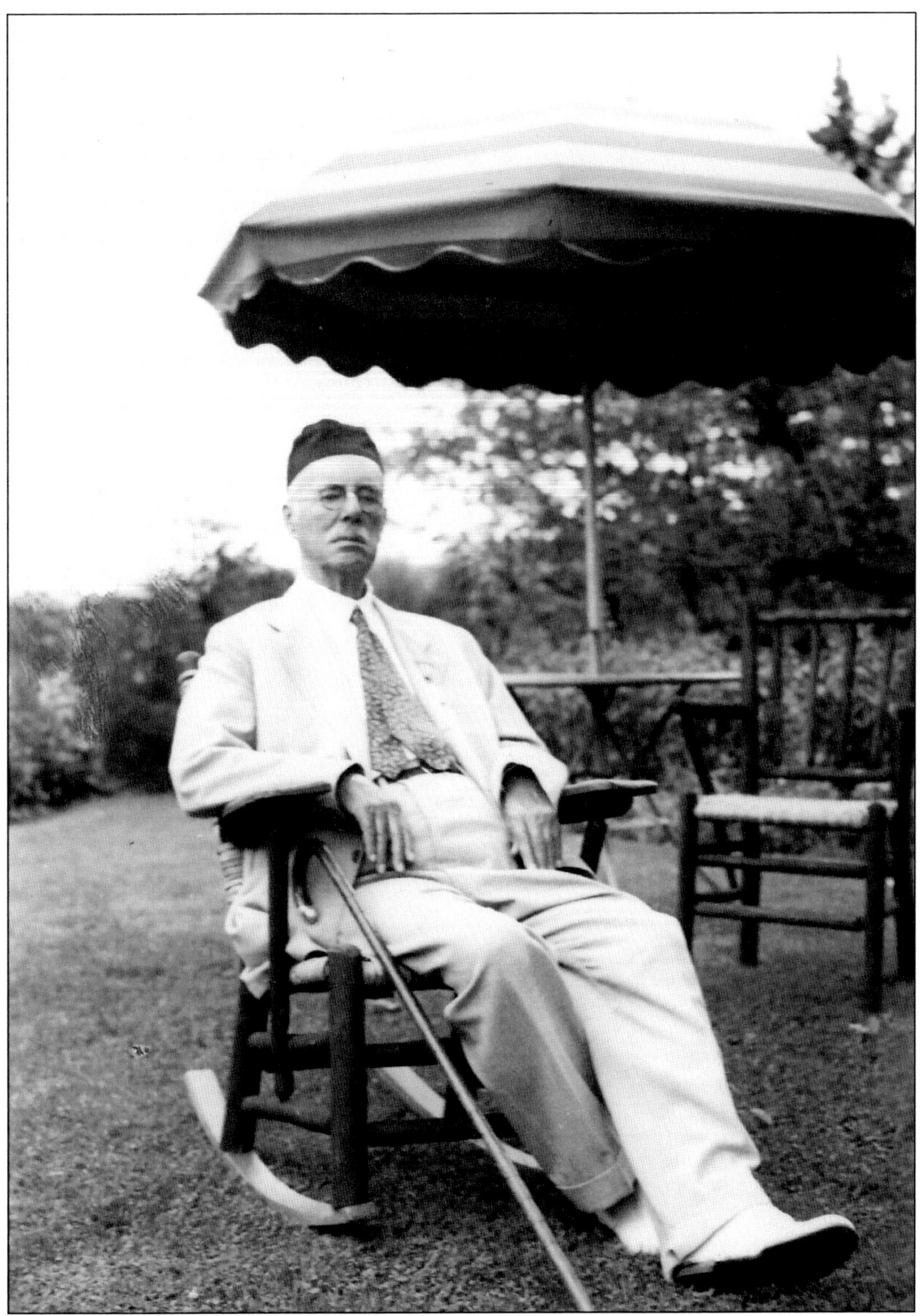

Arthur J. Stone on his ninetieth birthday, just after he had retired and sold his business to Henry Heywood.

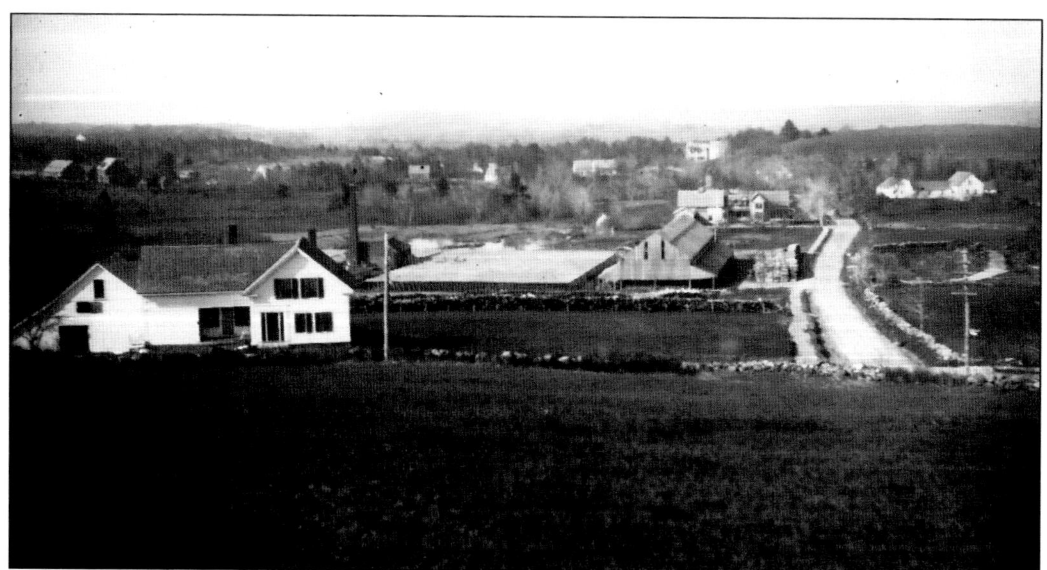

George N. Dyer came to Gardner from Templeton, with his father H.N. Dyer, and they commenced their brick manufacturing business in 1873. Products from this yard were used in the construction of the Levi Heywood Memorial Library and C.O. Bent's house. A million common bricks were being produced here each year during the late 1800s. The brickyard was sold to Cyril Caron in 1907. This is the present site of the Timpany Plaza Shopping Center.

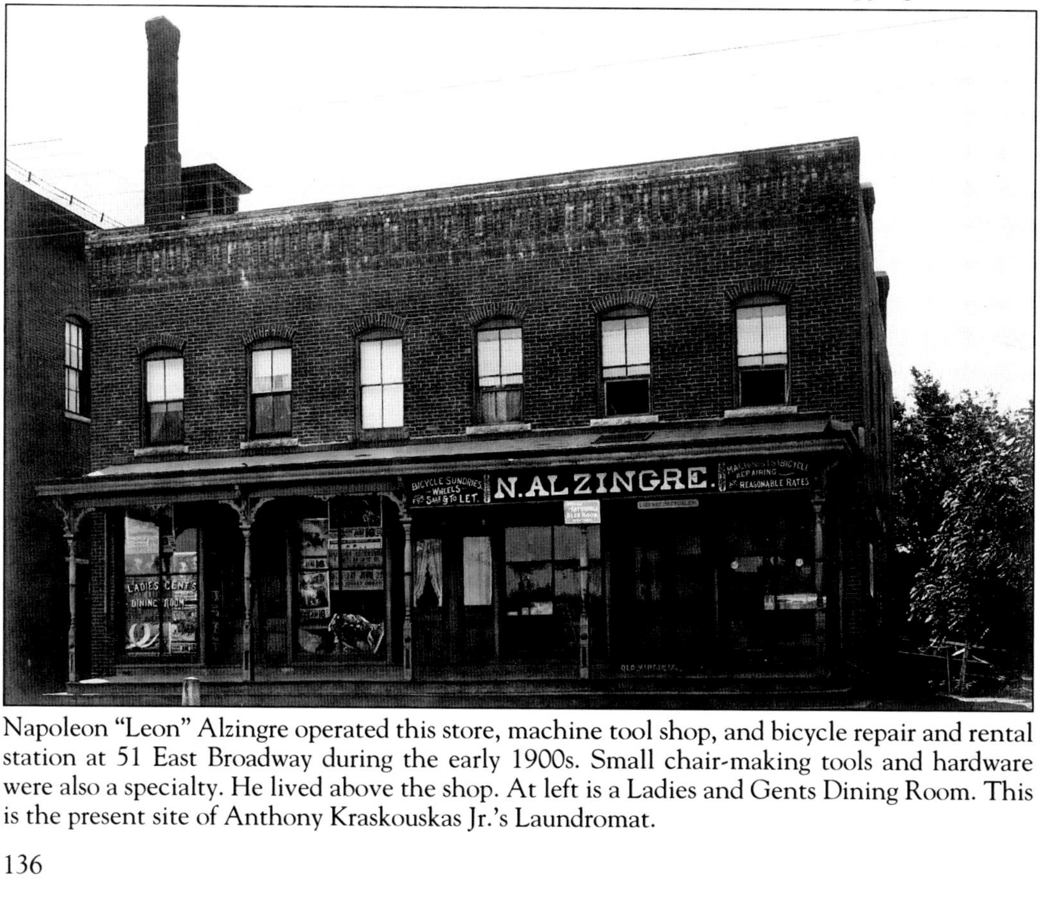

Napoleon "Leon" Alzingre operated this store, machine tool shop, and bicycle repair and rental station at 51 East Broadway during the early 1900s. Small chair-making tools and hardware were also a specialty. He lived above the shop. At left is a Ladies and Gents Dining Room. This is the present site of Anthony Kraskouskas Jr.'s Laundromat.

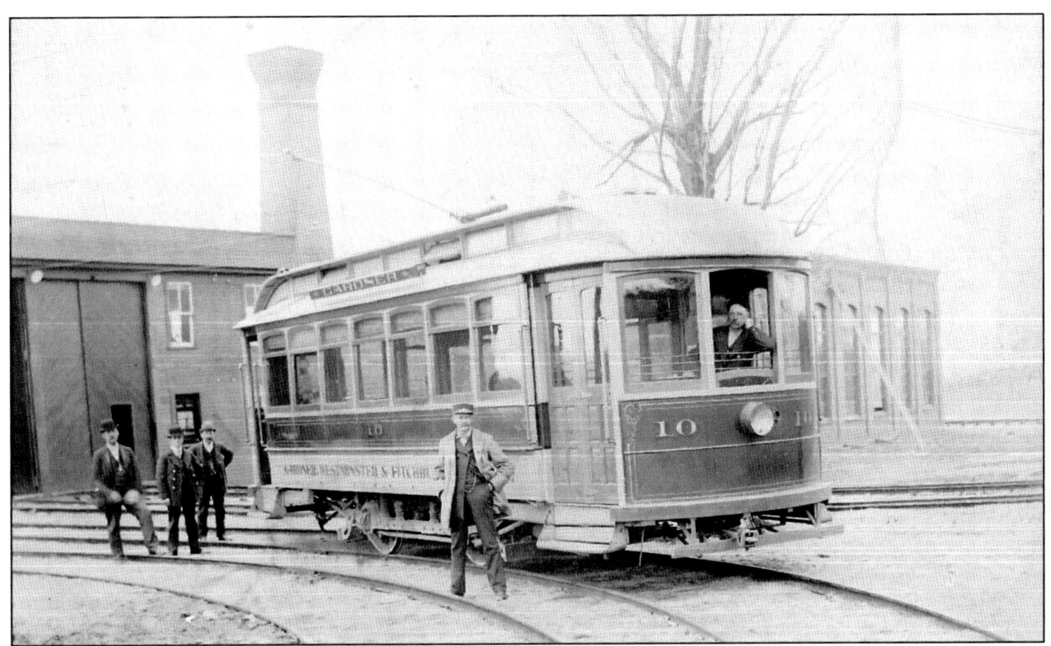

One of the early single truck trolley cars of the Gardner, Westminster, and Fitchburg Electric Street Railway shortly after 1900 with Winfy Sinclair, a motorman. The original company was called the Gardner Electric Street Railway, formed in 1894 to serve Gardner and later Crystal Lake Park. The early power house was situated on North Main Street near the present Collector Car Showroom. Expansion of the line saw the new car barn and power house moved to Westminster. The company closed after World War I.

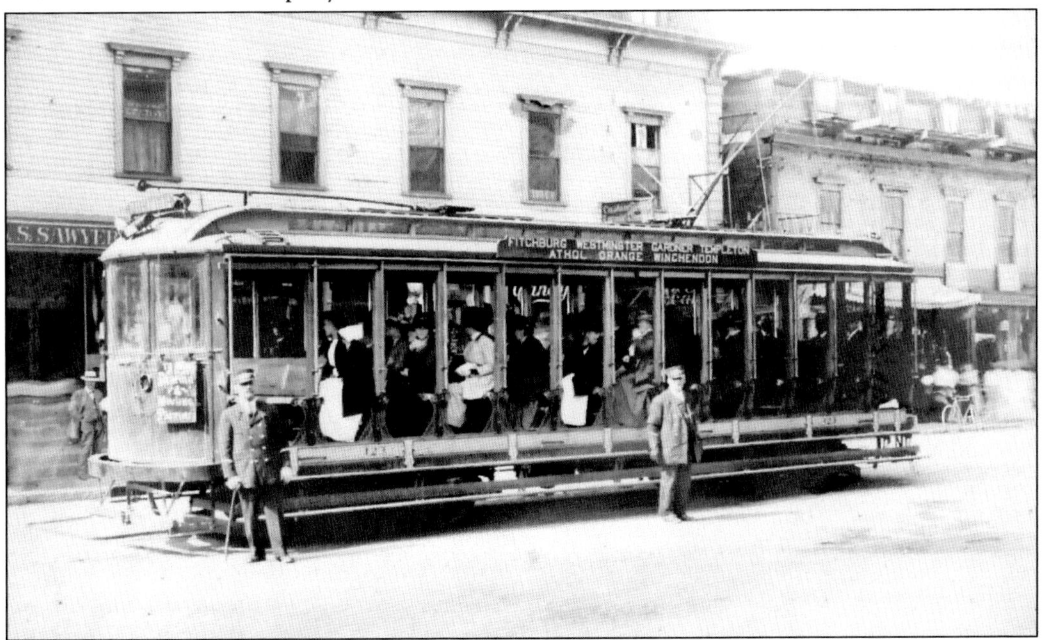

A double-truck open summer car of the Gardner, Westminster, and Fitchburg Street Railway in the mid-1910s on Parker Street next to the Garland Block. Note the Perley/Hillery Block being renovated in the rear right.

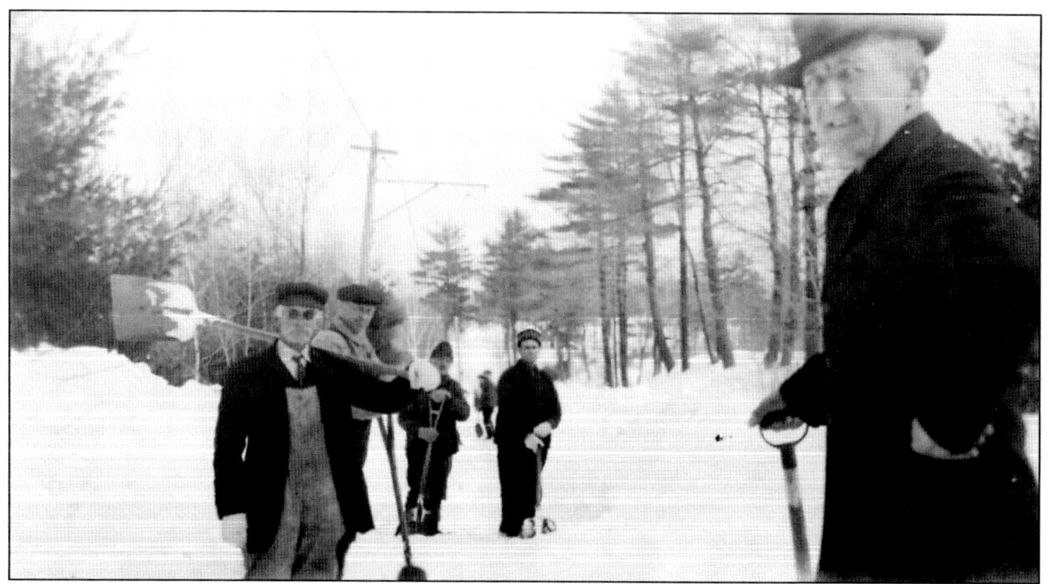

Members of the board of trade dig out the street railway tracks after a large snow storm. Phil Loughlin, electrical contractor, is on the right.

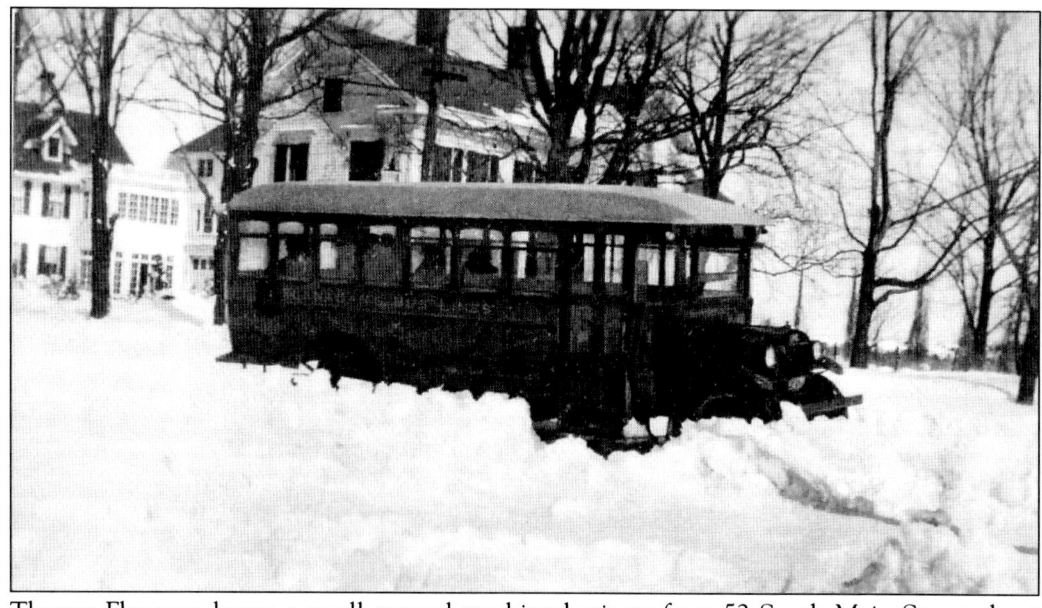

Thomas Flanagan began a small general trucking business from 52 South Main Street about 1922. Benches on the flat bed of a Reo Speedwagon carried chairmakers to work. A bus operation moved to the George Noonan property on Travers Street by the mid-1920s and George Marnane, mechanic, joined the firm. A garage was built on East Broadway, on the site of the old Bell Schoolhouse, and the line continued for many years. Buses were named, and among them were the "Chair City Queen" and "Miss Gardner."

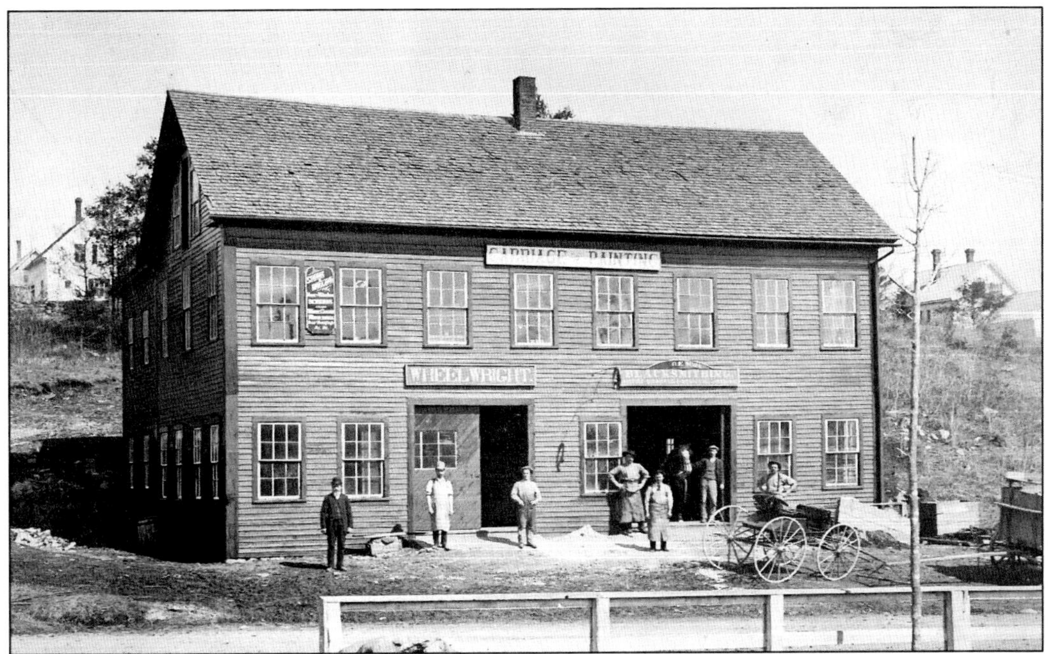

Darius Nims operated a blacksmith shop at 50 Chelsea Street near what is now the corner of Chelsea and Summer Streets. In 1884 he is listed with Avery on Chestnut Street. Shortly after he moved to Chelsea Street, to the reported location of a blacksmith shop set up by David Nichols on "Chelsea Lane" in South Gardner in the late 1700s.

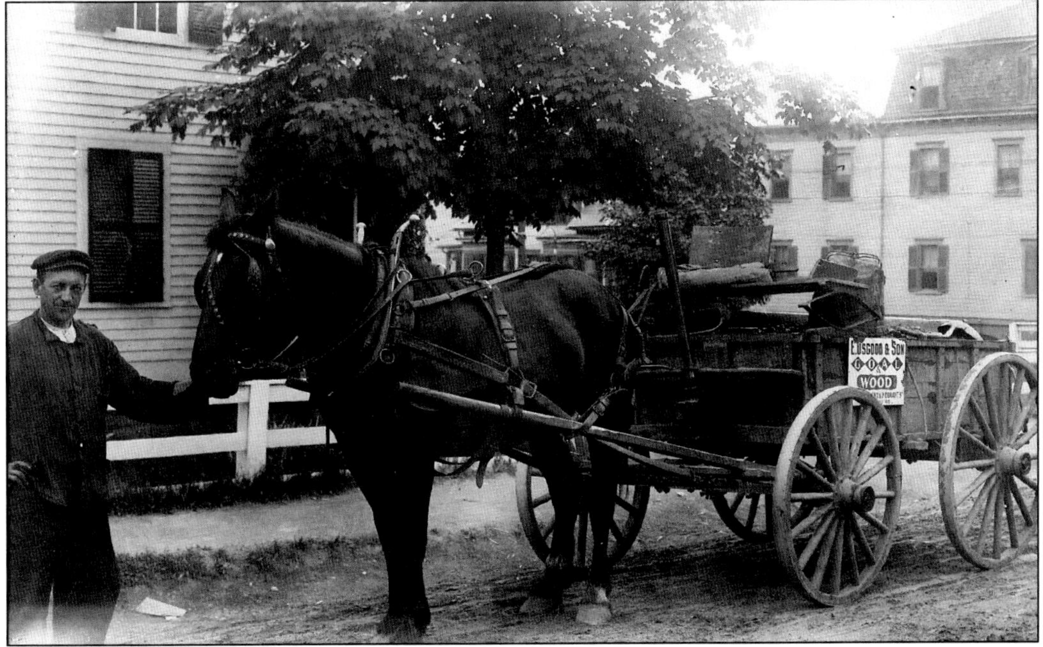

Ezra Osgood came to Gardner about 1848 from Barre. He worked in the chairs shop for fourteen years when he opened his coal business in 1858. He was the first retail dealer of coal in Gardner. He, and his son, operated their business from the depot. The area his business occupied is now under Route 2.

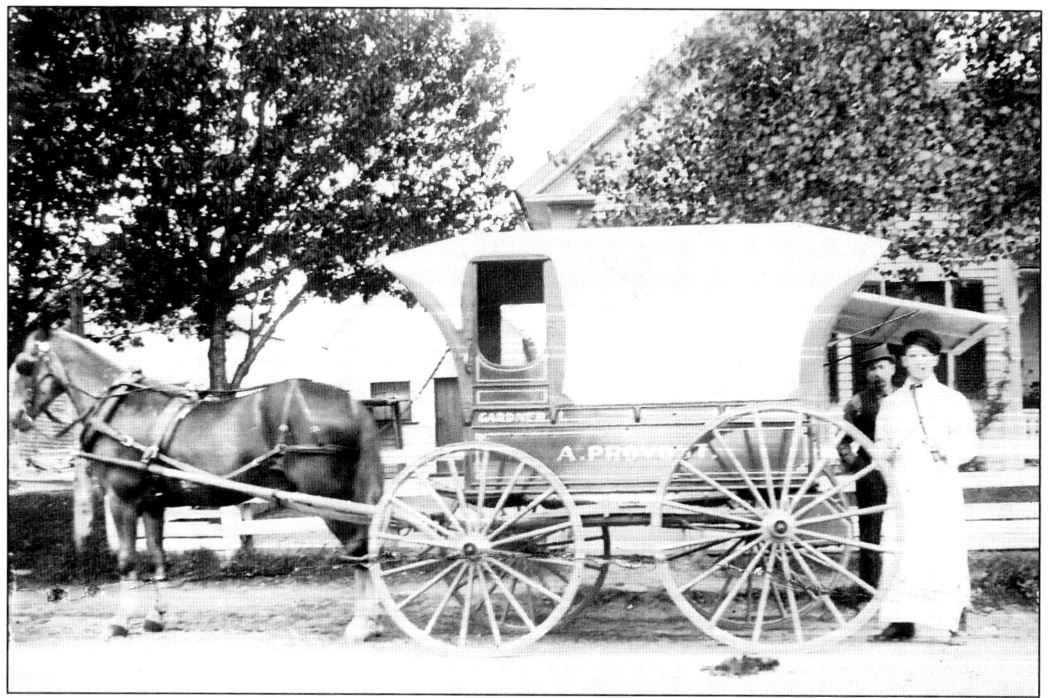

Alphonse Provost opened his meat market at 9 East Broadway in 1904, on what was later the site of markets run by George LaFortune, Ralph Ringer, Leroy "Bob" White, and his son Russell. In 1906 he moved to 28 East Broadway and continued until 1914, when he moved to Webster. His horse-drawn market cart made deliveries throughout South Gardner. A slaughter house once stood on Partridge Street just beyond the brook, serving local meat handlers.

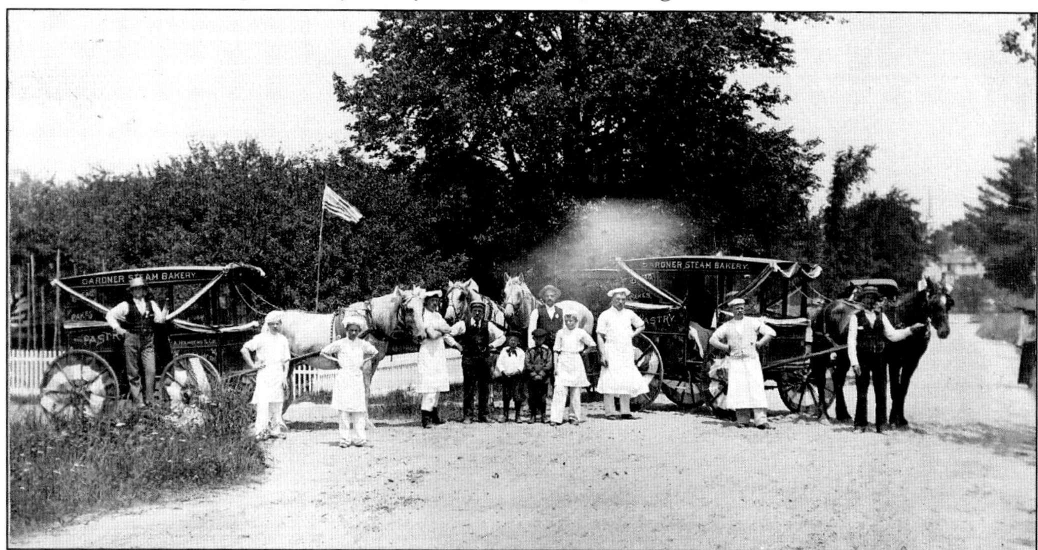

The Gardner Steam Bakery. Almer Holmberg took over Hoadley's branch bakery on the north corner of Pine and Jay Streets in 1897. The bakery specialized in bread, cake, and pastry, and if a postal card was sent, baked beans and brown bread would be delivered by their red carts on Sunday morning. The red carts were their trademark. Two of the drivers were Alfred Humphrey and Carl Anderson. In 1900 George N. Nichols bought the business and ran it until 1904.

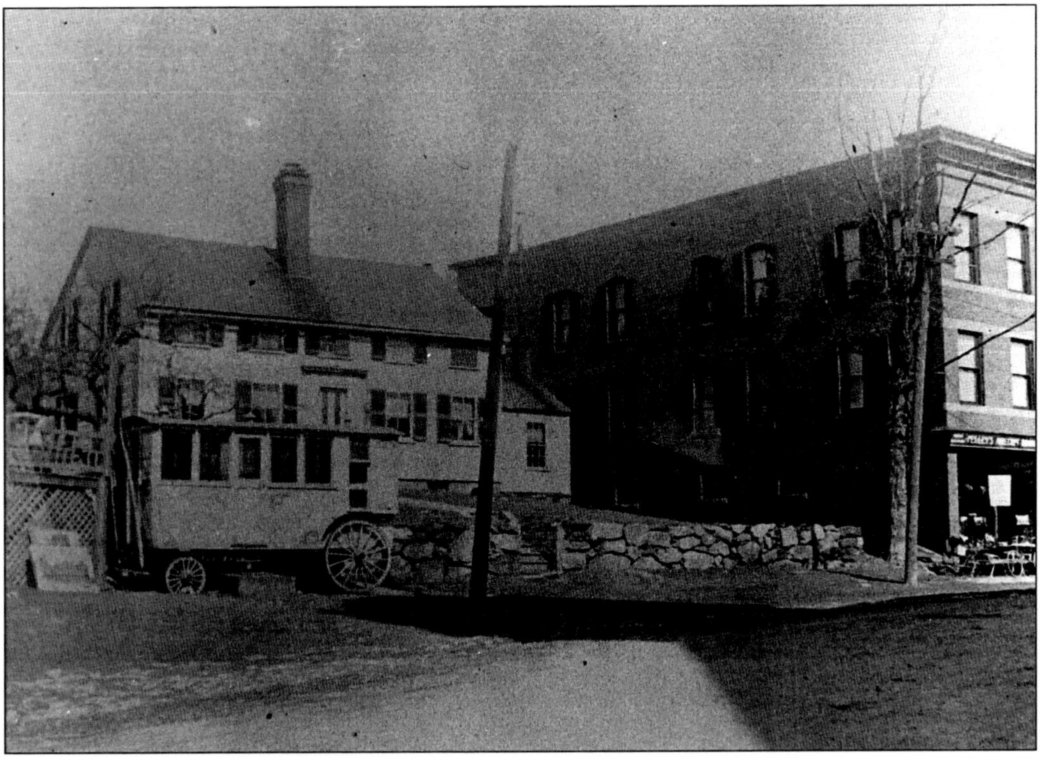

The Kelton house, where the *Gardner News* now stands, is seen behind Leather's Lunch wagon. Next to the Kelton house is the Greenwood Block, which still exists. Leather's Lunch eventually occupied a space next to the Greenwood Block and was a landmark of West Gardner for many years.

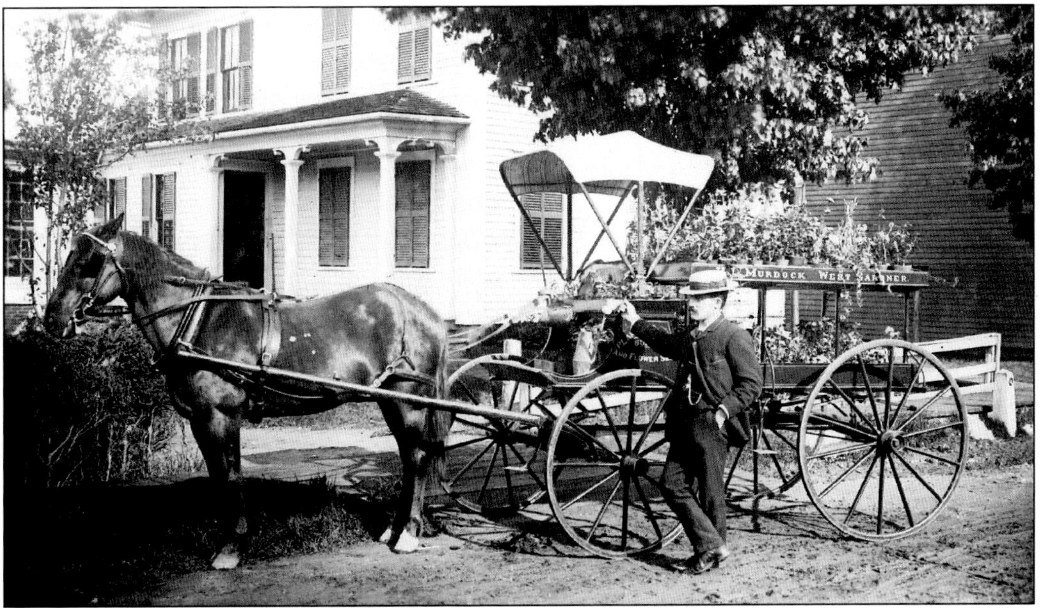

Murdock the florist operated a greenhouse complex off Pine Street near number 87, growing flowers and vegetables. His was the first such establishment in Gardner.

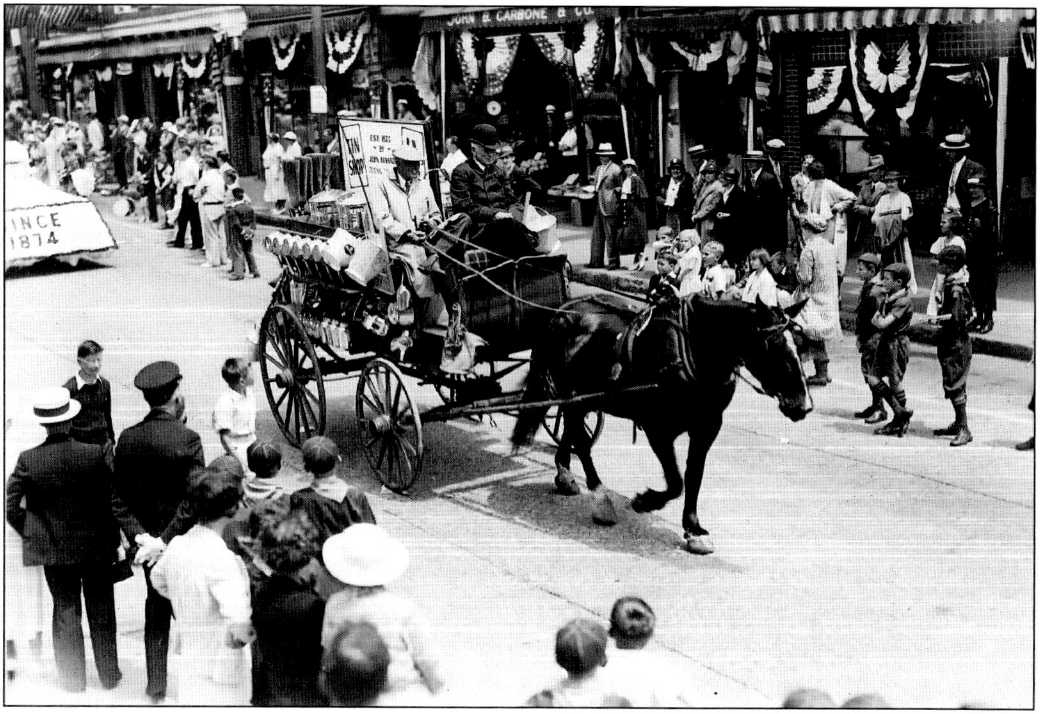

The tin peddler was a common site in the early days before stores. These itinerant peddler's came from town to town peddling not only tin ware but many different kinds of goods the citizens could get no where else. This was in the Sesquicentennial Parade in 1935. Jacquith and Richardson in 1877 made a variety of tin ware and later added paper stock and other sundries to their stock. Richard Symons later carried on the business.

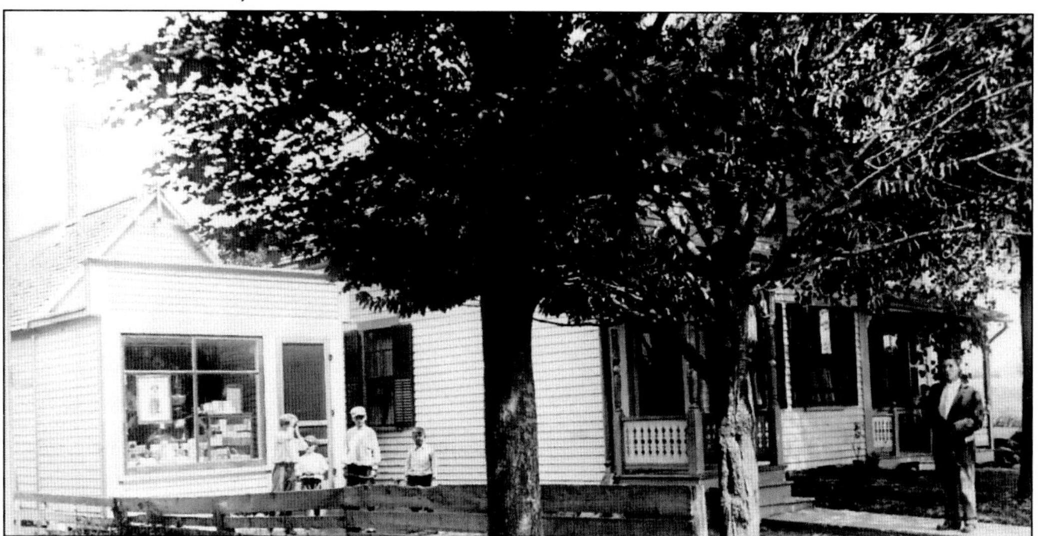

Fred Antaya ran this small grocery store during the early 1900s at 185 Union Street just beyond the present Winter Street Cemetery, and delivered orders throughout South Gardner, as well as parts of Greater Gardner. His horse Nellie knew every delivery stop and never required a horse weight. The store was a meeting place on Saturday night for fox hunters and fishermen who sat on cracker barrels and boxes to discuss their ventures.

In 1926 Leslie D. Hines moved his barber shop from the old Pepoon stand at 40 East Broadway, above the S.W.A. Stevens Store, to this site. His wife Florence operated a beauty parlor in the rear until her death in 1946. Les Hines moved his barber shop to 38 East Broadway in 1948. After Les Hines death, Stanley Hines, his son, continued the business until his death.

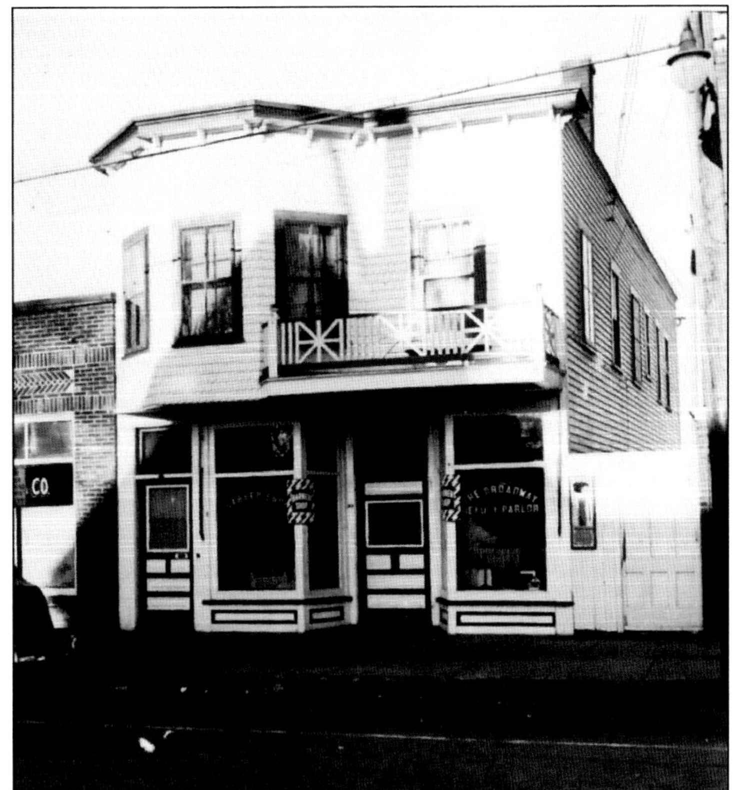

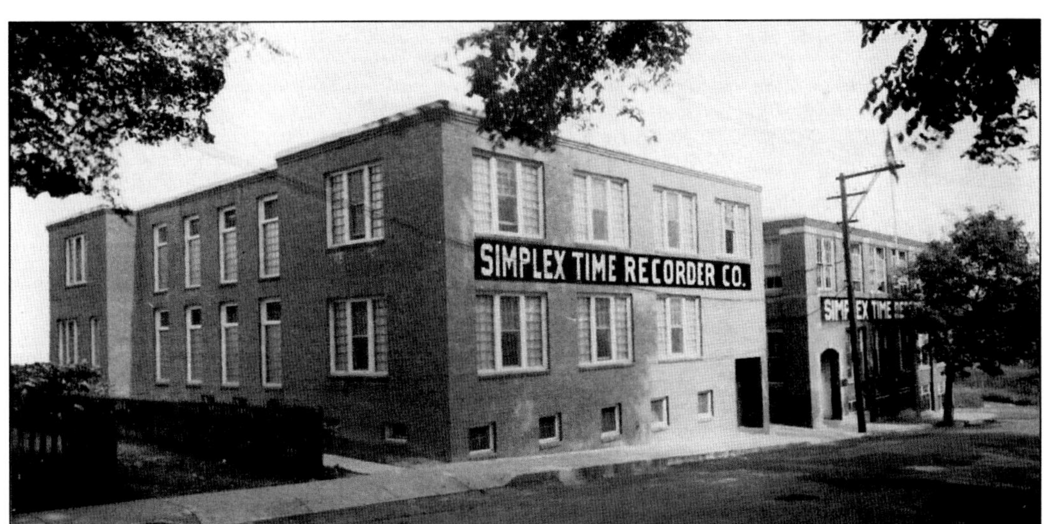

The Simplex Time Recorder Company. Edward G. Watkins developed a time recorder for the Heywood Brothers and Wakefield in 1894. In 1900 Mr. Watkins opened a small shop on Sanborn Street in the Royal Steam Heater Building. This shows the buildings as they looked in the mid-1950s. Today the company occupies all the area bounded by Cross, South Lincoln, and what was lower School Street. They have also renovated the old Florence Stove complex as part of their operation.

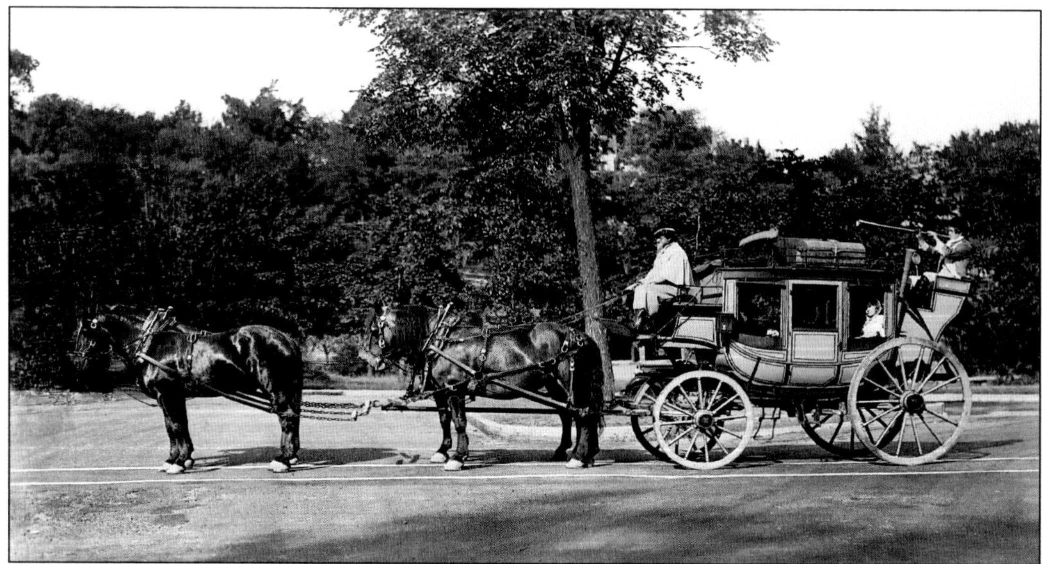

The stage coach in the Sesquicentennial Anniversary parade. In the parade Frank Pond and Milton Creed were on the front seat, with Roderic E. Bent as the postilion. Inside the coach were Mrs. Richard Udall, George Matthews, Lewis Travers, and Misses Marcia Dewey and Polly Stone. A "Concord" coach hanging on leather straps was operated by C.N. Howe, who carried passengers to and from the depot in 1880. C.B. Kendall also operated a stage line between Gardner and Hubbardston.

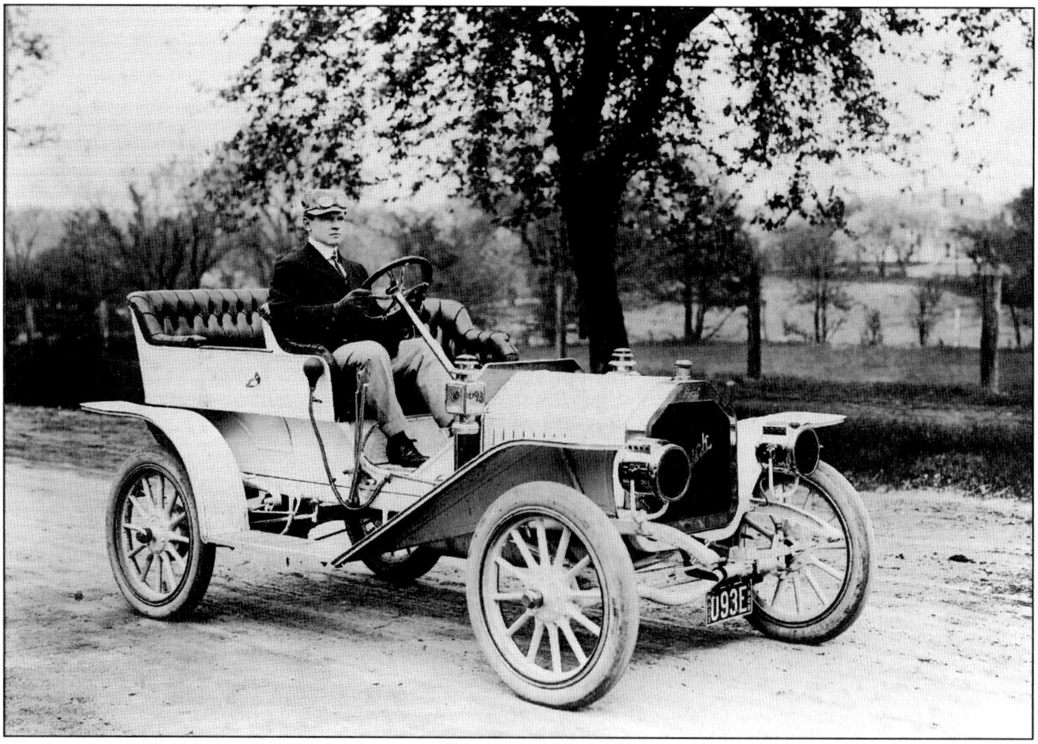

Stuart K. Pierce opened a Buick Agency in 1908. Here Mr. Pierce sits in one of his 1908 Buick cars.